EPISODE ONE: DIVE

STORY
BILL JEMAS

SCRIPT
JENN SODINI
JOHN FLYNN
BILL JEMAS

LAYOUTS
YOUNG HELLER
KURT TIEDE

PENCILS
DERLIS SANTACRUZ

COLORS
MARTA MARTINEZ

COVER
CHARLOTTE GREENBAUM

EDITOR
CHARLOTTE GREENBAUM

EPISODE TWO: UNDERTOW

STORY
BILL JEMAS

SCRIPT
JENN SODINI
JOHN FLYNN
BILL JEMAS

LAYOUTS
YOUNG HELLER

PENCILS
DERLIS SANTACRUZ

COLORS
SANDRA MOLINA

COVER
JEFF DEKAL

LETTERS
CHARLOTTE GREENBAUM
KYLE FUREY

EDITOR
CHARLOTTE GREENBAUM

EPISODE THREE: SINK OR SWIM

STORY
BILL JEMAS

SCRIPT
JENN SODINI
JOHN FLYNN
BILL JEMAS
CHARLOTTE GREENBAUM

LAYOUTS
YOUNG HELLER

PENCILS
DERLIS SANTACRUZ

COLORS
SANDRA MOLINA

COVER
ANDREY VASILCHENKO

LETTERS
CHARLOTTE GREENBAUM

EDITOR
CHARLOTTE GREENBAUM

EPISODE FOUR: LEVEL UP

STORY
BILL JEMAS
YOUNG HELLER

SCRIPT
BILL JEMAS
CHARLOTTE GREENBAUM

LAYOUTS
YOUNG HELLER

PENCILS
DERLIS SANTACRUZ

COLORS
SANDRA MOLINA

COVER
FEDERICA MANFREDI

LETTERS
CHARLOTTE GREENBAUM

EDITOR
CHARLOTTE GREENBAUM

EPISODE FIVE: TORRENT

STORY
BILL JEMAS
STAN CHOU

SCRIPT
BILL JEMAS

LAYOUTS
STAN CHOU
JONATHAN ASHLEY
ALLEN WATSON

PENCILS
DERLIS SANTACRUZ
JETHRO MORALES

COLORS
SANDRA MOLINA

COVER
NEWSHA GHASEMI

LETTERS
MICHAEL PFEIFFER

EDITOR
CHARLOTTE GREENBAUM

Premieres

	TV SHOWS	HIT MOVIES	TOP SINGLES
1960	The Flintstones The Andy Griffith Show My Three Sons	Spartacus Psycho Exodus	Theme from A Summer Place He'll Have to Go
1961	The Dick Van Dyke Show ABC's Wide World of Sports The Avengers	The Gun of Navarone West Side Story El Cid	Tossin' and Turnin I Fall to Pieces Michael
1962	The Jetsons The Beverly Hillbillies Tonight Show: Johnny Carson	Lawrence of Arabia The Longest Day In Search of the Castaways	Stranger on the Shore I Can't Stop Loving You Mashed Potato Time
1963	Doctor Who General Hospital Let's Make a Deal	Cleopatra How the West Was Won It's a Mad, Mad, Mad, Mad, World	Sugar Shack Surfin' U.S.A. The End of the World
1964	The Addams Family Gilligan's Island Jeopardy!	Mary Poppins Goldfinger My Fair Lady	I Want to Hold Your Hand She Loves You Hello, Dolly!
1965	I Dream of Jeannie Get Smart Hogan's Heroes	The Sound of Music Thunderball Dr. Zhivago	Wooly Bully I Can't Help Myself Satisfaction
1966	Batman Mission: Impossible Star Trek	The Bible: In the Beginning Hawaii Who's Afraid of Virginia Woolf?	Ballad of the Green Berets Cherish Soul and Inspiration
1967	The Smothers Brothers The Newlywed Game The Prisoner	The Graduate The Jungle Book Doctor Dolittle	To Sir With Love The Letter Ode to Billie Joe
1968	Hawaii Five-O The Mod Squad 60 Minutes	Rosemary's Baby 2001: A Space Odyssey Planet of the Apes	Hey Jude Love is Blue Honey
1969	Sesame Street The Brady Bunch Monty Python's Flying Circus	Easy Rider Midnight Cowboy Butch Cassidy and the Sundance Kid	Sugar, Sugar Aquarius I Can't Get Next to You

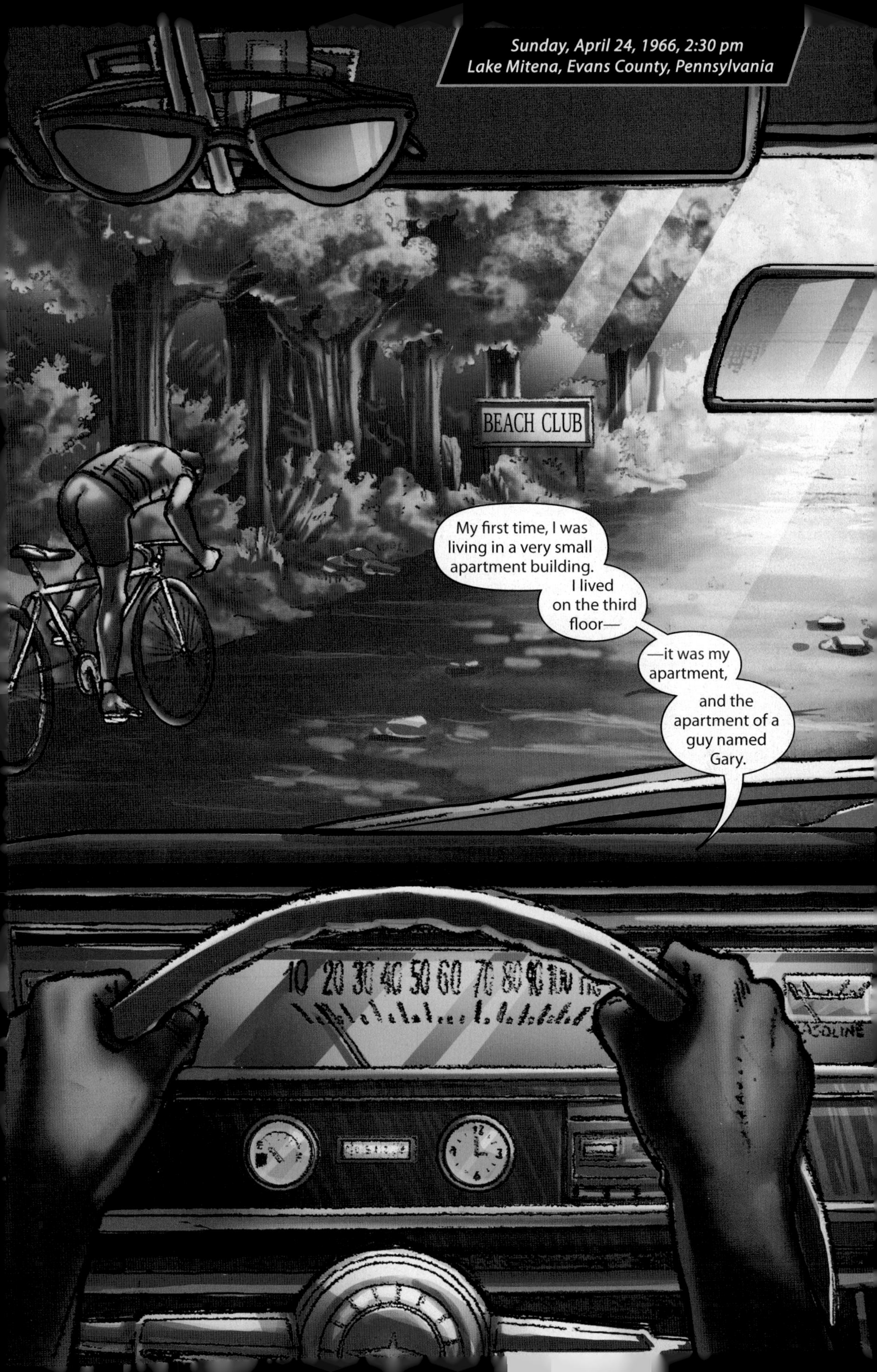
Sunday, April 24, 1966, 2:30 pm
Lake Mitena, Evans County, Pennsylvania
BEACH CLUB
My first time, I was living in a very small apartment building.
I lived on the third floor—
—it was my apartment,
and the apartment of a guy named Gary.

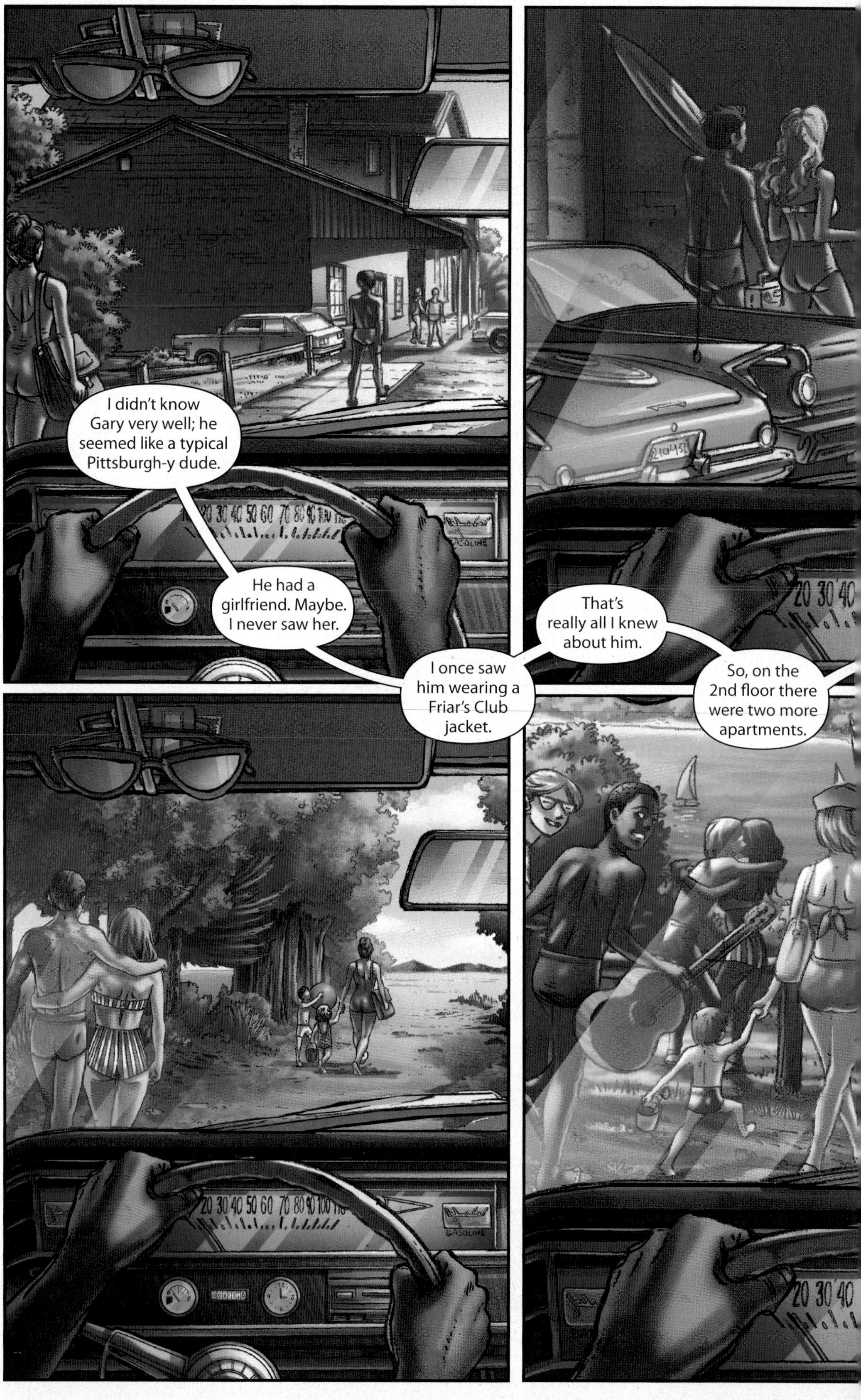
I didn't know Gary very well; he seemed like a typical Pittsburgh-y dude.
He had a girlfriend. Maybe. I never saw her.
I once saw him wearing a Friar's Club jacket.
That's really all I knew about him.
So, on the 2nd floor there were two more apartments.
GASOLINE
GASOLINE

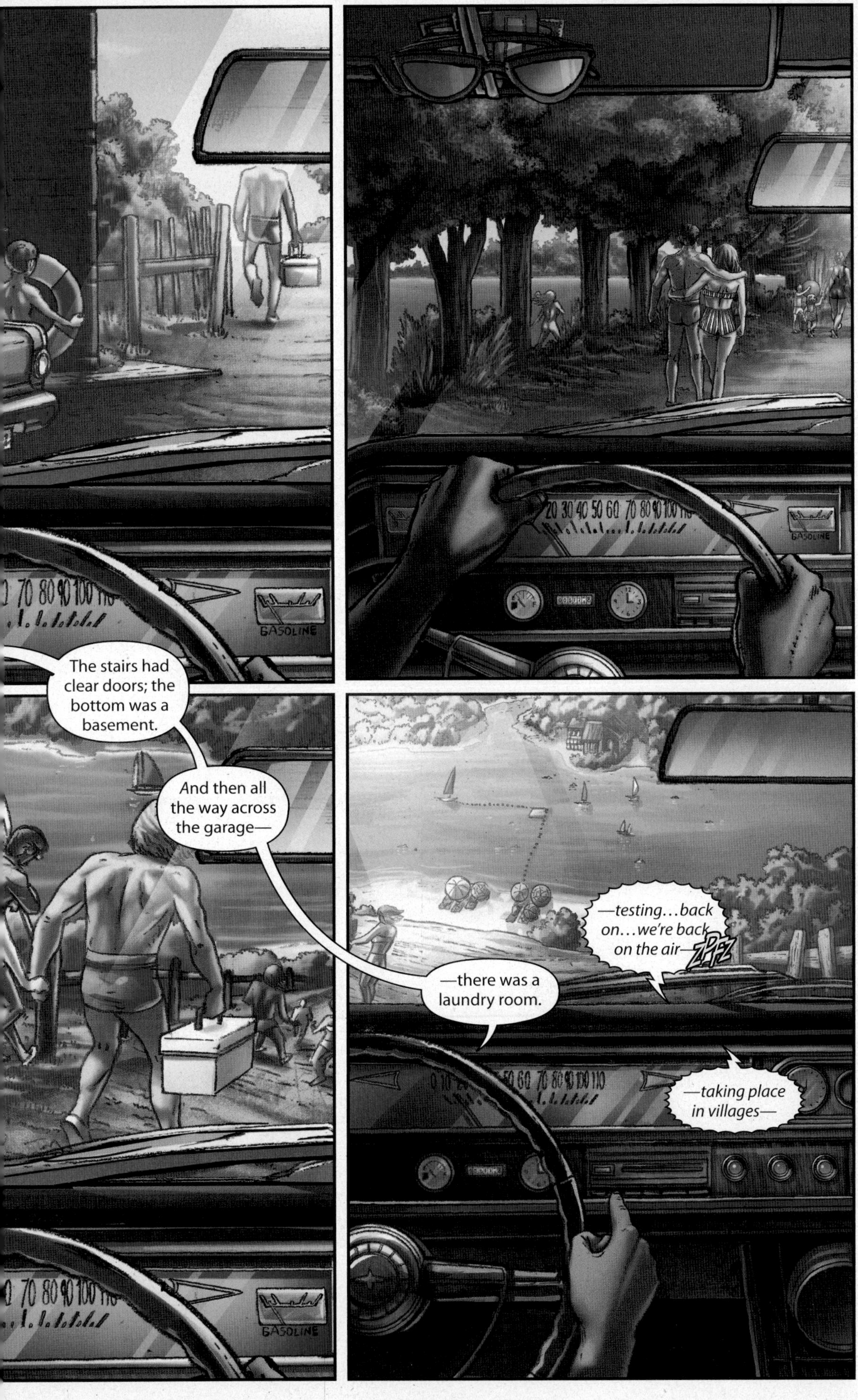
GASOLINE
The stairs had clear doors; the bottom was a basement.
And then all the way across the garage—
—there was a laundry room.
—testing…back on…we're back on the air—
—taking place in villages—

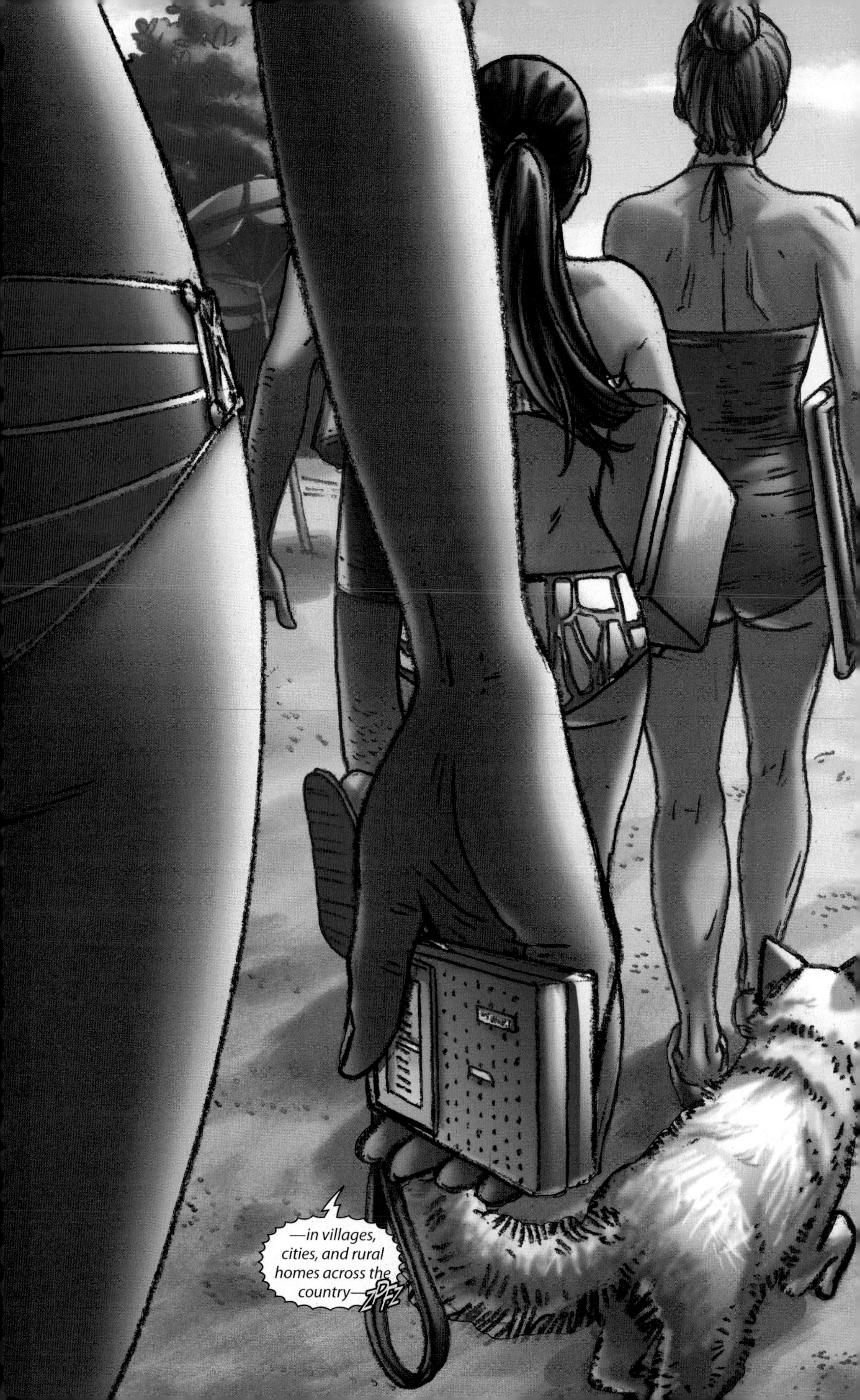
—in villages, cities, and rural homes across the country—
ZPFZ

EXPERIMENTAL SUBSCRIPTION TO THE **2T BOOK-OF-THE-DECADE CLUB** WILL DEMONSTRATE HOW DEVOTED MEMBERSHIP IS THE BEST INSURANCE AGAINST MISSING OUT ON THE BEST BOOKS FROM BYGONE DECADES.

YOUR CHOICE OF ANY 3 FOR ONLY $1

TO KILL A
Mockingbird
HARPER LEE

An idiot's guide.

Cat's Cradle
a novel by KURT VONNEGUT, JR.

Yes, humans can cause climate change.

The
Godfather
A NOVEL
Mario
Puzo

Guaranteed to include zero references to *The Godfather III.*

SLAUGHTERHOUSE-FIVE
OR
The Children's Crusade
A NEW NOVEL BY
KURT VONNEGUT, JR.

The most hilarious book about firebombing that you'll ever read.

An illustrated guide to conquering nature.

Tom Wolfe
The Electric Kool-Aid
Acid Test

Makes for great reading on any trip.

THE
AGONY
AND THE
ECSTASY
IRVING
STONE

50 shades of marble.

Please enroll me as a member. I am to receive for $1 the three books I've selected below. I will pay $300 for each book-of-the-decade I buy after. I agree to purchase at least 6 books-of the-decade from 2T each year I am a member. I may cancel the subscription only if I pay 2T $1 million and give 2T the soul of my firstborn child.

SELECT THREE BOOKS ☐ ☐ ☐

NAME ______________________

Please do not actually

ADDRESS ______________________

fill this out and send it in.

CITY ________ POSTAL ZONE No. ________ STATE ________

Valley
of the
Dolls
A NOVEL BY
Jacqueline Susann

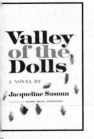

Downers are a girl's best friend.

Portnoy's
Complaint
Philip
Roth

Includes new liver recipe.

JAMES AND
THE GIANT PEACH
by ROALD DAHL

Story of the first GMO.

MAIL TO:

2T BOOK-OF-THE-DECADE CLUB
38 W. 39TH STREET 2ND FLOOR,
NEW YORK, NY 10018

Signing and mailing the coupon enrolls you into the 2T Book of the Decade Club ("2T Club") for life. You start with three books of your choice for $1 but thereafter are obligated to purchase at least six books-of-the-decade for $300 each within a twelve-month period after you enroll. You do not have the right to cancel your membership at any point until you have given us $1 million and the soul of your firstborn child, plus postage, handling, and any other expenses 2T feels like tacking onto your bill. We understand money can be tight so we accept payment plans. Any payment plans will be subject to a 15 percent interest to account for inflation and the ever depreciating value of your child's soul as your child ages. Please note, under no circumstances will 2T actually send you any books.

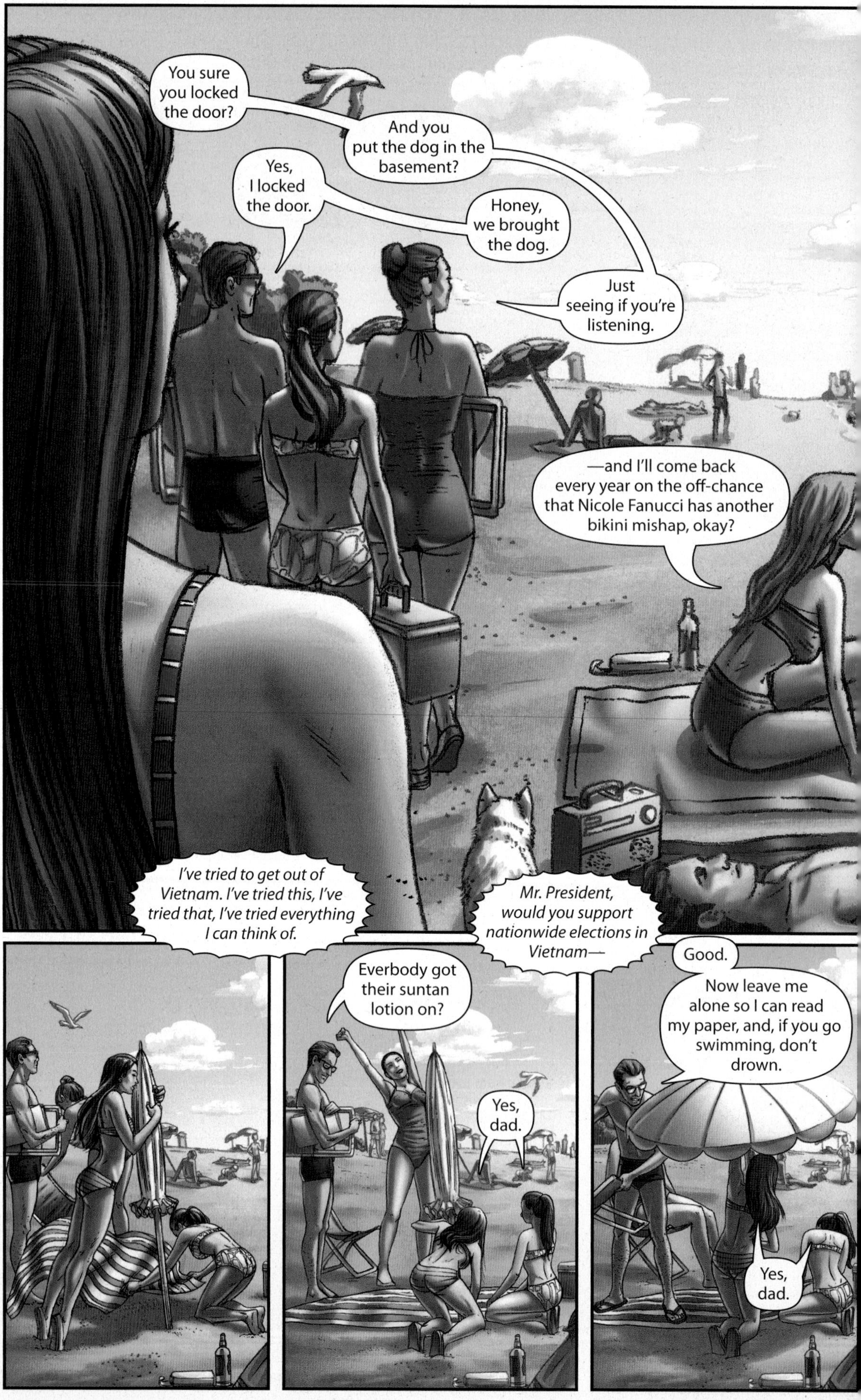
You sure you locked the door?
And you put the dog in the basement?
Yes, I locked the door.
Honey, we brought the dog.
Just seeing if you're listening.
—and I'll come back every year on the off-chance that Nicole Fanucci has another bikini mishap, okay?
I've tried to get out of Vietnam. I've tried this, I've tried that, I've tried everything I can think of.
Mr. President, would you support nationwide elections in Vietnam—
Everbody got their suntan lotion on?
Yes, dad.
Good.
Now leave me alone so I can read my paper, and, if you go swimming, don't drown.
Yes, dad.

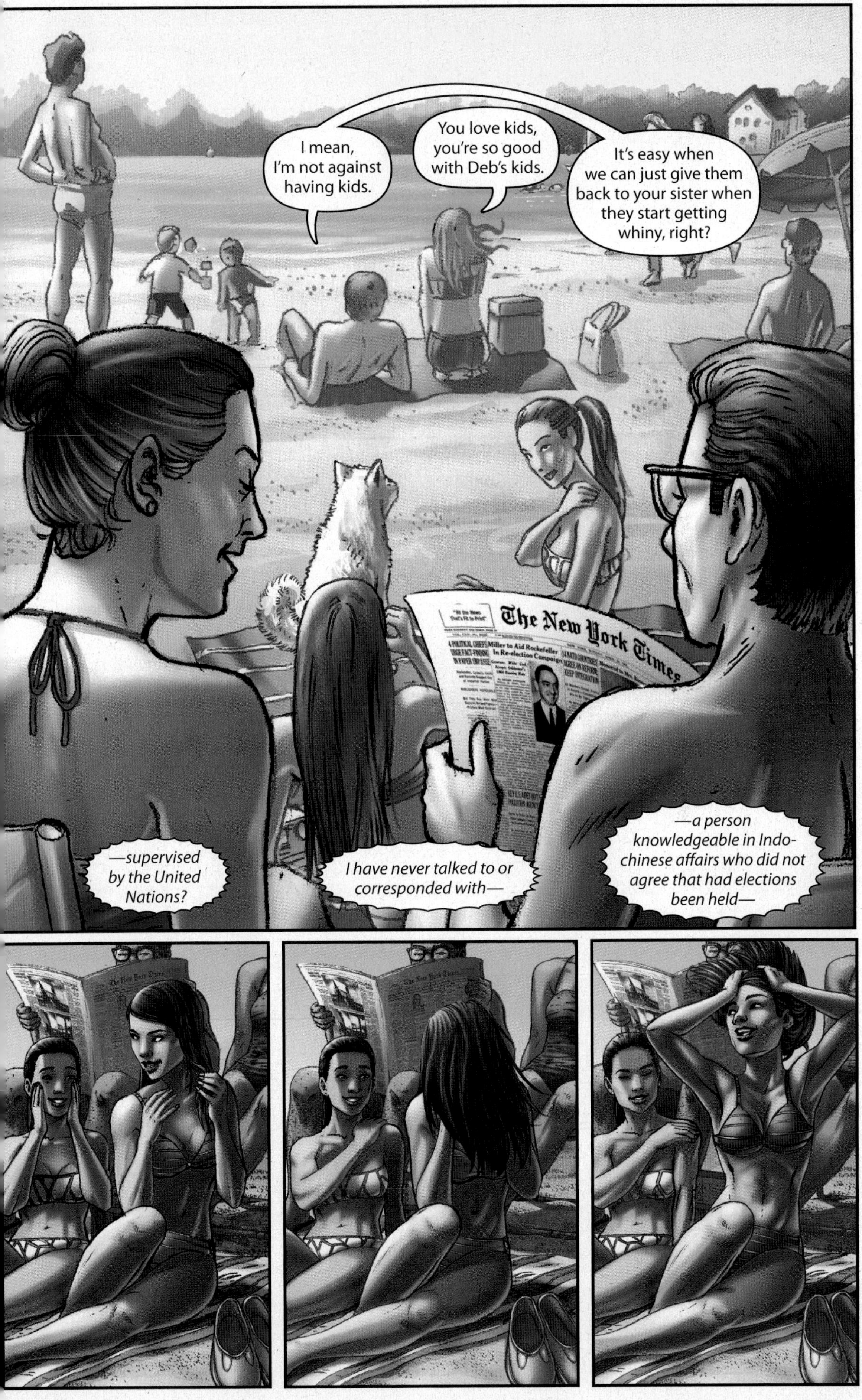
I mean, I'm not against having kids.
You love kids, you're so good with Deb's kids.
It's easy when we can just give them back to your sister when they start getting whiny, right?
The New York Times
—supervised by the United Nations?
I have never talked to or corresponded with—
—a person knowledgeable in Indo-chinese affairs who did not agree that had elections been held—

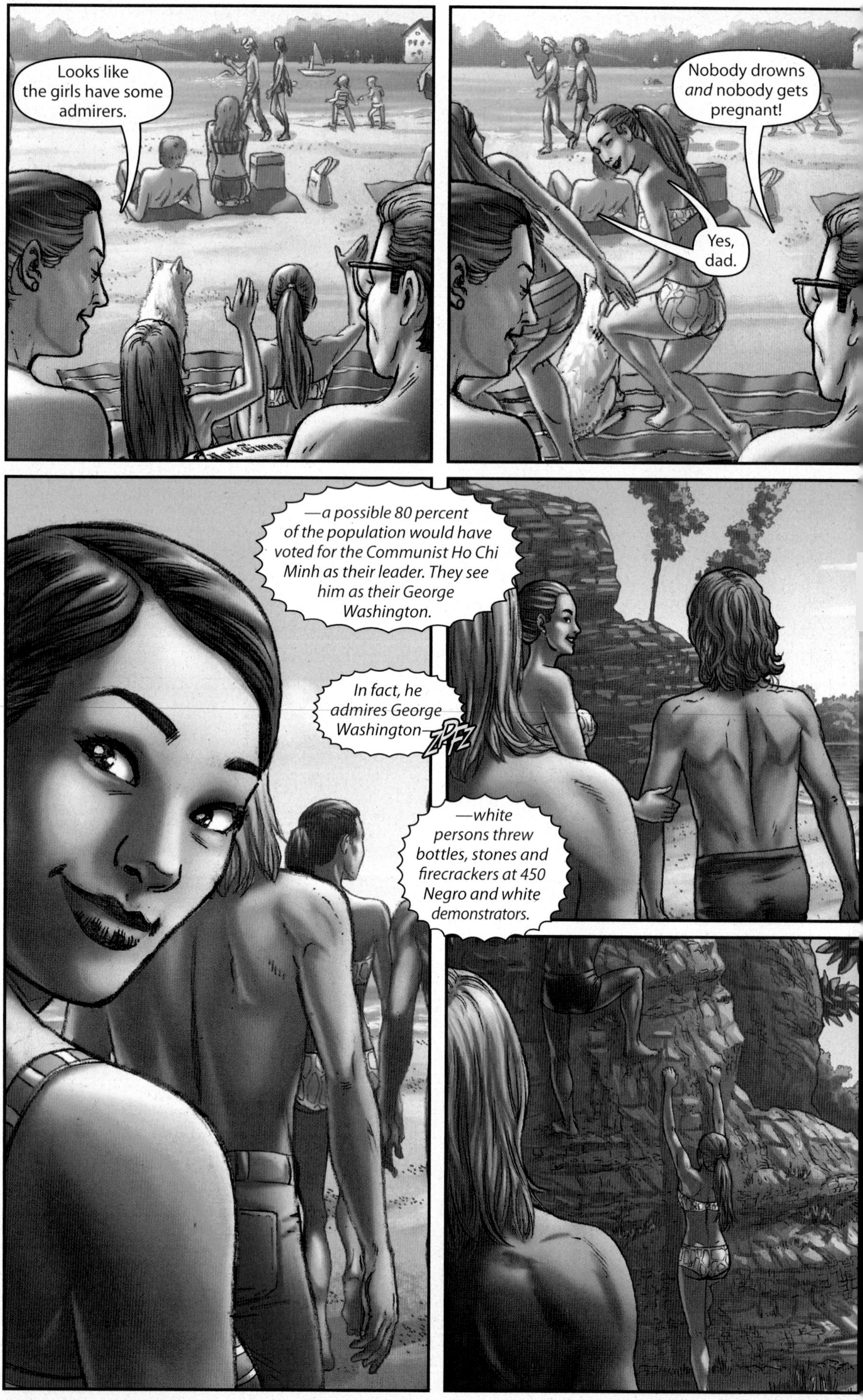
Looks like the girls have some admirers.
Nobody drowns *and* nobody gets pregnant!
Yes, dad.
—a possible 80 percent of the population would have voted for the Communist Ho Chi Minh as their leader. They see him as their George Washington.
In fact, he admires George Washington—
ZPFZ
—white persons threw bottles, stones and firecrackers at 450 Negro and white demonstrators.

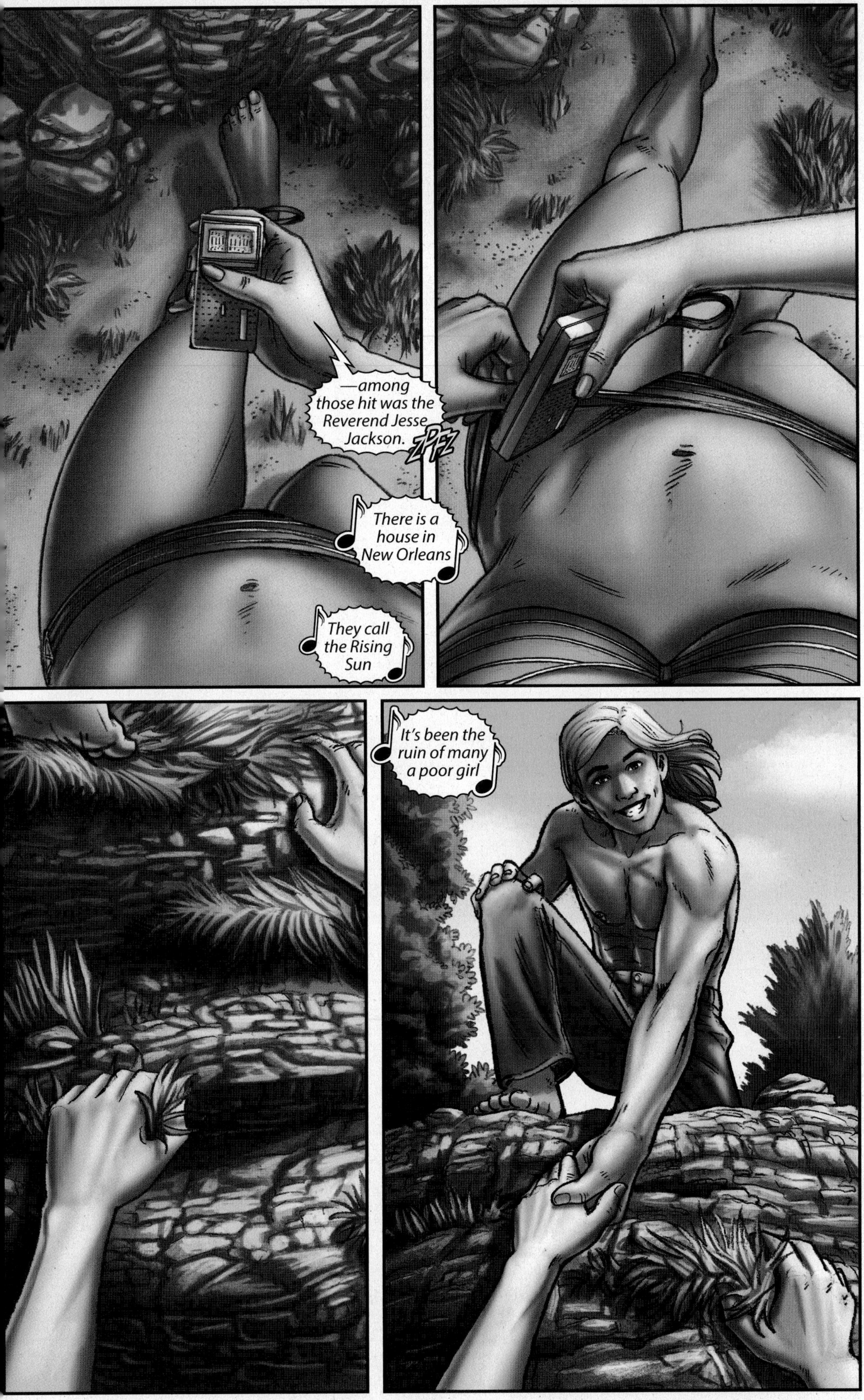
—among those hit was the Reverend Jesse Jackson.
There is a house in New Orleans
They call the Rising Sun
It's been the ruin of many a poor girl

1960s Music Festivals

Blank Archives/Contributor/Getty Images

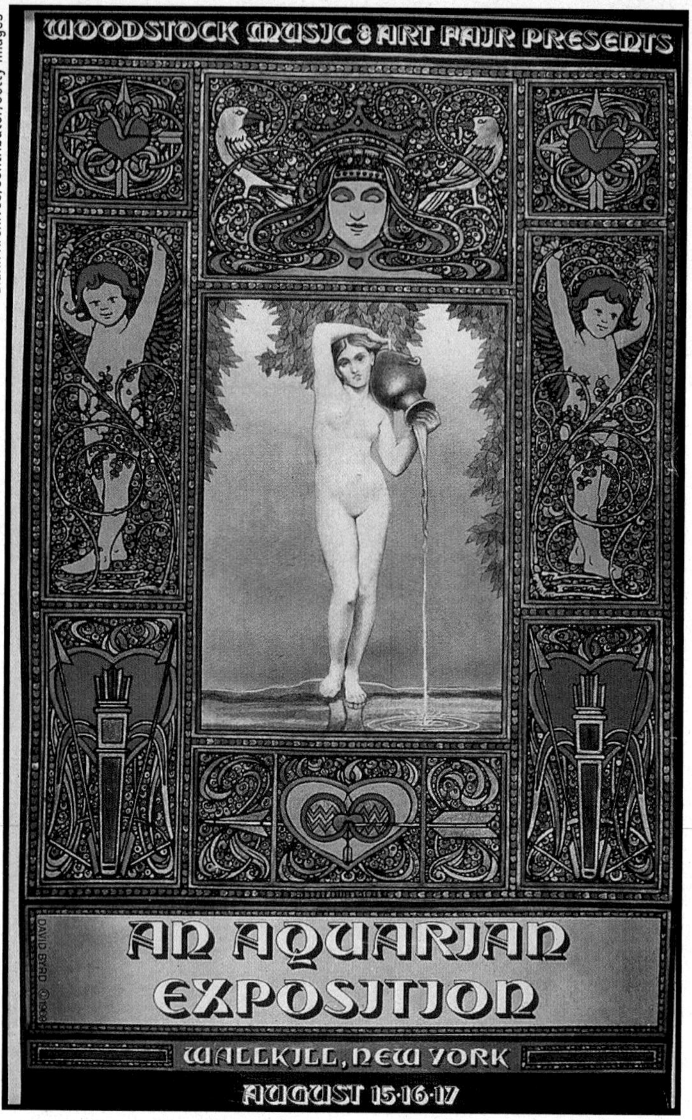
WOODSTOCK MUSIC & ART FAIR PRESENTS
AN AQUARIAN EXPOSITION
WALLKILL, NEW YORK
AUGUST 15-16-17

The original poster by David Byrd for Woodstock. Note the festival was moved from Wallkill, NY to Max Yasgur's farm in Bethel, NY.

TRIPS FESTIVAL

January 21–23, 1966
ATTENDANCE: 6,000
LOCATION: San Francisco, CA
TICKET: $2-$5
KEY ACTS: Grateful Dead, Big Brother and the Holding Company, Jefferson Airplane

MIAMI POP FESTIVAL II

December 28–30, 1968
ATTENDANCE: 100,000
LOCATION: Hallandale, FL
TICKET: $7
KEY ACTS: Chuck Berry, Marvin Gaye, Steppenwolf

MONTEREY INTERNATIONAL POP MUSIC FESTIVAL

June 16–18, 1967
ATTENDANCE: 25,000 to 90,000
LOCATION: Monterey, CA
TICKET: $3-$6.50
KEY ACTS: The Jimi Hendrix Experience, The Who, Janis Joplin

MANTRA-ROCK DANCE

January 29, 1967
ATTENDANCE: 3,000
LOCATION: San Francisco, CA
TICKET: $2.50 (proceeds went to a local Hare Krishna temple)
KEY ACTS: Grateful Dead, Swami Bhaktivedanta, Allen Ginsberg

FANTASY FAIR AND MAGIC MOUNTAIN MUSIC FESTIVAL

June 10–11, 1967
ATTENDANCE: 36,000
LOCATION: Mount Tamalpais in Marin County, CA
TICKET: $2, donated to the nearby Hunters Point Child Care Center in San Francisco.
KEY ACTS: The Doors, The Byrds, Jefferson Airplane

NEWPORT JAZZ FESTIVAL

July 3–6, 1969
ATTENDANCE: 80,000
LOCATION: Newport, RI
TICKET: $5.50-$10
KEY ACTS: Led Zeppelin, Frank Zappa, James Brown

ATLANTIC CITY POP FESTIVAL

August 1–3, 1969
ATTENDANCE: over 100,000
LOCATION: Atlantic City, NJ
TICKET: $15
KEY ACTS: Creedence Clearwater Revival, Little Richard, Santana

WOODSTOCK: AN AQUARIAN EXPOSITION

August 15–18, 1969
ATTENDANCE: 400,000
LOCATION: Max Yasgur's 600-acre dairy farm near White Lake in Bethel, NY
TICKET: Free
KEY ACTS: The Jimi Hendrix Experience, The Who, Creedence Clearwater Revival

TEXAS INTERNATIONAL POP FESTIVAL

August 30–September 1, 1969
ATTENDANCE: Estimated 120,000 to 150,000
LOCATION: Lewisville, TX
TICKET PRICE: $6-$7
KEY ACTS: BB King, Grand Funk Railroad, Janis Joplin

ALTAMONT SPEEDWAY FREE FESTIVAL

December 6, 1969
ATTENDANCE: 300,000
LOCATION: Altamont Speedway, CA
TICKET: Free
KEY ACTS: Rolling Stones, Grateful Dead, Jefferson Airplanes

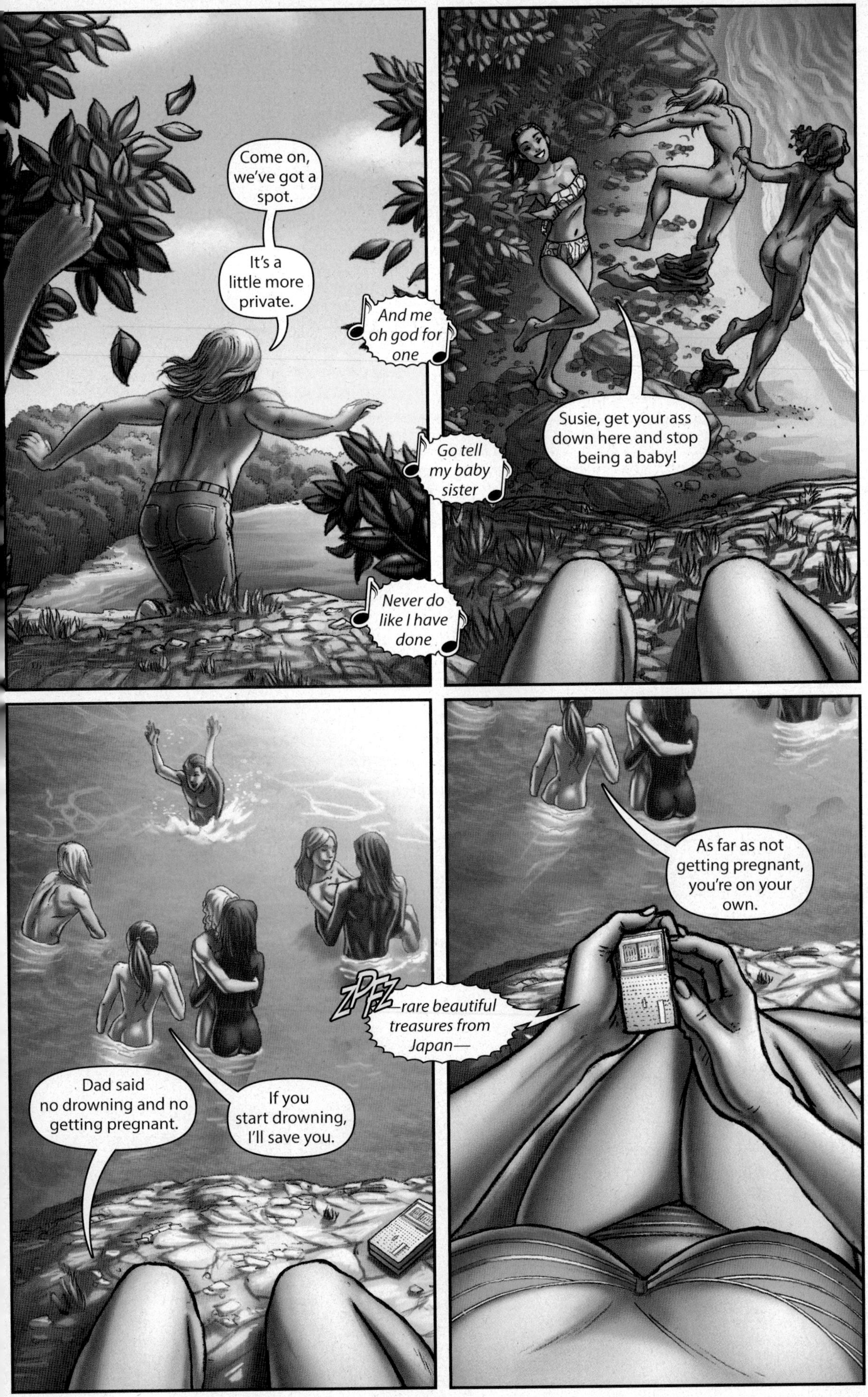
Come on, we've got a spot.
It's a little more private.
And me oh god for one
Susie, get your ass down here and stop being a baby!
Go tell my baby sister
Never do like I have done
Dad said no drowning and no getting pregnant.
If you start drowning, I'll save you.
As far as not getting pregnant, you're on your own.
ZPFZ
—rare beautiful treasures from Japan—

—from Japan are now on exhibit at the ZPZ

At the time, I was working a lot of different jobs. Going from one job to the next.

I had an internship, and then I worked as a waitress.

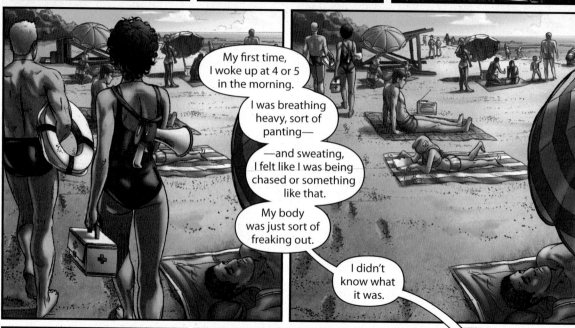

My first time, I woke up at 4 or 5 in the morning.

I was breathing heavy, sort of panting—

—and sweating, I felt like I was being chased or something like that.

My body was just sort of freaking out.

I didn't know what it was.

As I was waking up, I sort of absentmindedly, as one will do—

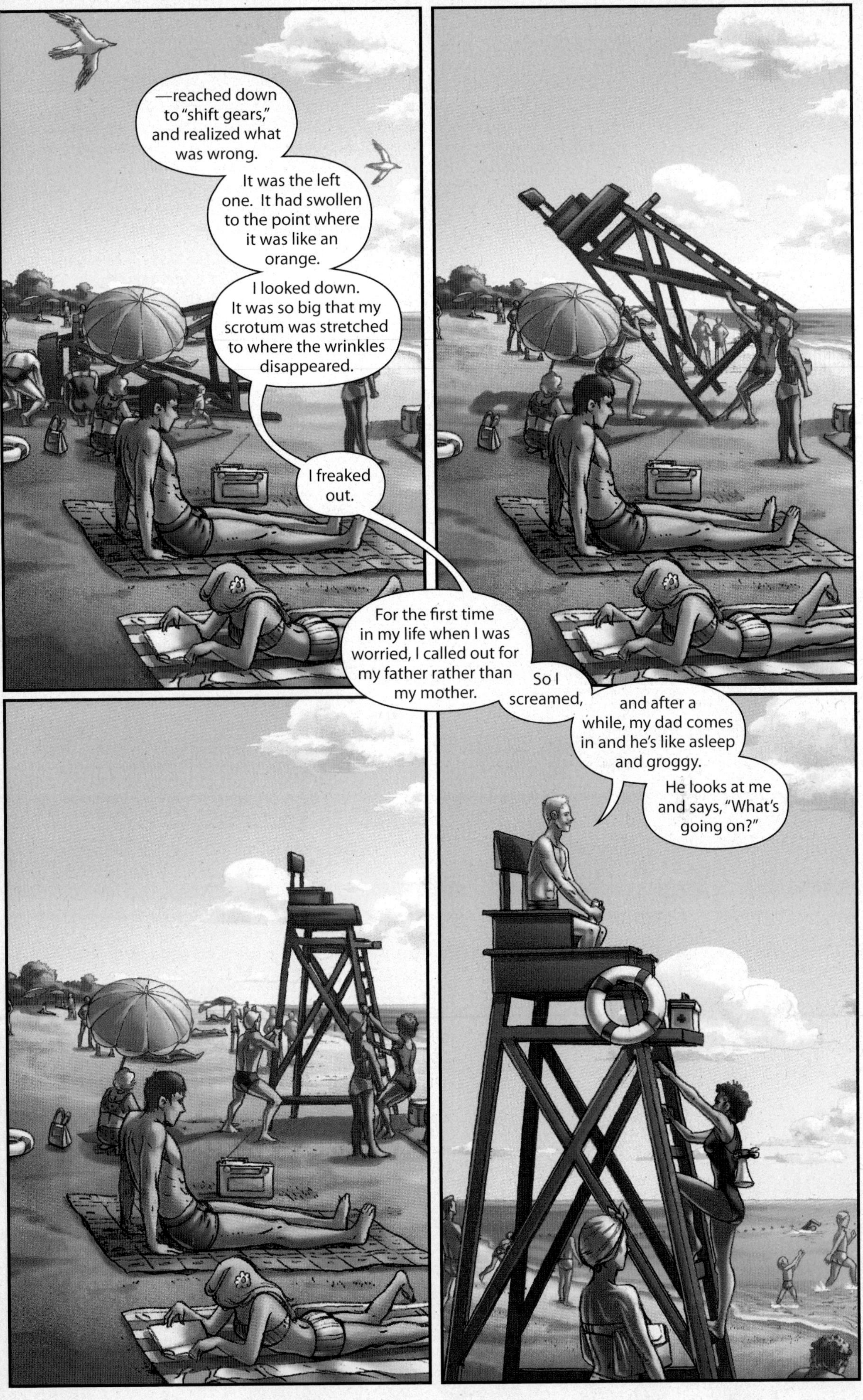
—reached down to "shift gears," and realized what was wrong.
It was the left one. It had swollen to the point where it was like an orange.
I looked down. It was so big that my scrotum was stretched to where the wrinkles disappeared.
I freaked out.
For the first time in my life when I was worried, I called out for my father rather than my mother.
So I screamed,
and after a while, my dad comes in and he's like asleep and groggy.
He looks at me and says, "What's going on?"

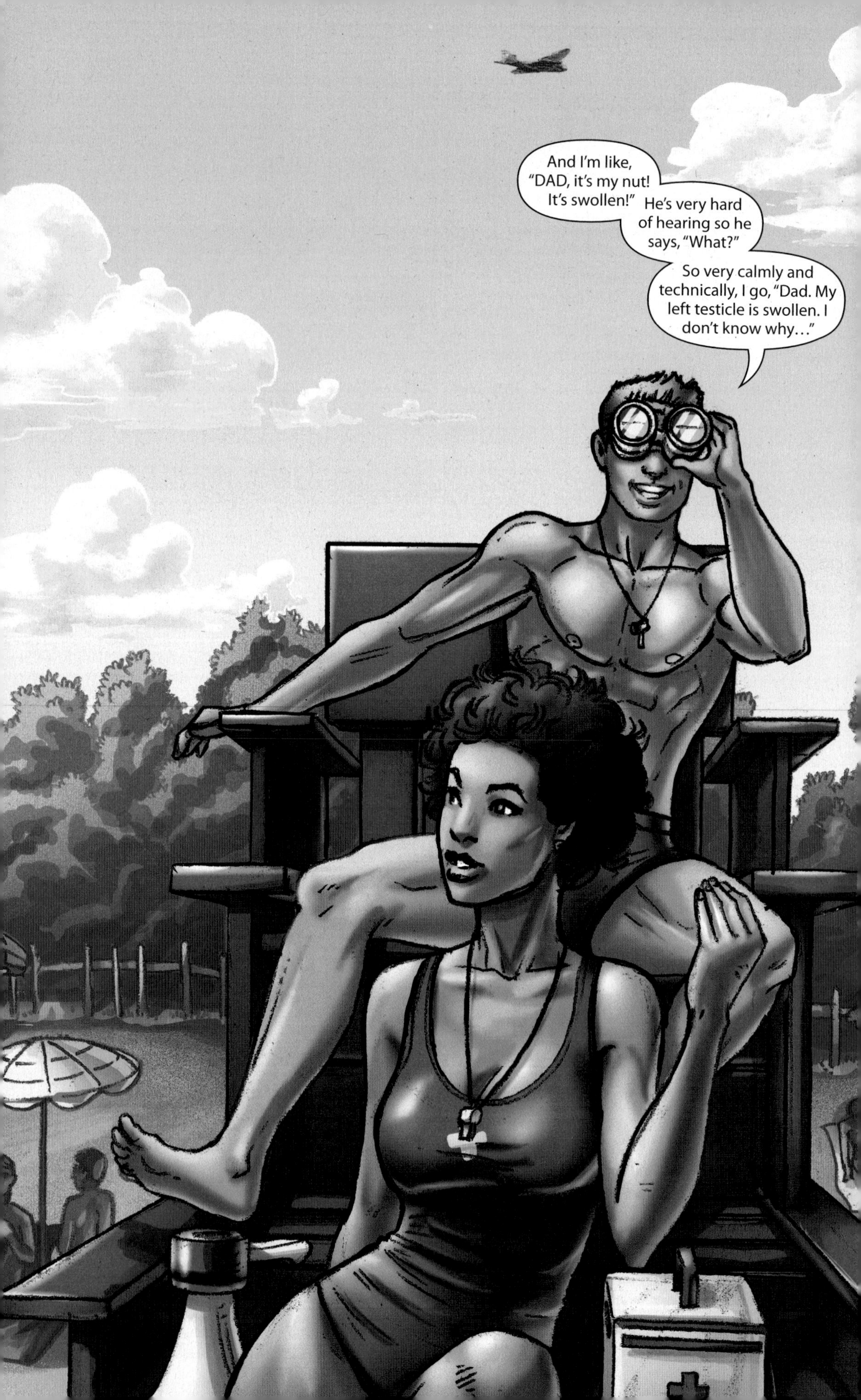
And I'm like, "DAD, it's my nut! It's swollen!"
He's very hard of hearing so he says, "What?"
So very calmly and technically, I go, "Dad. My left testicle is swollen. I don't know why…"

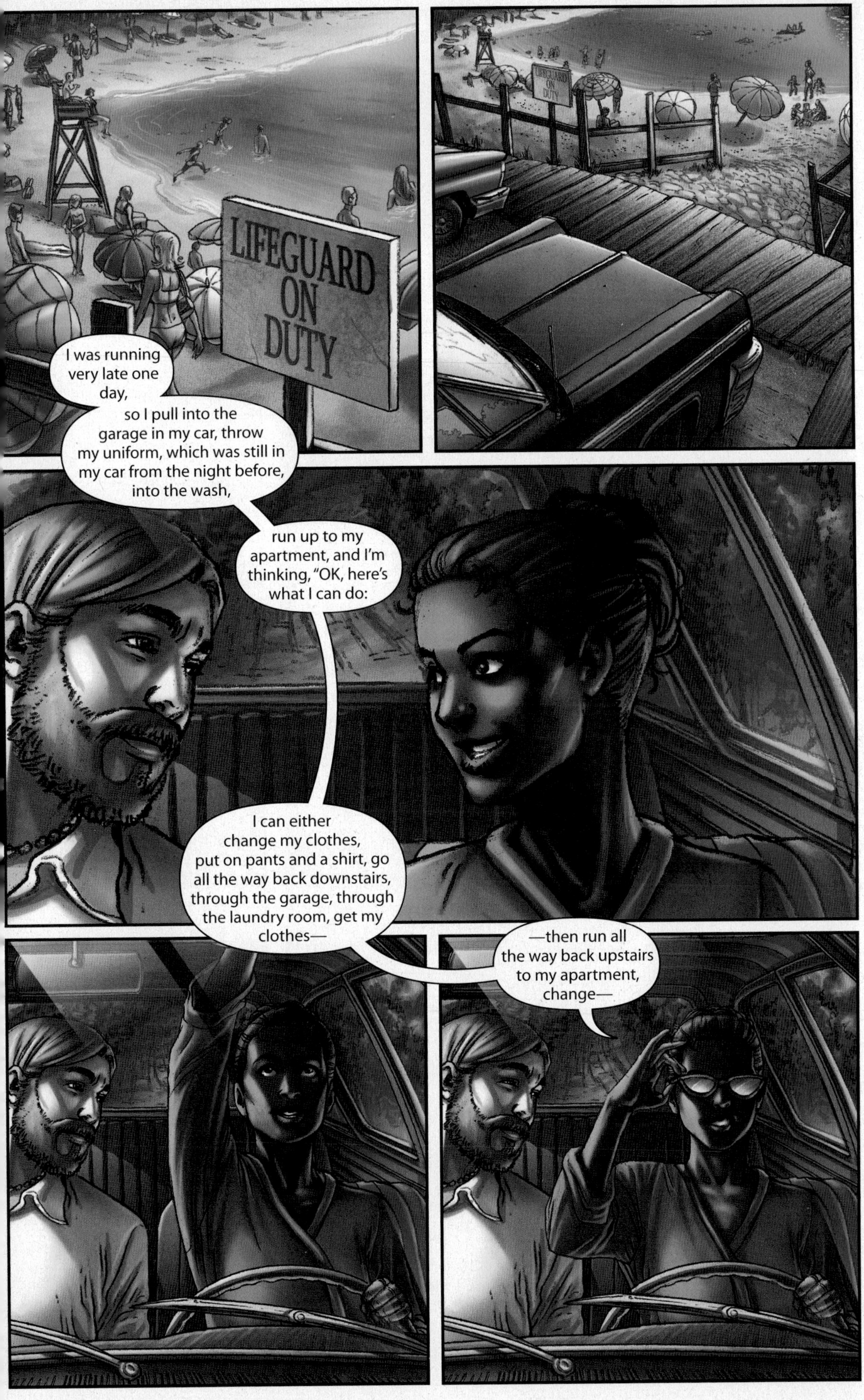
LIFEGUARD ON DUTY
LIFEGUARD ON DUTY
I was running very late one day,
so I pull into the garage in my car, throw my uniform, which was still in my car from the night before, into the wash,
run up to my apartment, and I'm thinking, "OK, here's what I can do:
I can either change my clothes, put on pants and a shirt, go all the way back downstairs, through the garage, through the laundry room, get my clothes—
—then run all the way back upstairs to my apartment, change—

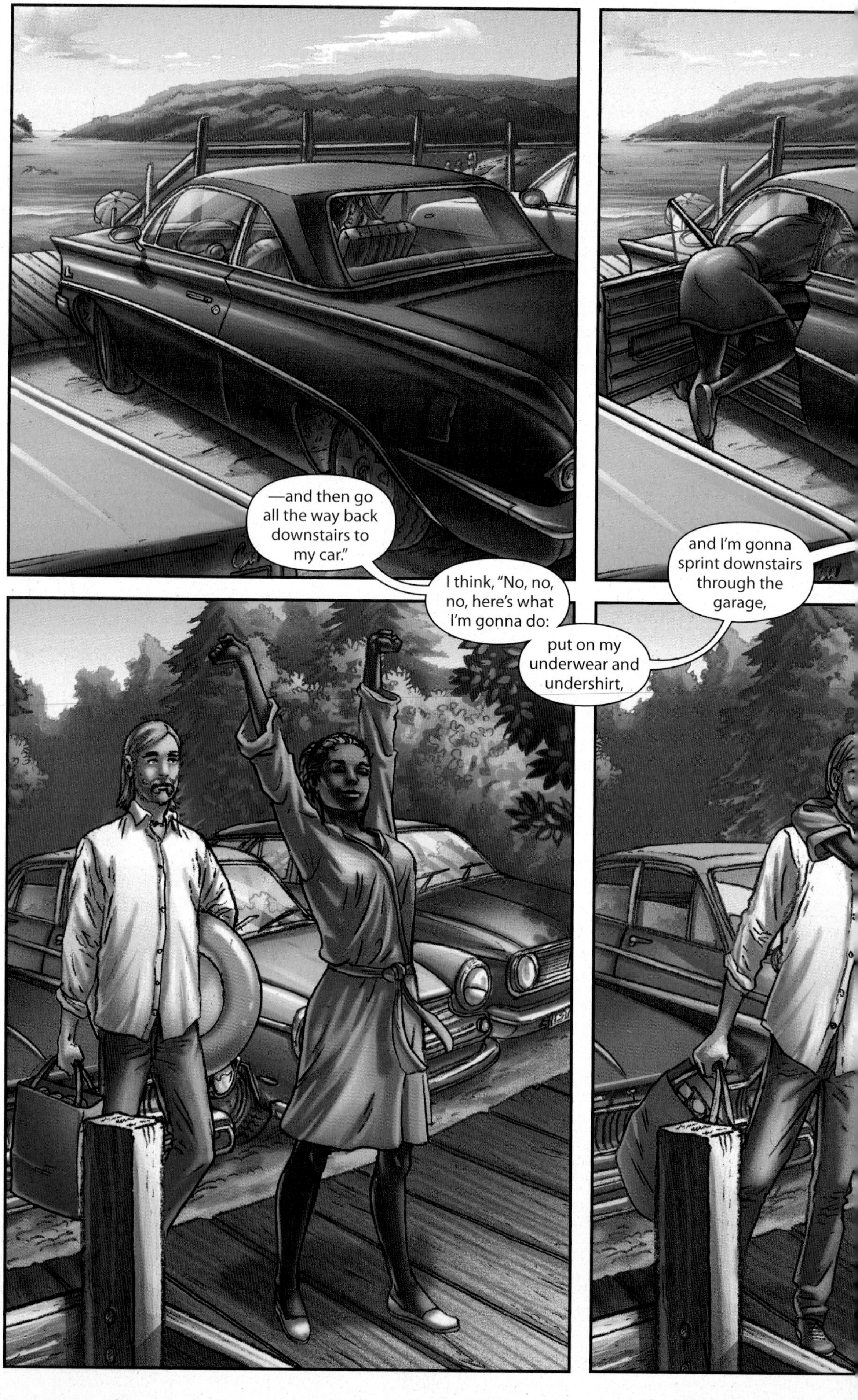
—and then go all the way back downstairs to my car."
I think, "No, no, no, here's what I'm gonna do:
put on my underwear and undershirt,
and I'm gonna sprint downstairs through the garage,

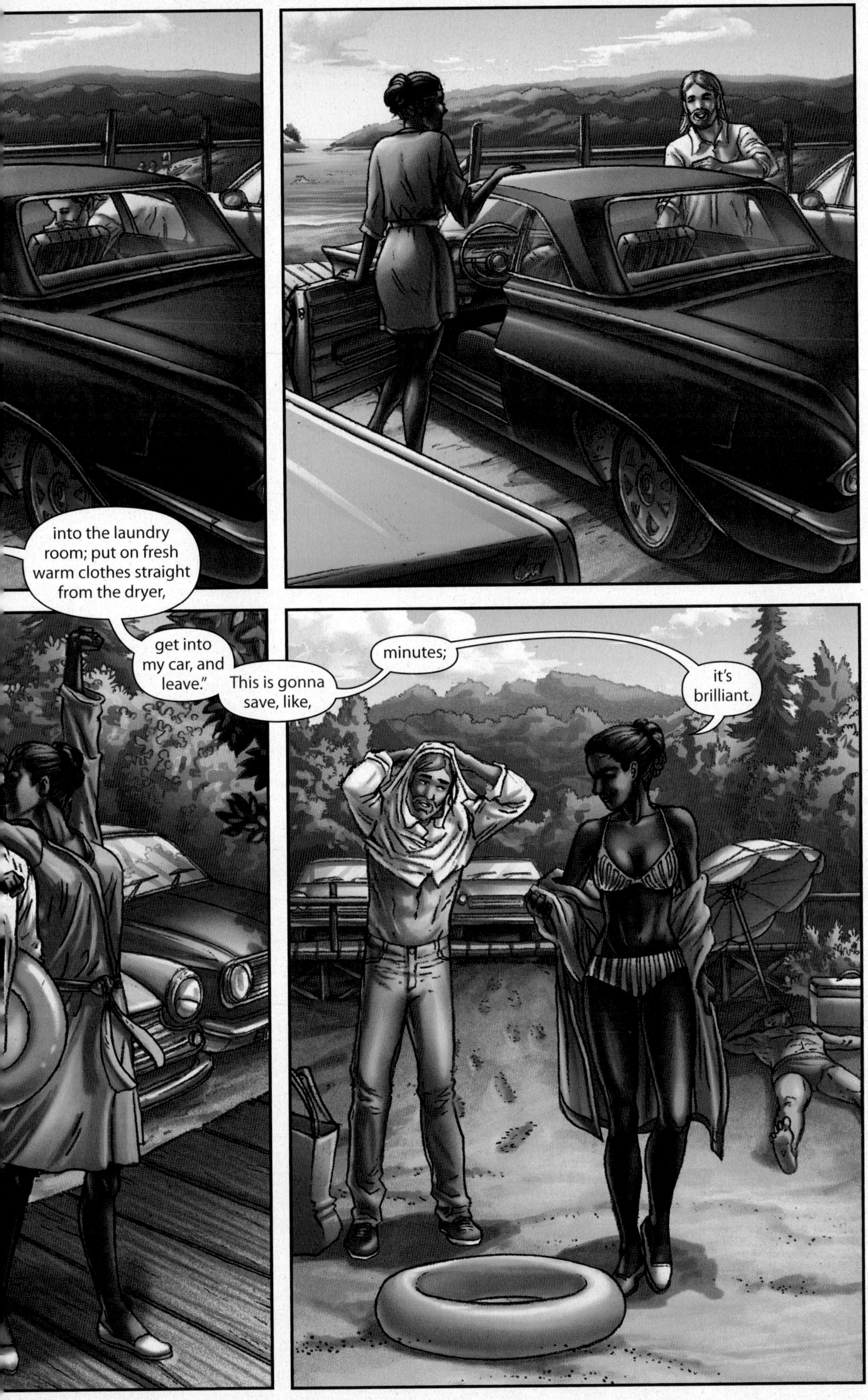
into the laundry room; put on fresh warm clothes straight from the dryer,
get into my car, and leave."
This is gonna save, like,
minutes;
it's brilliant.

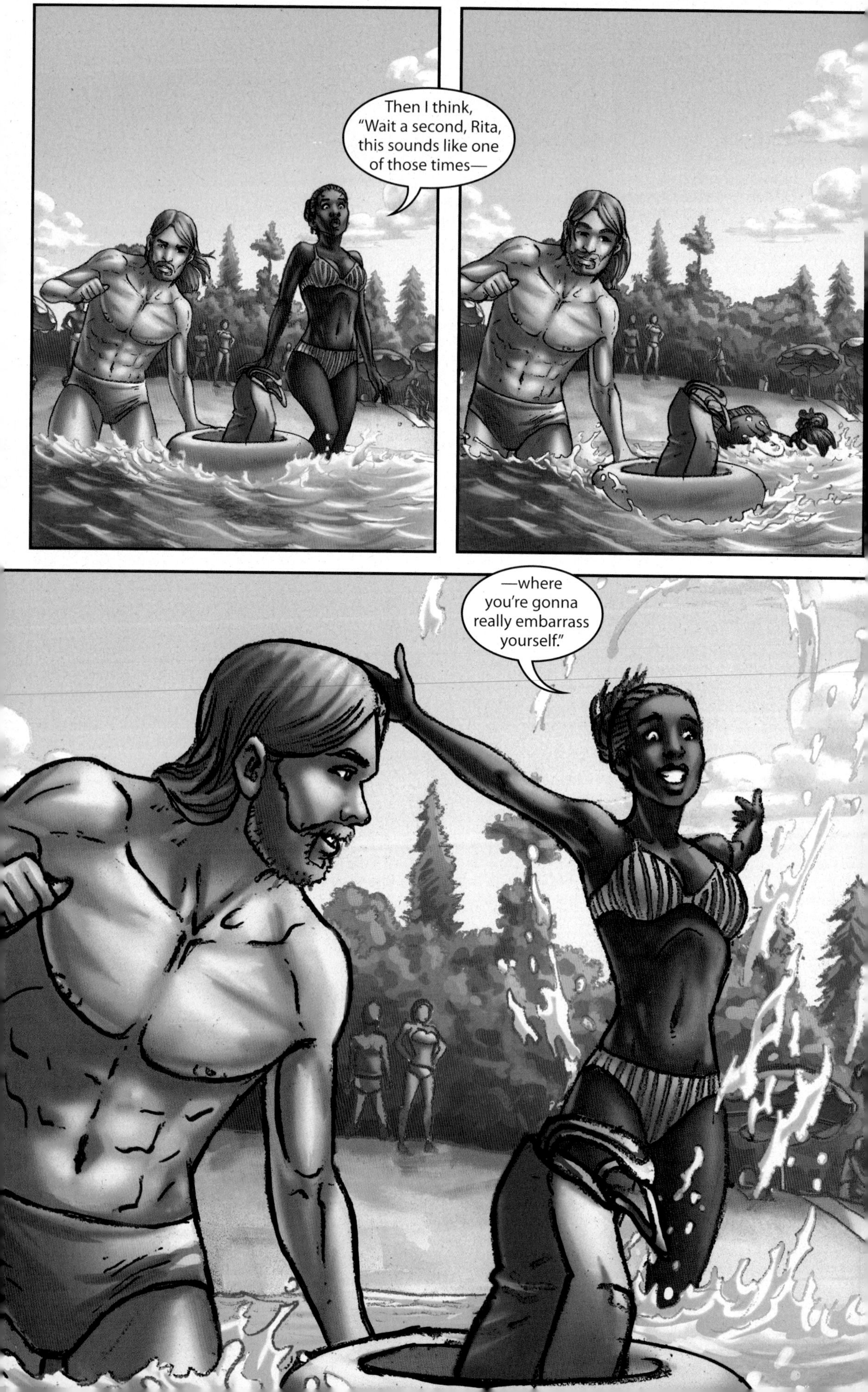
Then I think, "Wait a second, Rita, this sounds like one of those times—
—where you're gonna really embarrass yourself."

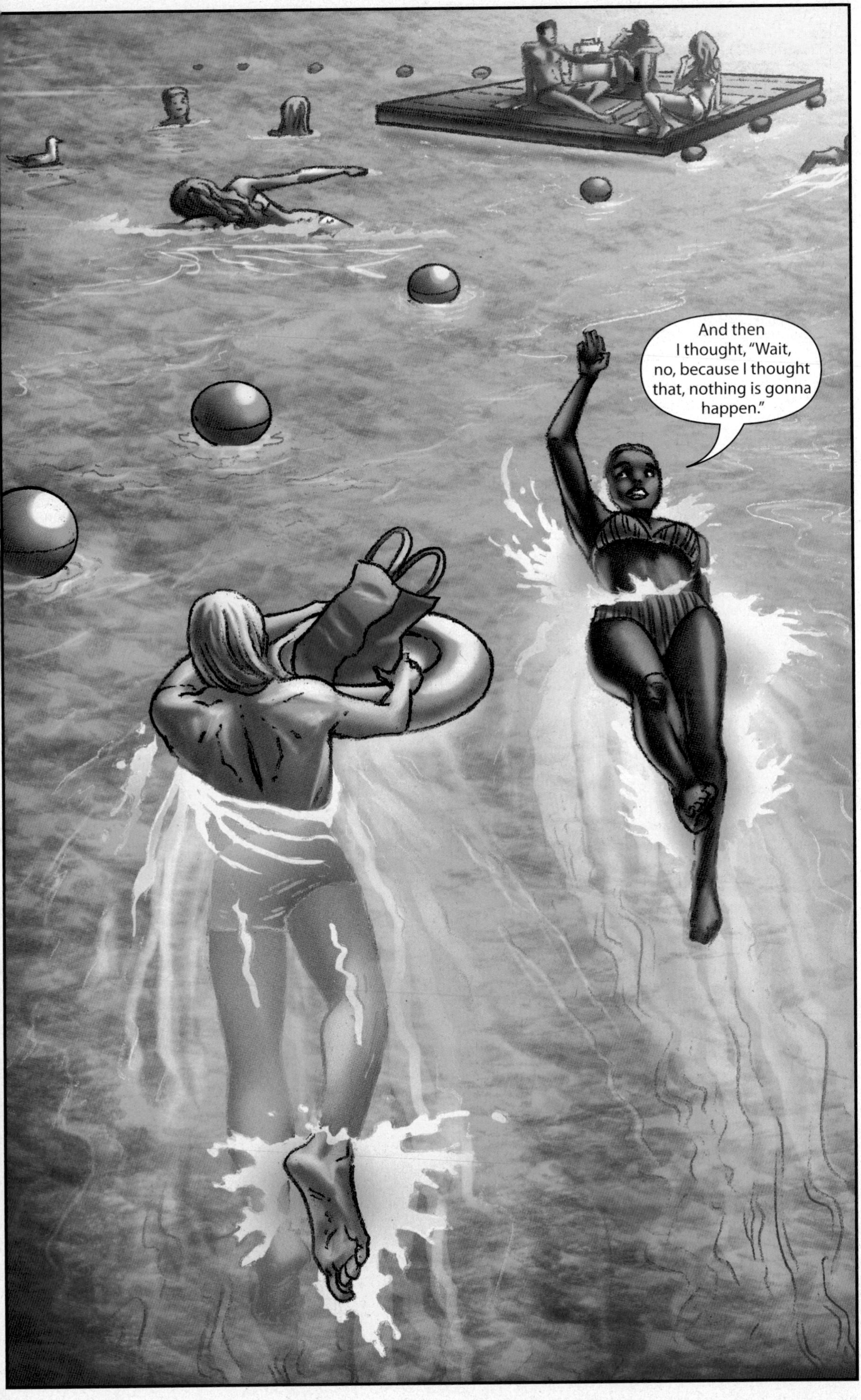
And then I thought, "Wait, no, because I thought that, nothing is gonna happen."

DOUBLE TAKE RECORD HOUSE

SUMMER SELECTION

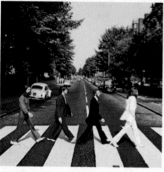

Finally you'll be able to understand all those album cover parodies!

STEREO
BEACH BOYS CONCERT

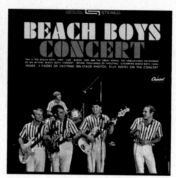

Sunburn for the soul!

JOHNNY CASH AT SAN QUENTIN

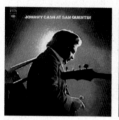

Perfectly captures the feeling of being in prison!

STEREO
RAY CHARLES
MODERN SOUNDS IN COUNTRY AND WESTERN MUSIC

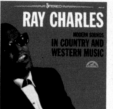

Maybe it will remind you how much you like Jamie Foxx!

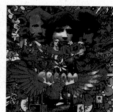

Consider it an Eric Clapton prequel!

BOBBIE GENTRY
ODE TO BILLIE JOE

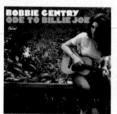

Really close to being 'Billy Joel!'

THE GRADUATE
PAUL SIMON
SIMON & GARFUNKEL

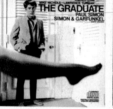

Why bother seeing the movie? Use this musical Cliff Notes!

MY SON, THE NUT
allan SHERMAN

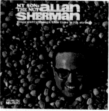

Like Weird Al without the fun!

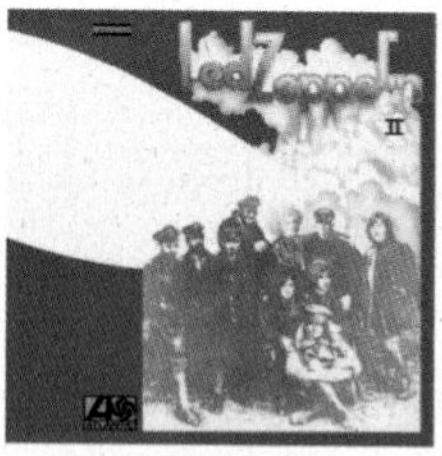

In case your local classic rock station isn't already playing Zeppelin twice an hour!

MORE OF THE

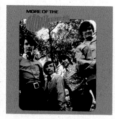

12 tracks, 19 credited songwriters – Now that's value!

the doors

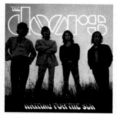

Even the worst poets can find success in this world!

ANY 3 RECORDS FOR ONLY $5.95

A LIFETIME PURCHASE! You may have any three of the best-selling records shown here—for ONLY $5.95! That's the fantastic bargain the Double Take Record House is offering new members who join and commit to purchasing as few as four additional records from our Buying Guide in the next year.

FREE SUBSCRIPTION TO THE RECORD BUYING GUIDE! You'll have no problem selecting four more records with our quarterly Buying Guide, which you'll get for free. With all the movie and musical soundtracks your heart desires, you'll only struggle with your choices!

YOUR OWN CHARGE ACCOUNT! Upon enrollment, the Double Take Record House will open a charge account in your name (or your husband's name, ladies). You pay for your records only after you've received them. They will be mailed and billed to you at the regular service price of $66.95.*

YOU GET FREE RECORDS! Once you've signed on, you'll groove on with a FREE record of your choice for every two records purchased! That's a 33 1/3% discount for your lifetime and post-mortem membership!

Please note under no circumstances will Double Take Record House send you any records.

SEND NO MONEY NOW!

Just fill in and mail the coupon to:

DOUBLE TAKE RECORD HOUSE
38 W. 39th Street, 2nd Floor
New York, New York 10018

Please enroll me as a member of the Double Take Record House. I've indicated here the 3 records I wish to receive for $5.95, plus postage and handling, etc. I agree to purchase four more selections in the next 12 months at the regular service price of $66.95,* and I may try to cancel my membership any time thereafter.** If I continue, I am to receive a FREE record of my choice for every two additional records purchased.

SELECT THREE RECORDS ☐ ☐ ☐

NAME ______________________

Please do not actually

ADDRESS ______________________

fill this out and send it in.

CITY __________ POSTAL ZONE No. __________ STATE __________

*Additional charges include a penalizing upcharge for buying British albums, plus postage, handling, and other charges Double Take Record House will tack on your charge account. **Good luck. Even death won't cancel your membership.

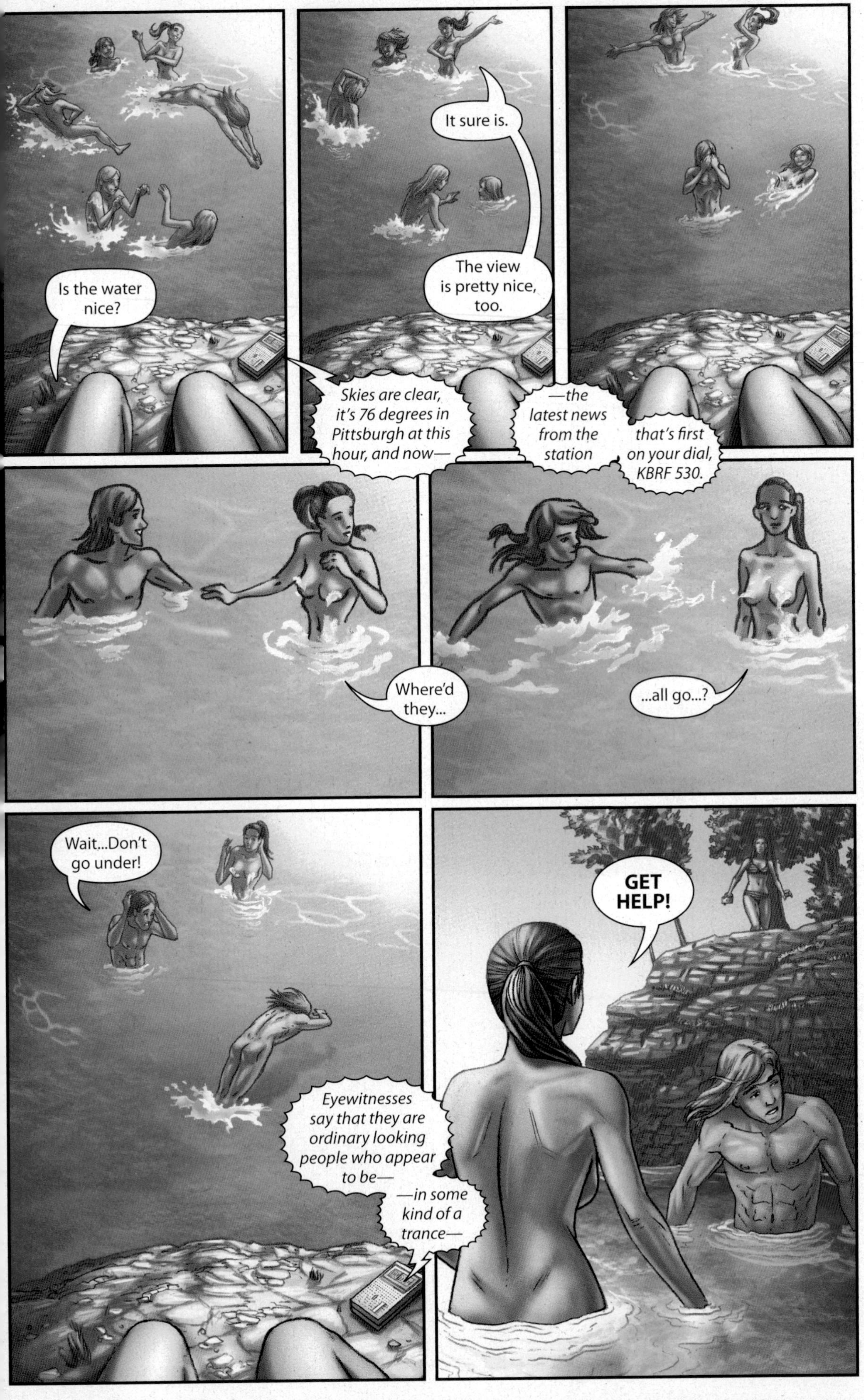
Is the water nice?
It sure is.
The view is pretty nice, too.
Skies are clear, it's 76 degrees in Pittsburgh at this hour, and now—
—the latest news from the station
that's first on your dial, KBRF 530.
Where'd they...
...all go...?
Wait...Don't go under!
Eyewitnesses say that they are ordinary looking people who appear to be—
—in some kind of a trance—
GET HELP!

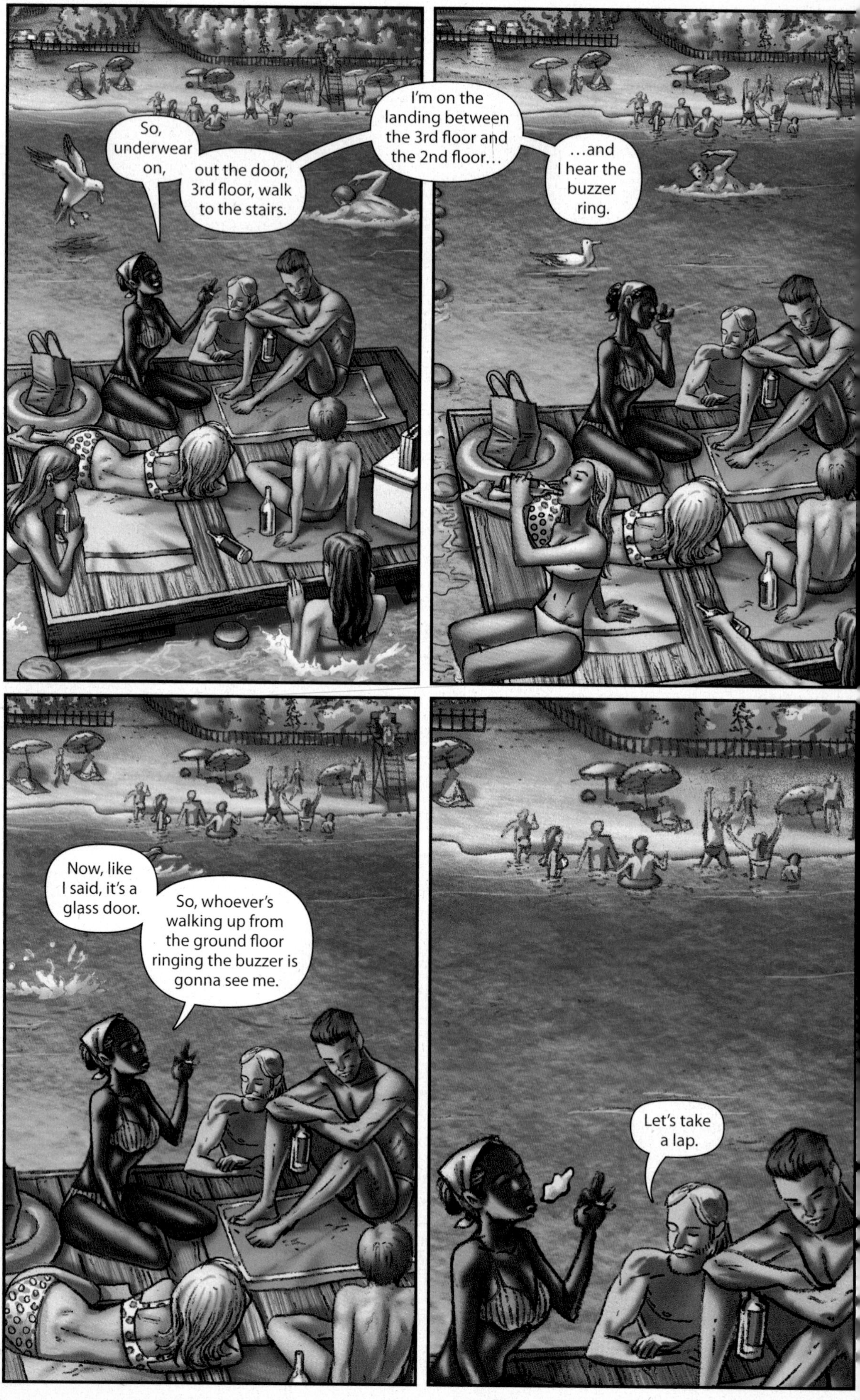
So, underwear on,
out the door, 3rd floor, walk to the stairs.
I'm on the landing between the 3rd floor and the 2nd floor…
…and I hear the buzzer ring.
Now, like I said, it's a glass door.
So, whoever's walking up from the ground floor ringing the buzzer is gonna see me.
Let's take a lap.

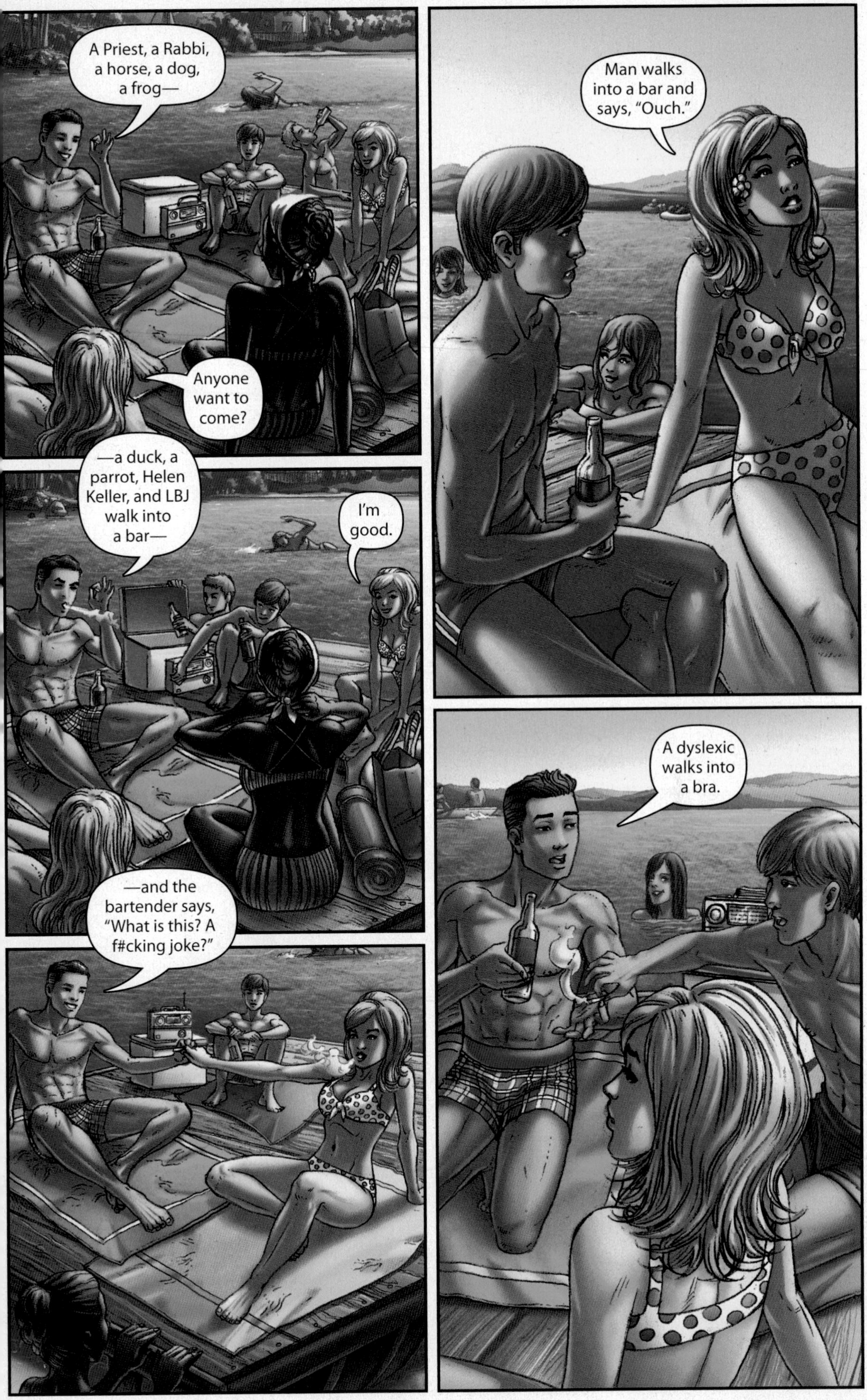
A Priest, a Rabbi, a horse, a dog, a frog—
Anyone want to come?
—a duck, a parrot, Helen Keller, and LBJ walk into a bar—
I'm good.
—and the bartender says, "What is this? A f#cking joke?"
Man walks into a bar and says, "Ouch."
A dyslexic walks into a bra.

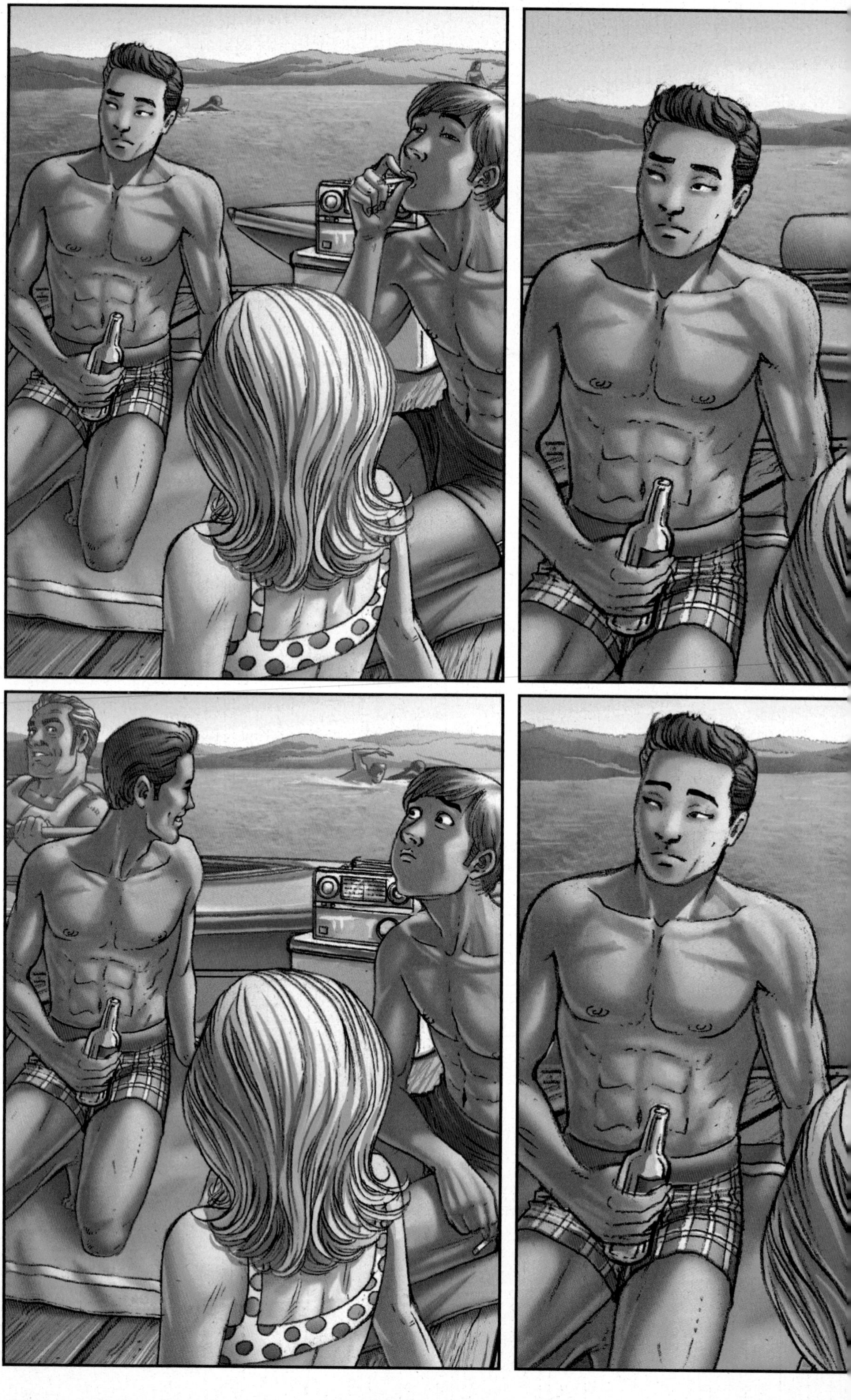

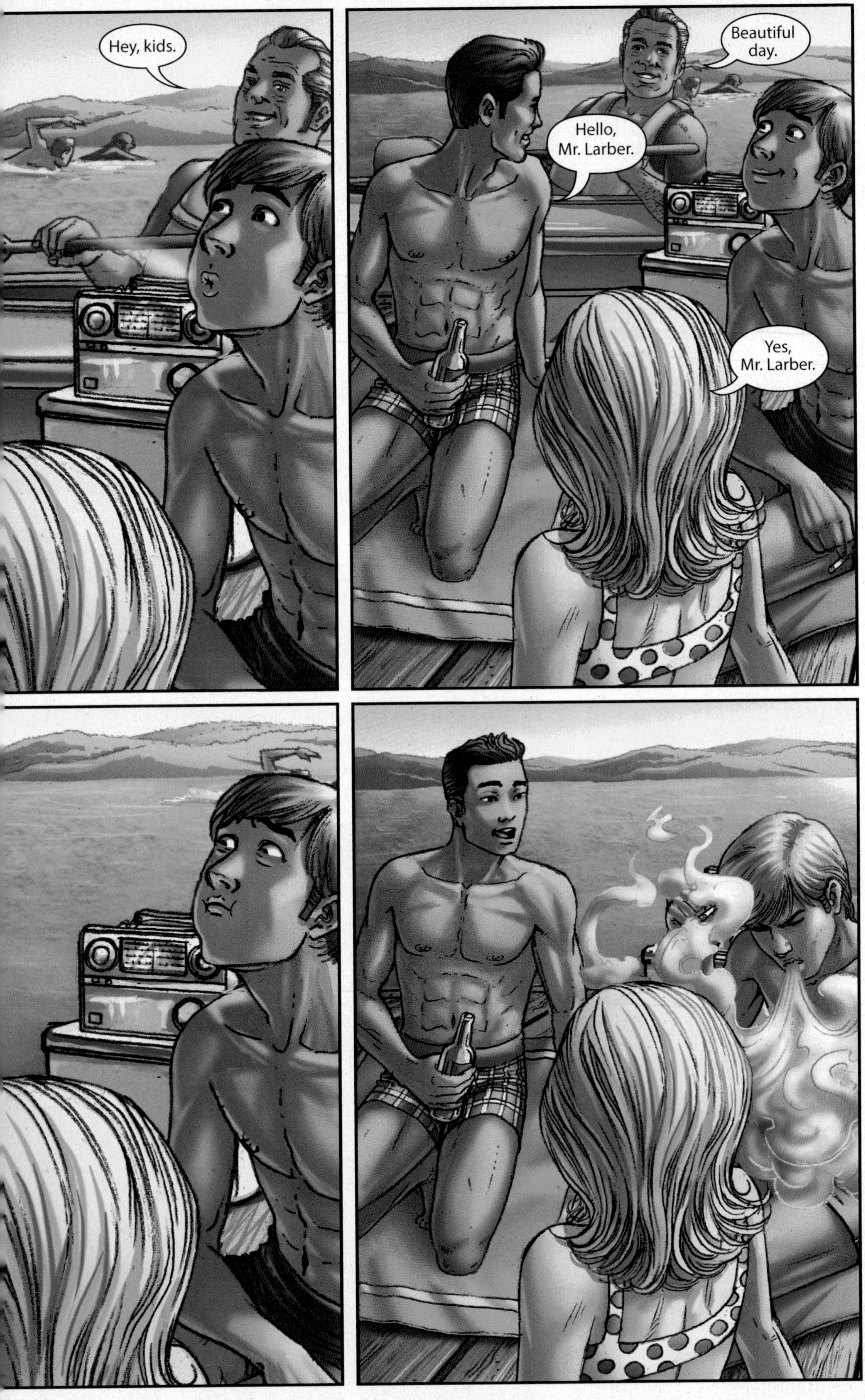
Hey, kids.
Beautiful day.
Hello, Mr. Larber.
Yes, Mr. Larber.

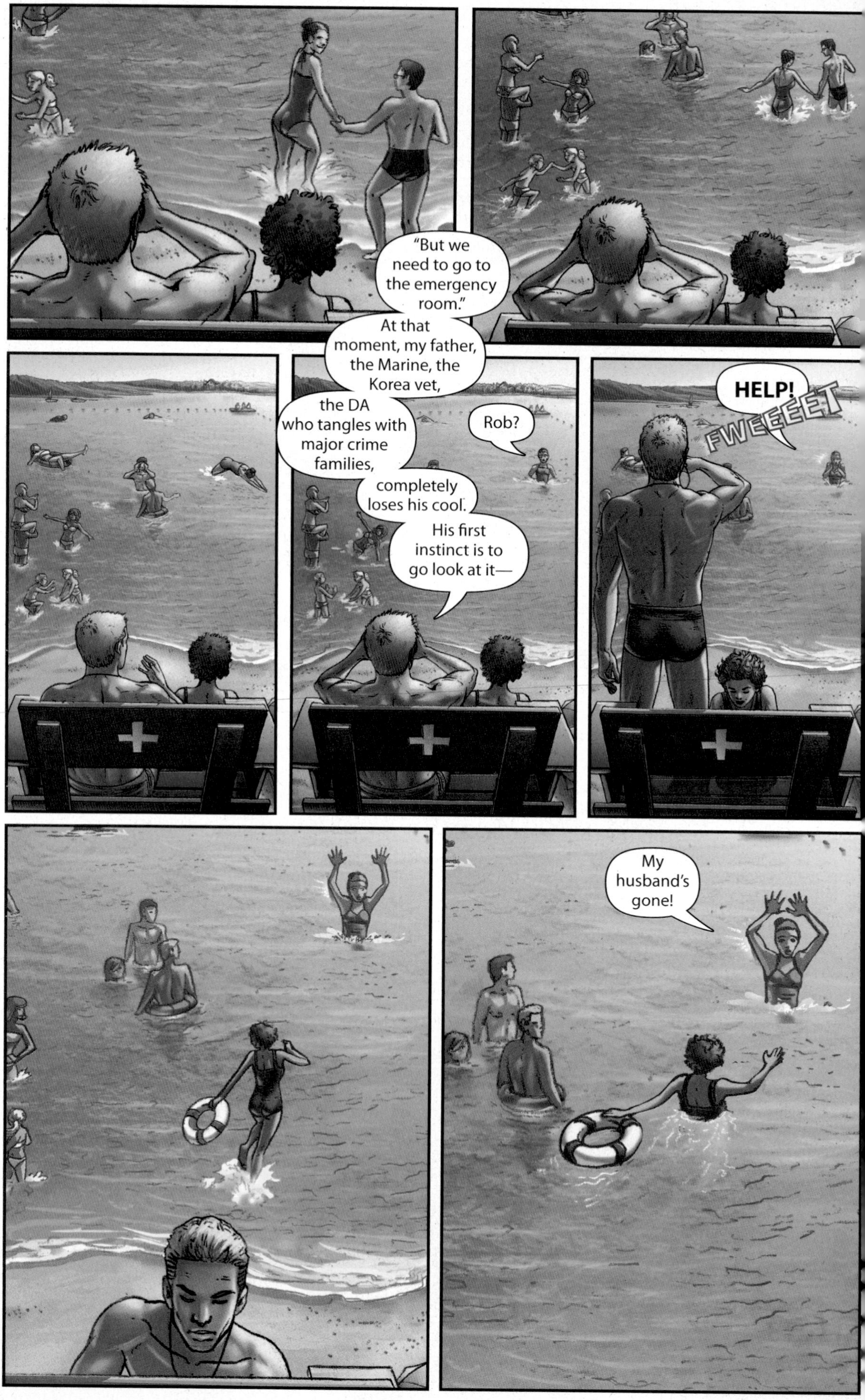
"But we need to go to the emergency room."
At that moment, my father, the Marine, the Korea vet,
the DA who tangles with major crime families,
completely loses his cool.
His first instinct is to go look at it—
Rob?
HELP!
FWEEEET
My husband's gone!

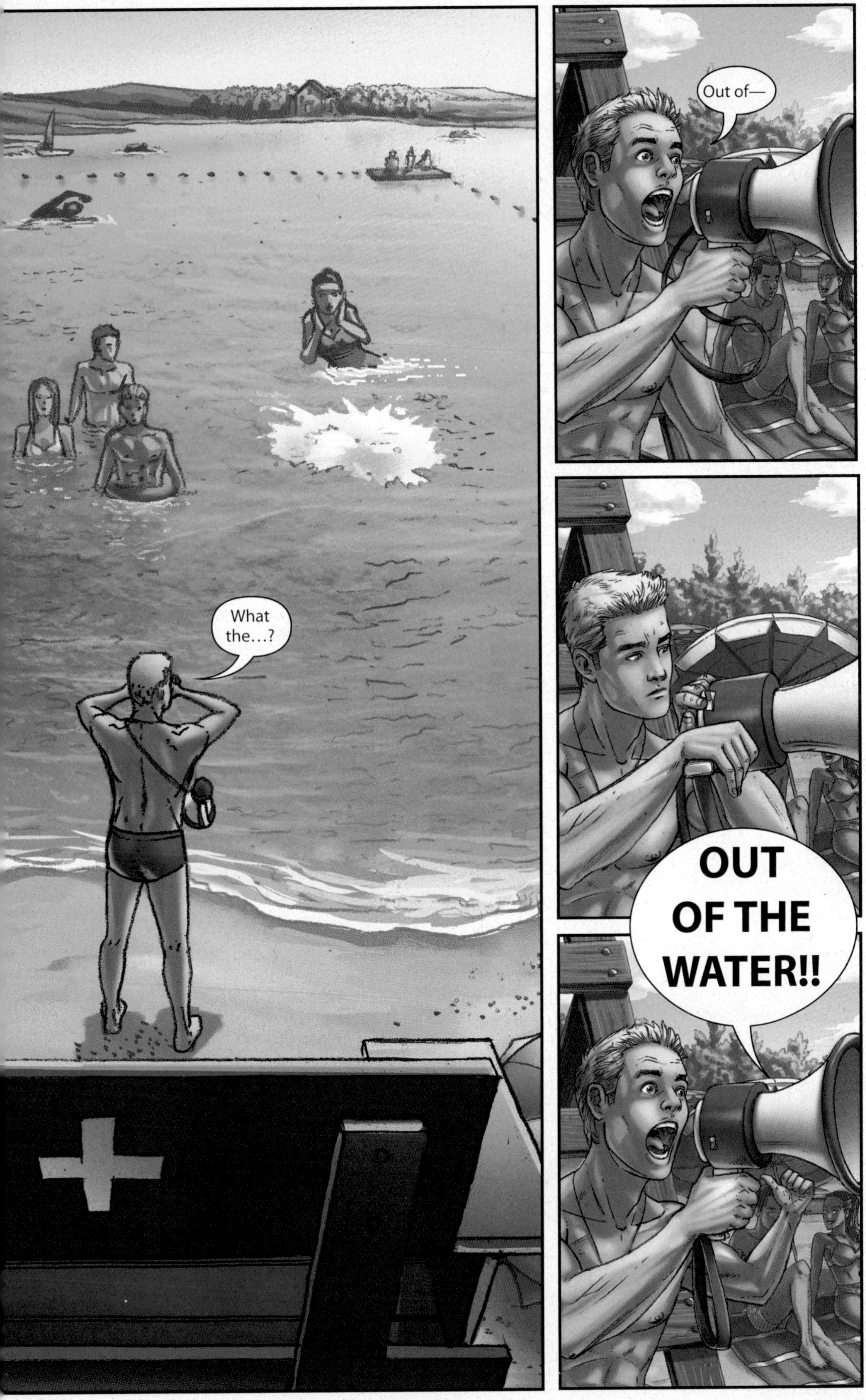
What the…?
Out of—
OUT OF THE WATER!!

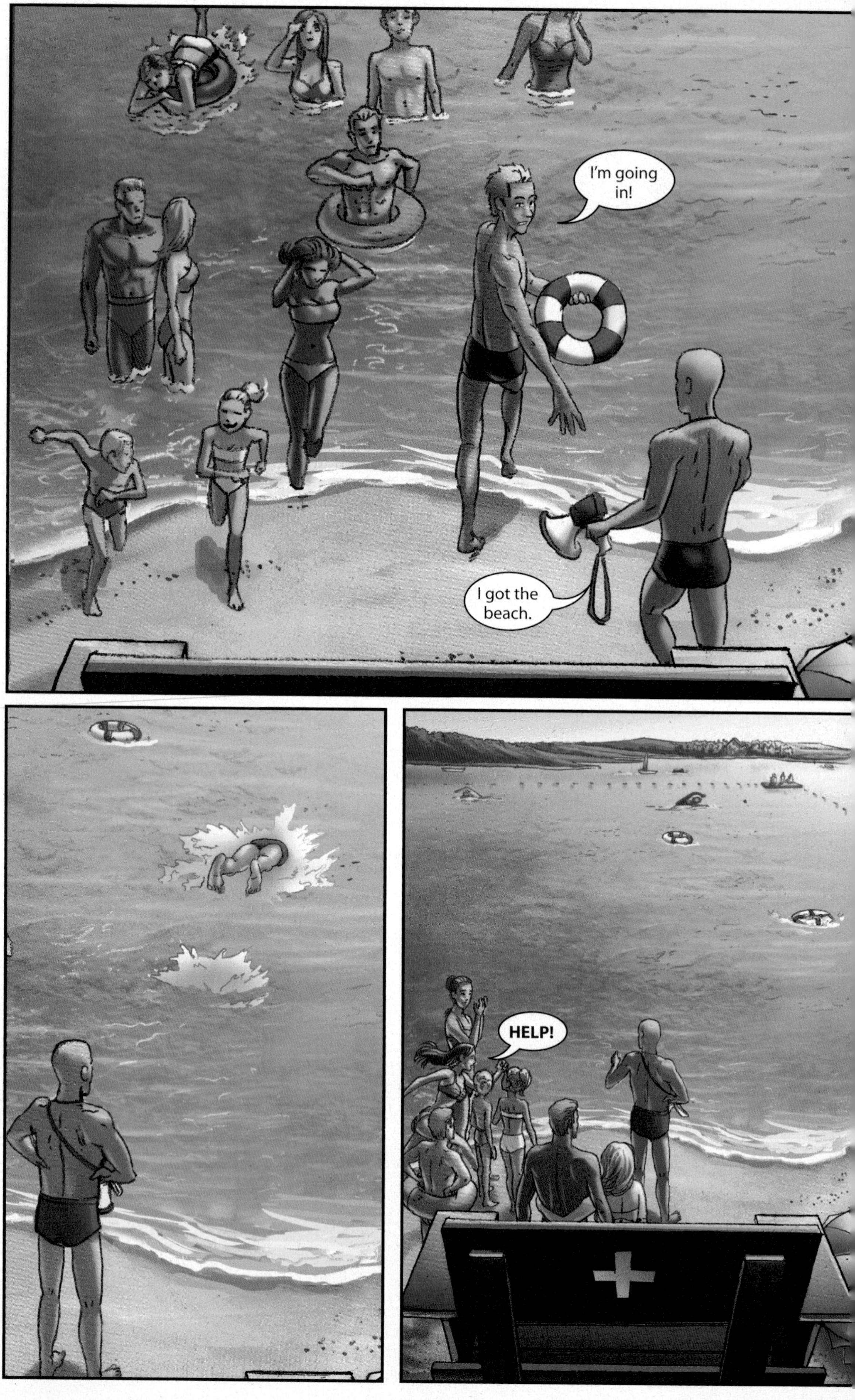
I'm going in!
I got the beach.
HELP!

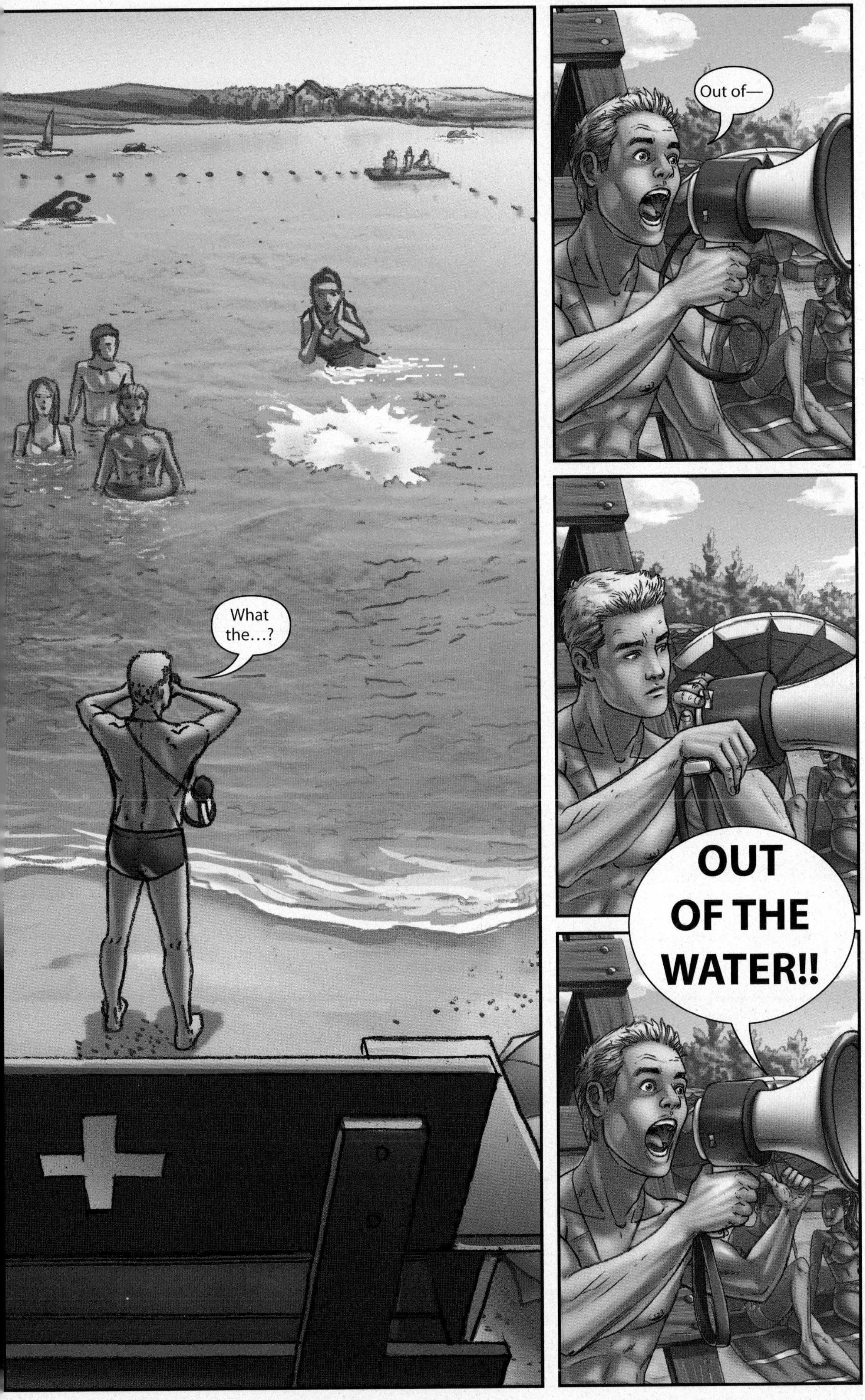
What the…?
Out of—
OUT OF THE WATER!!

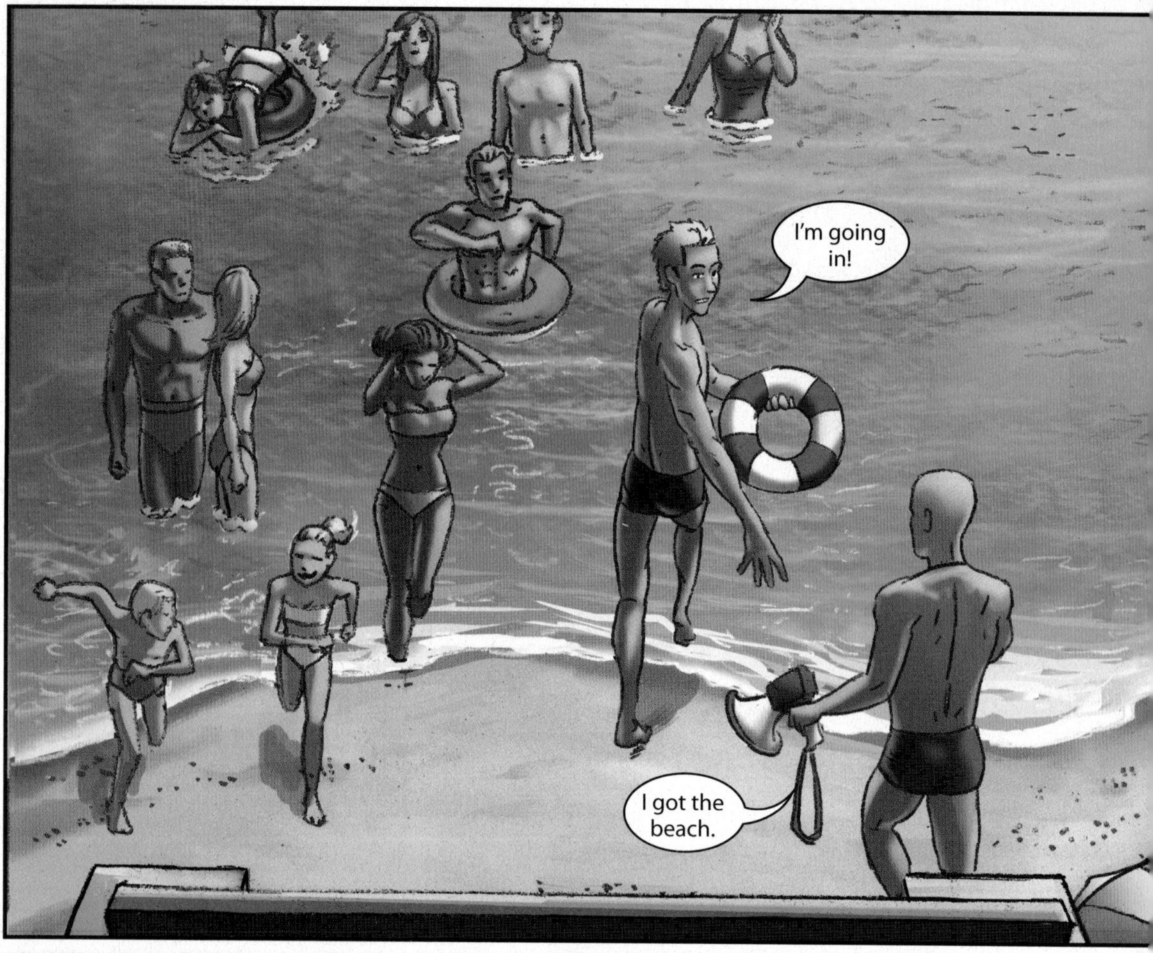
I'm going in!
I got the beach.

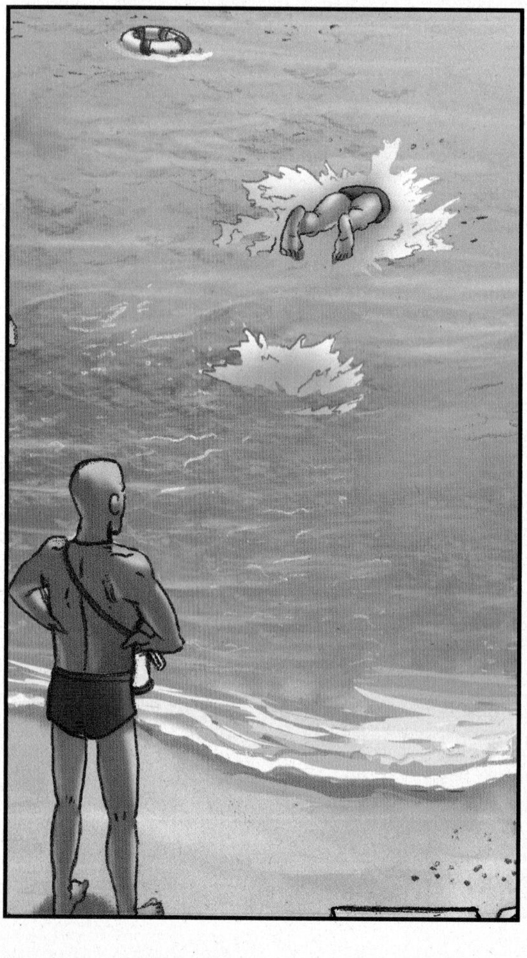

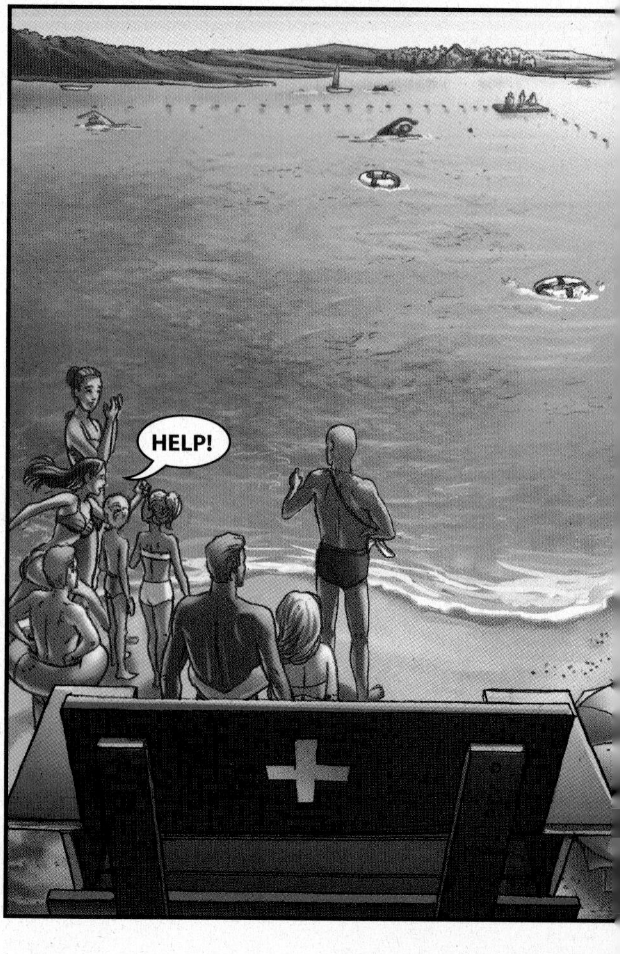
HELP!

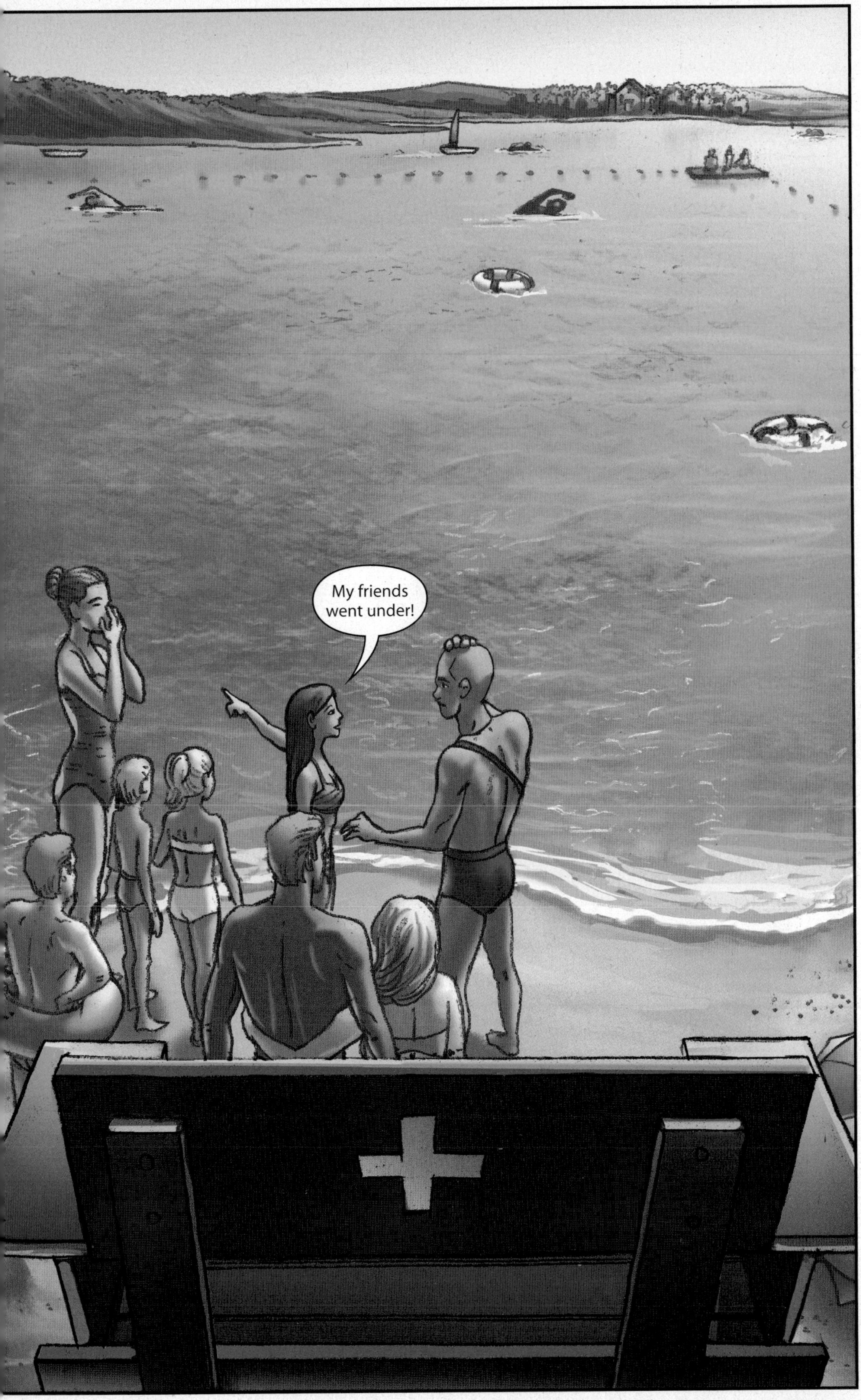
My friends went under!

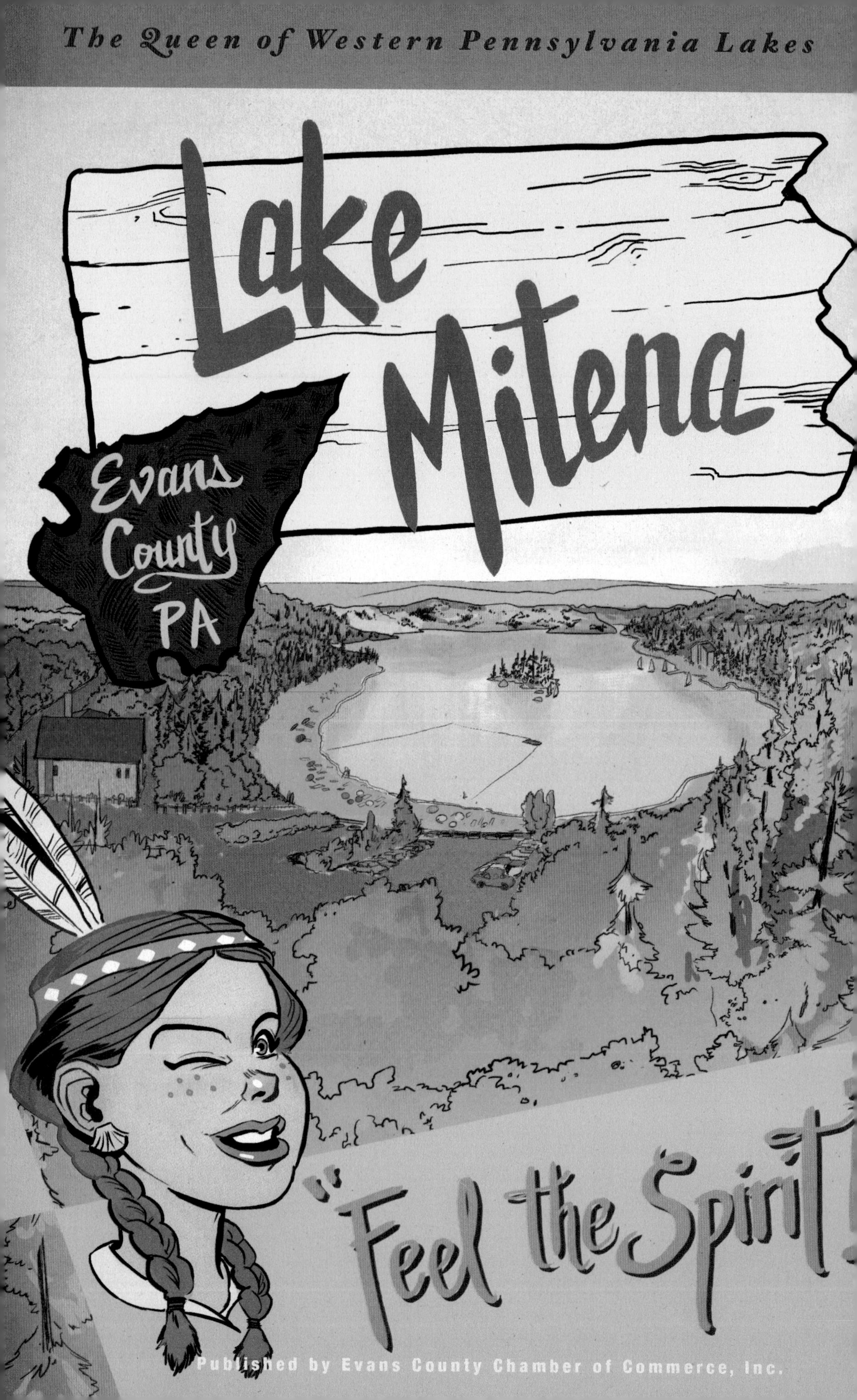
The Queen of Western Pennsylvania Lakes
Lake Mitena
Evans County PA
"Feel the Spirit!"
Published by Evans County Chamber of Commerce, Inc.

2

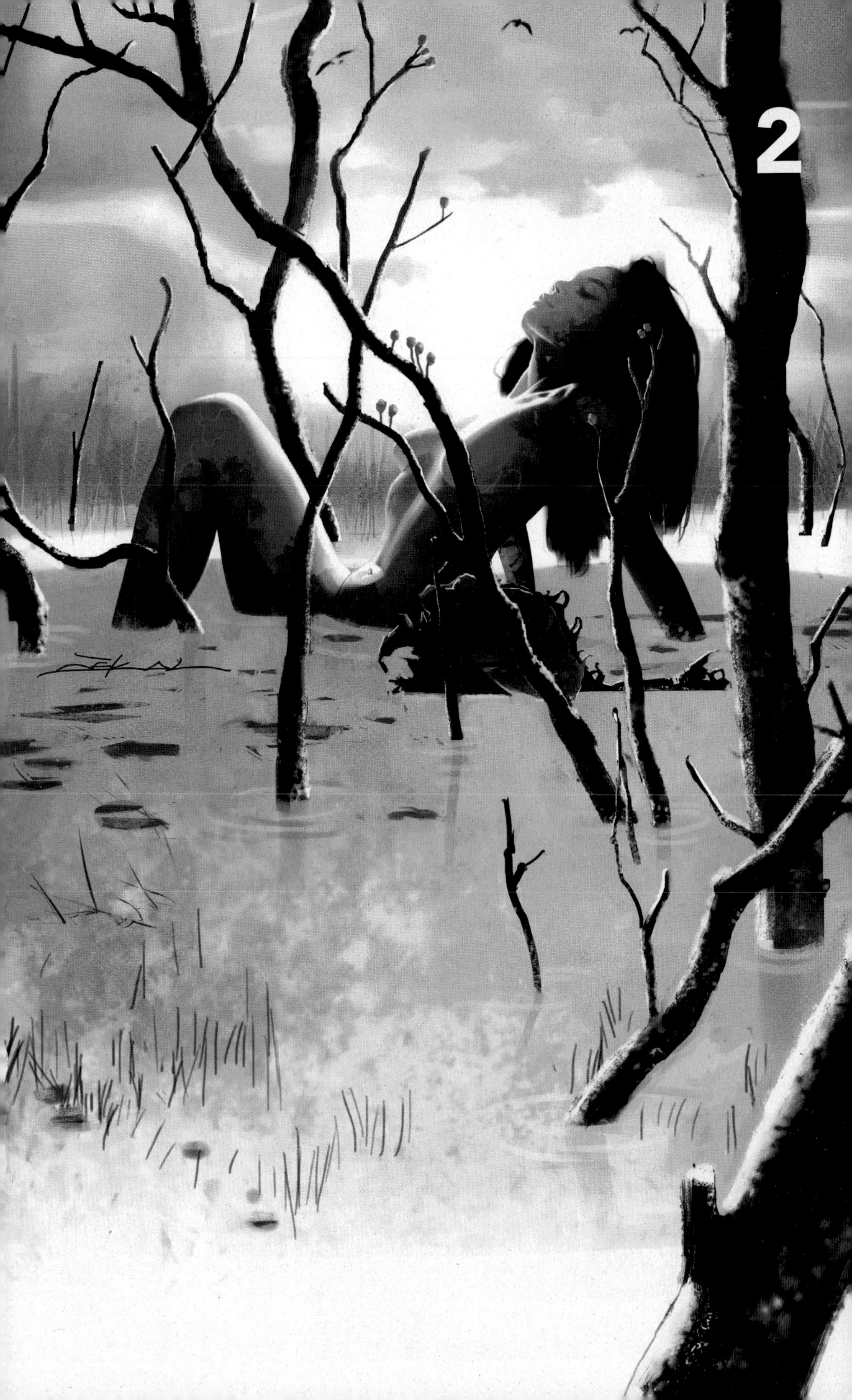

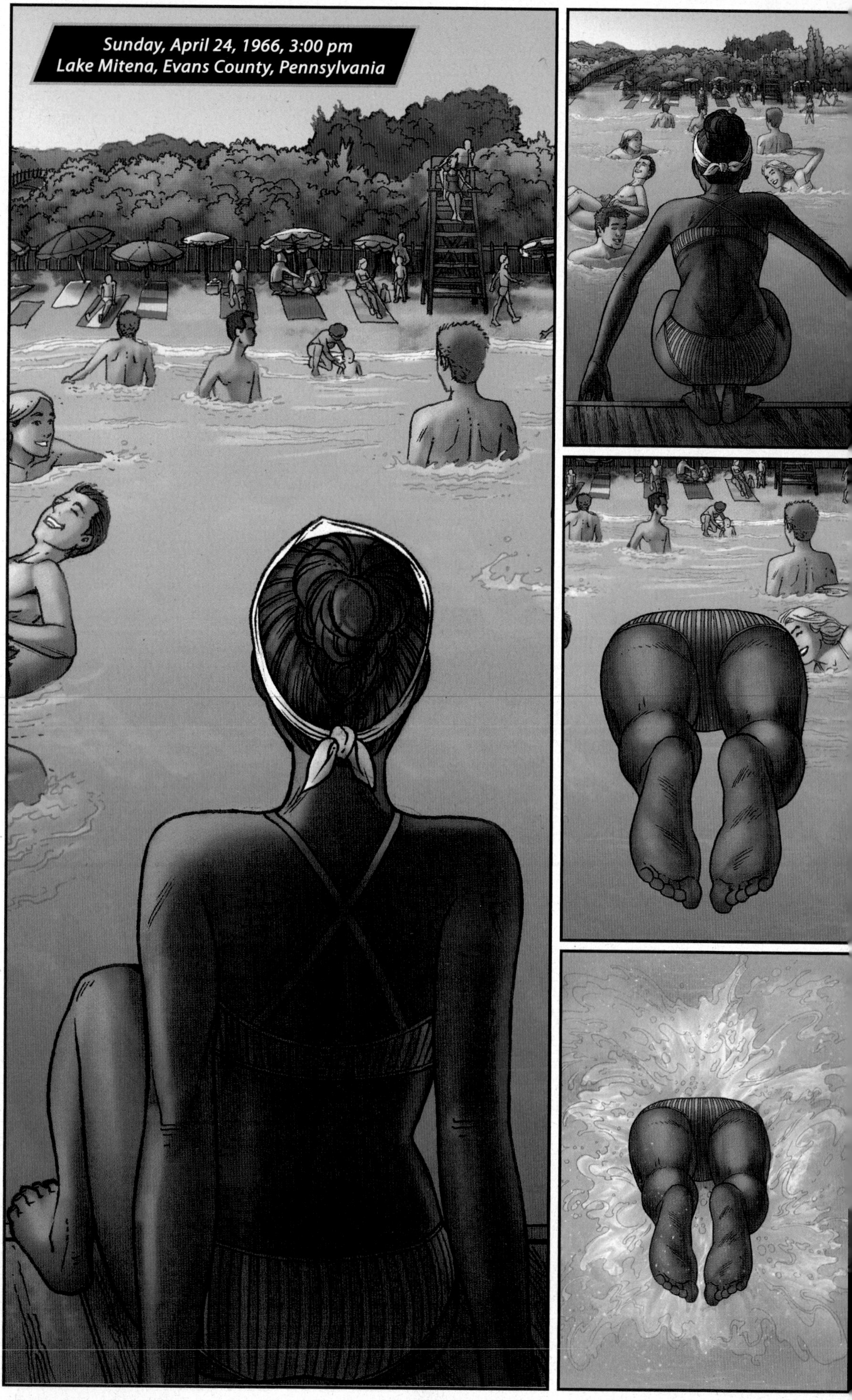
Sunday, April 24, 1966, 3:00 pm
Lake Mitena, Evans County, Pennsylvania

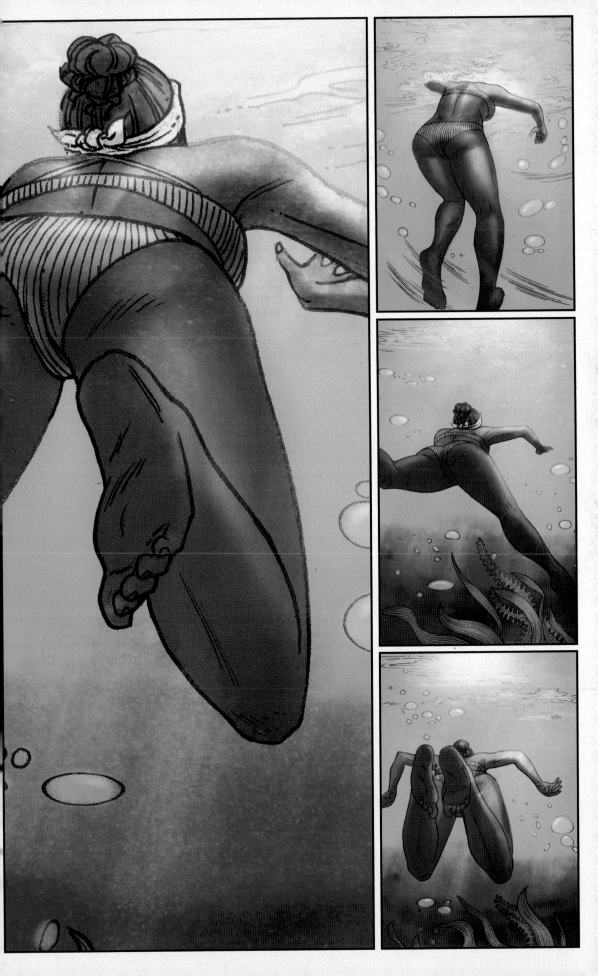

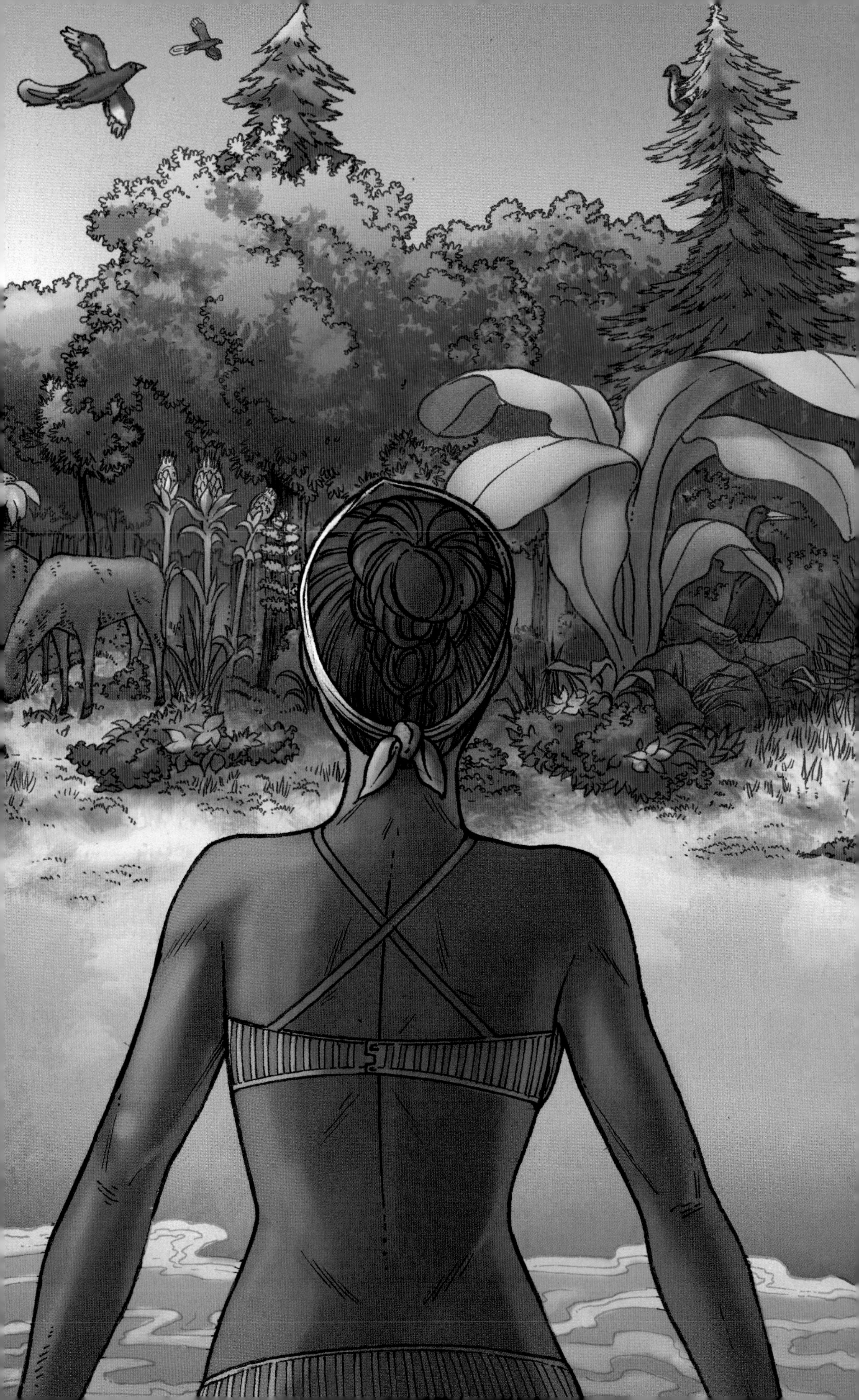

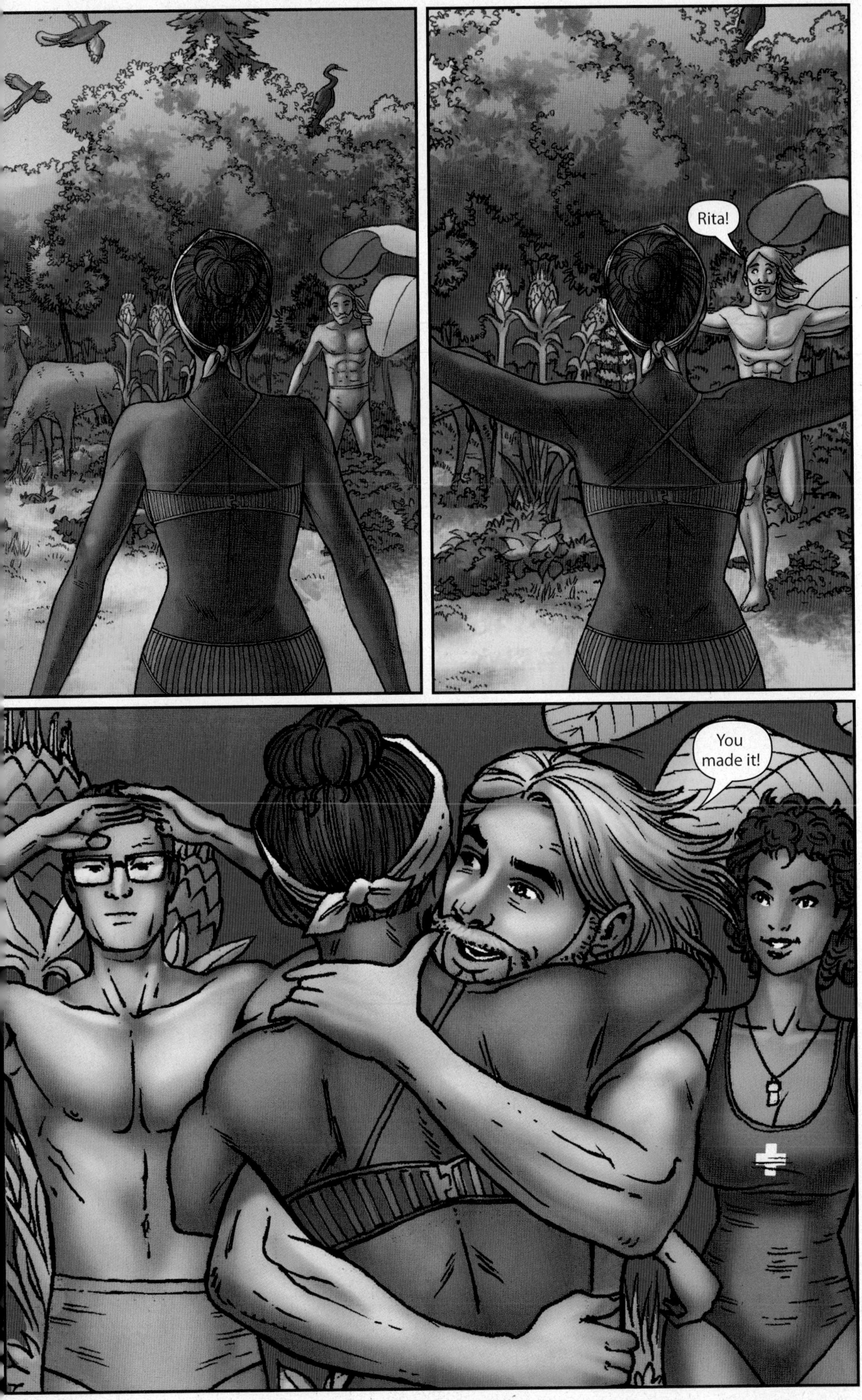
Rita!
You made it!

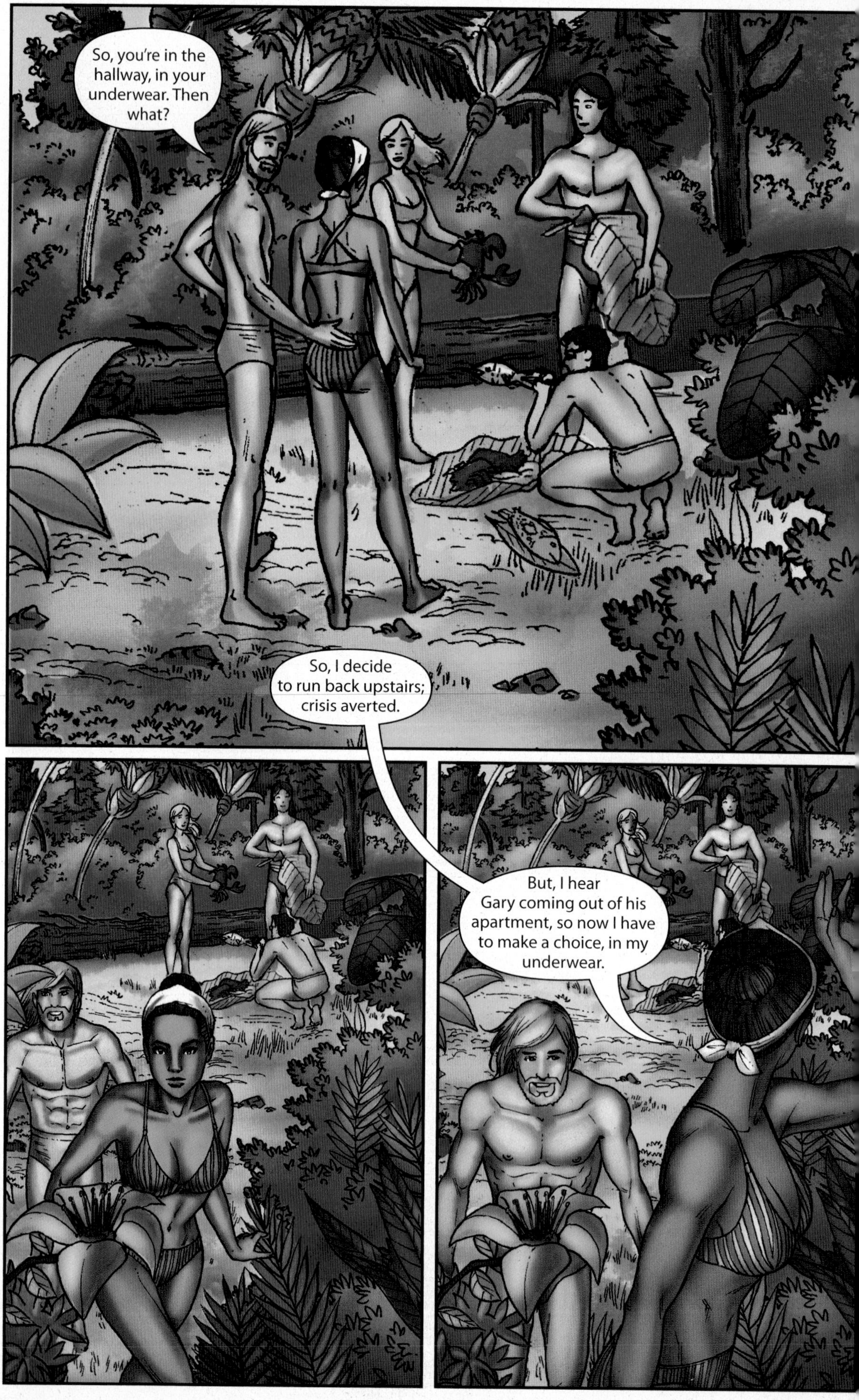
So, you're in the hallway, in your underwear. Then what?
So, I decide to run back upstairs; crisis averted.
But, I hear Gary coming out of his apartment, so now I have to make a choice, in my underwear.

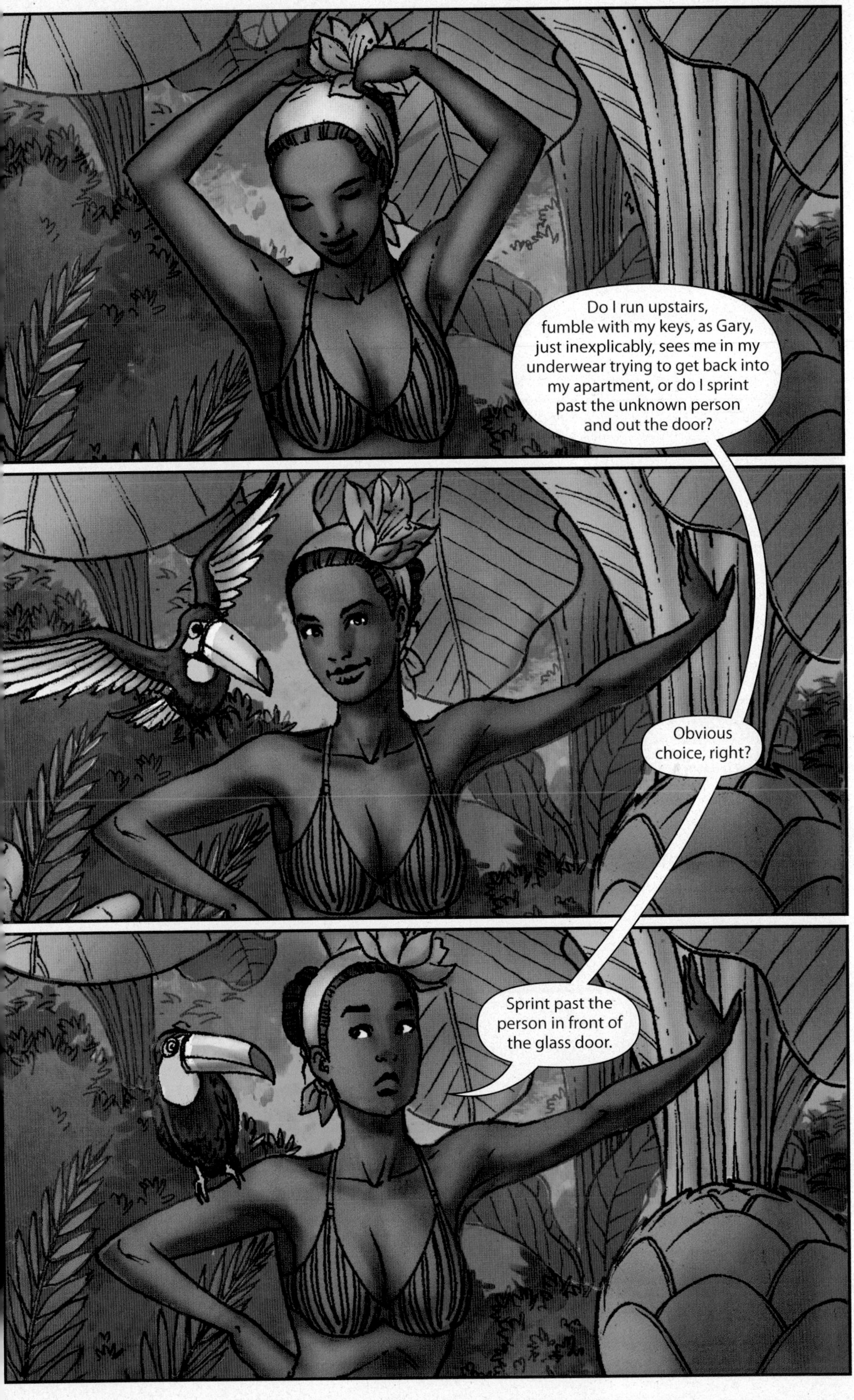
Do I run upstairs, fumble with my keys, as Gary, just inexplicably, sees me in my underwear trying to get back into my apartment, or do I sprint past the unknown person and out the door?
Obvious choice, right?
Sprint past the person in front of the glass door.

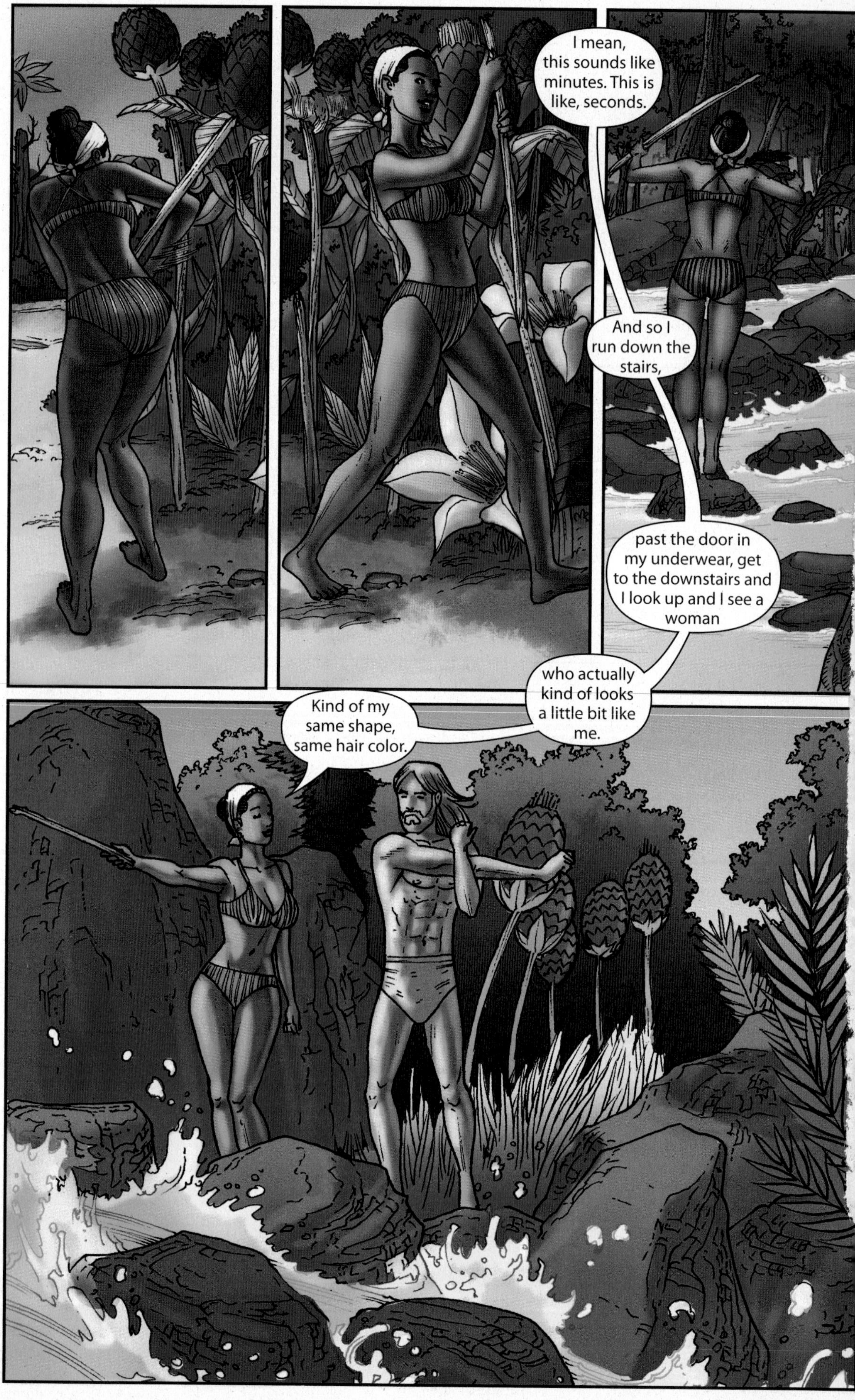
I mean, this sounds like minutes. This is like, seconds.
And so I run down the stairs,
past the door in my underwear, get to the downstairs and I look up and I see a woman
who actually kind of looks a little bit like me.
Kind of my same shape, same hair color.

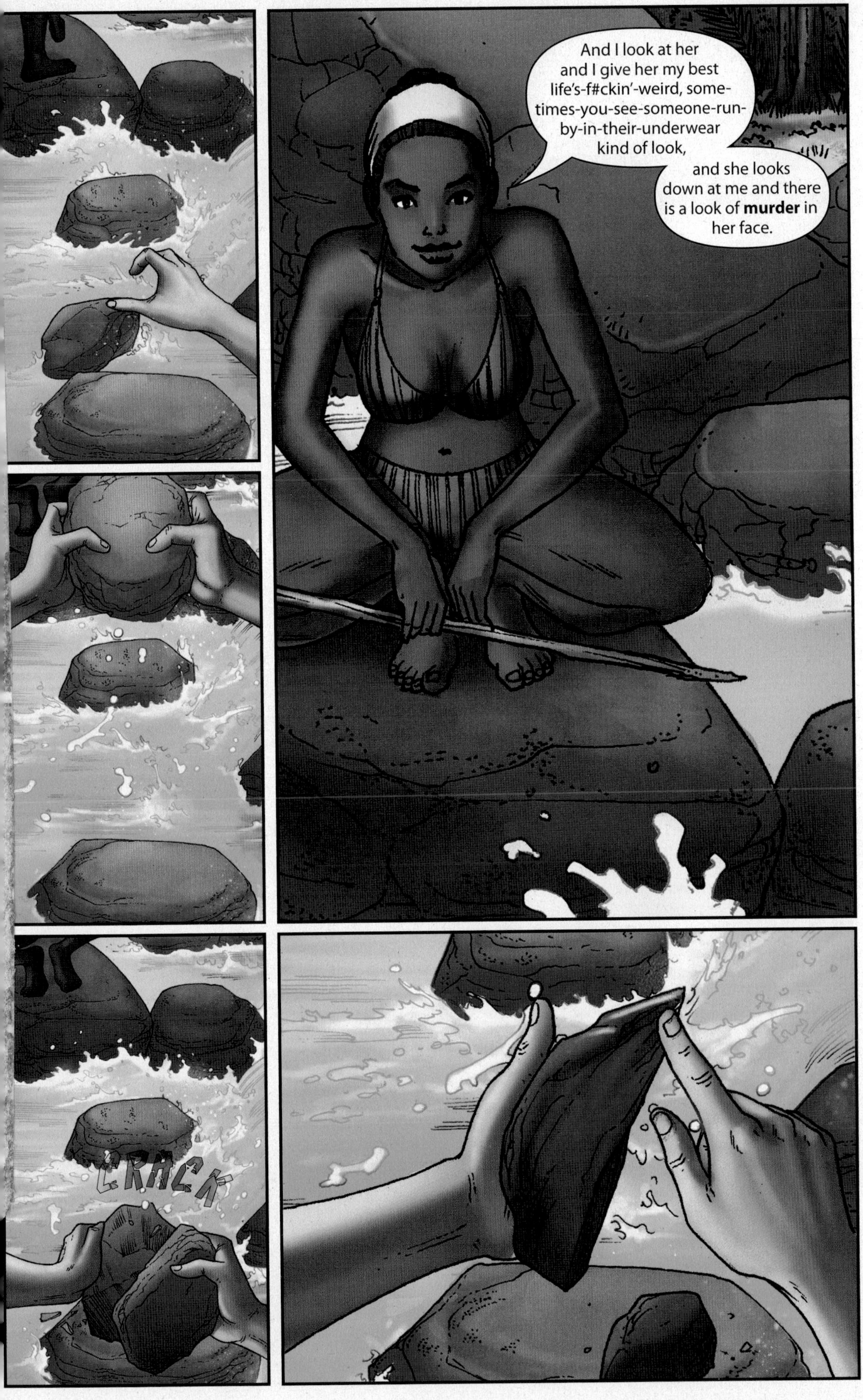
And I look at her and I give her my best life's-f#ckin'-weird, some-times-you-see-someone-run-by-in-their-underwear kind of look,
and she looks down at me and there is a look of **murder** in her face.
CRACK

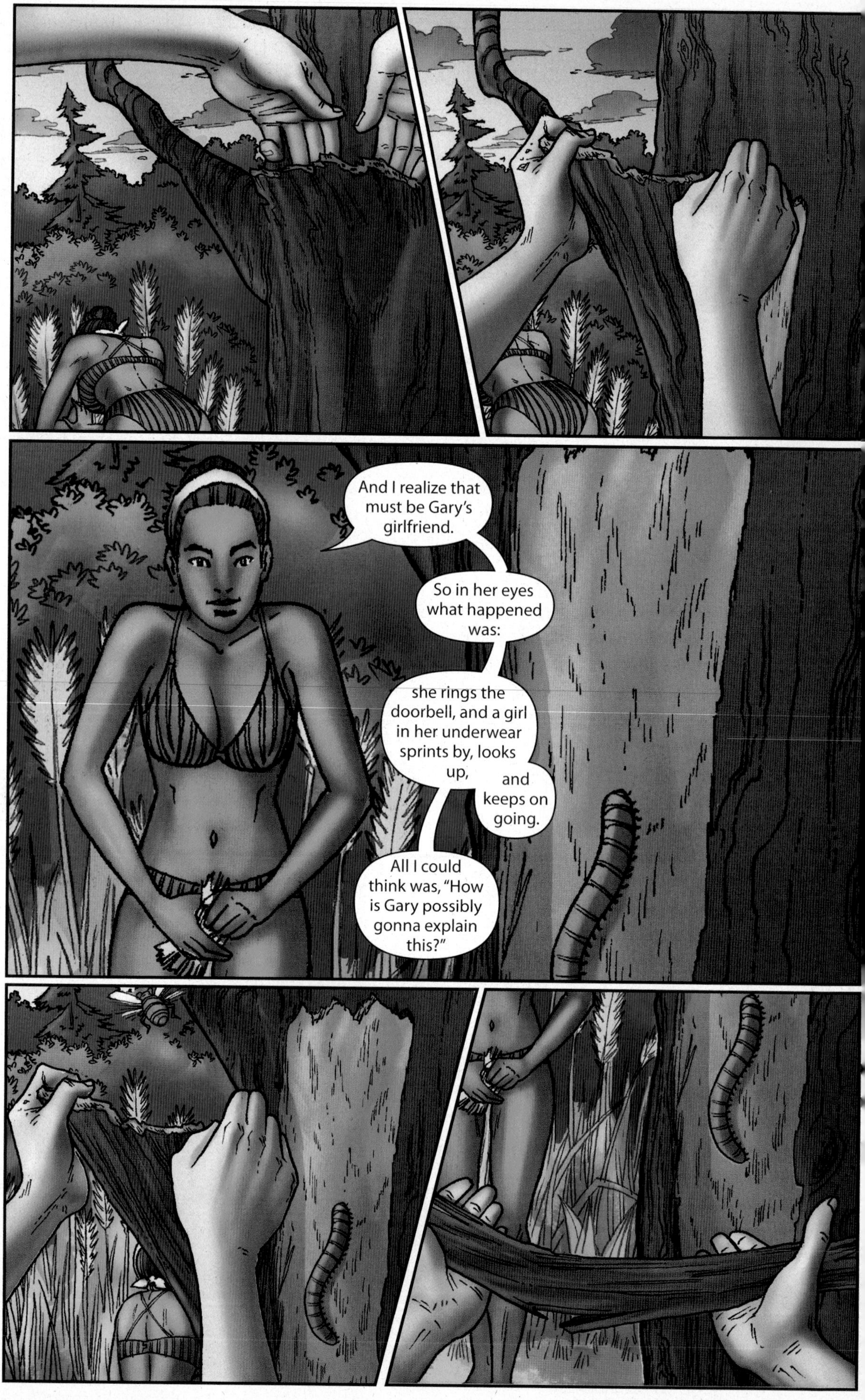
And I realize that must be Gary's girlfriend.
So in her eyes what happened was:
she rings the doorbell, and a girl in her underwear sprints by, looks up,
and keeps on going.
All I could think was, "How is Gary possibly gonna explain this?"

THE ★ ★ SKINNY

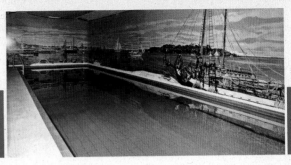

In 1668, Thomas Guidott set up the practice of nude swimming in the English town of Bath, believing in the curative properties of the waters. Doctors and quacks set up spa towns around mineral springs and guaranteed a cure by dipping naked in the cold mineral water.

In America, Benjamin Franklin and John Quincy Adams were also interested in nude swimming. Franklin was an avid swimmer and owned a book about the art of swimming, which had pictures of nude swimmers. As part of his morning ritual, John Quincy Adams would skinny-dip in the Potomac. A number of our presidents in the 20th century also spent time skinny-dipping. Sometimes for recreation—and sometimes, to break down political barriers.

THEODORE ROOSEVELT: Lifelong naturalist Teddy Roosevelt enjoyed recreational skinny-dipping. He also skinny-dipped for diplomacy. In 1903, Teddy Roosevelt invited the French Ambassador to a nude swim in the Potomac. The shy ambassador joined him but kept his gloves on in case they met ladies.

JOHN F. KENNEDY: JFK also enjoyed taking relaxing nude dips in the White House pool. Sometimes his brothers joined him. And on at least one occasion two young female assistants kept him company in the pool.

FRANKLIN DELANO ROOSEVELT: Taking a cue from his older cousin, FDR also stripped down to build political relationships. In 1937, he invited Congressional Democrats to a "stag party" to win over their good will. Activities included fishing, clay pigeon shooting, and skinny-dipping. The first White House pool was also built in 1933 for FDR's therapeutic use. It was located in the West Wing, enclosed, and easily accessible from the Oval Office.

LYNDON B. JOHNSON: Shortly after being sworn in, LBJ invited Christian evangelist Billy Graham to skinny-dip in the White House pool. LBJ used the White House pool almost daily. He even sometimes held meetings with senior staff in the shallow end of the pool, while in the nude with his "Jumbo" out.

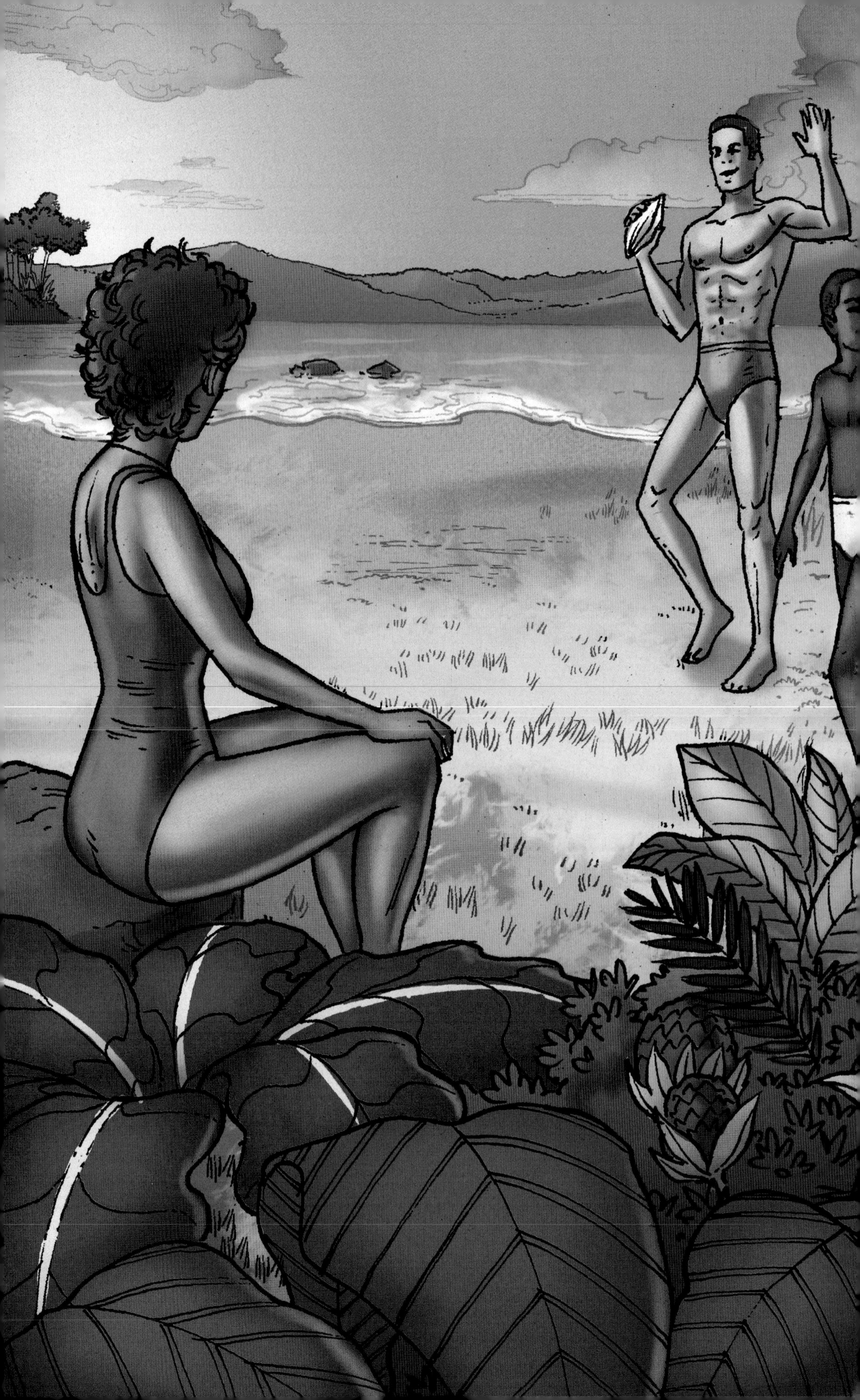

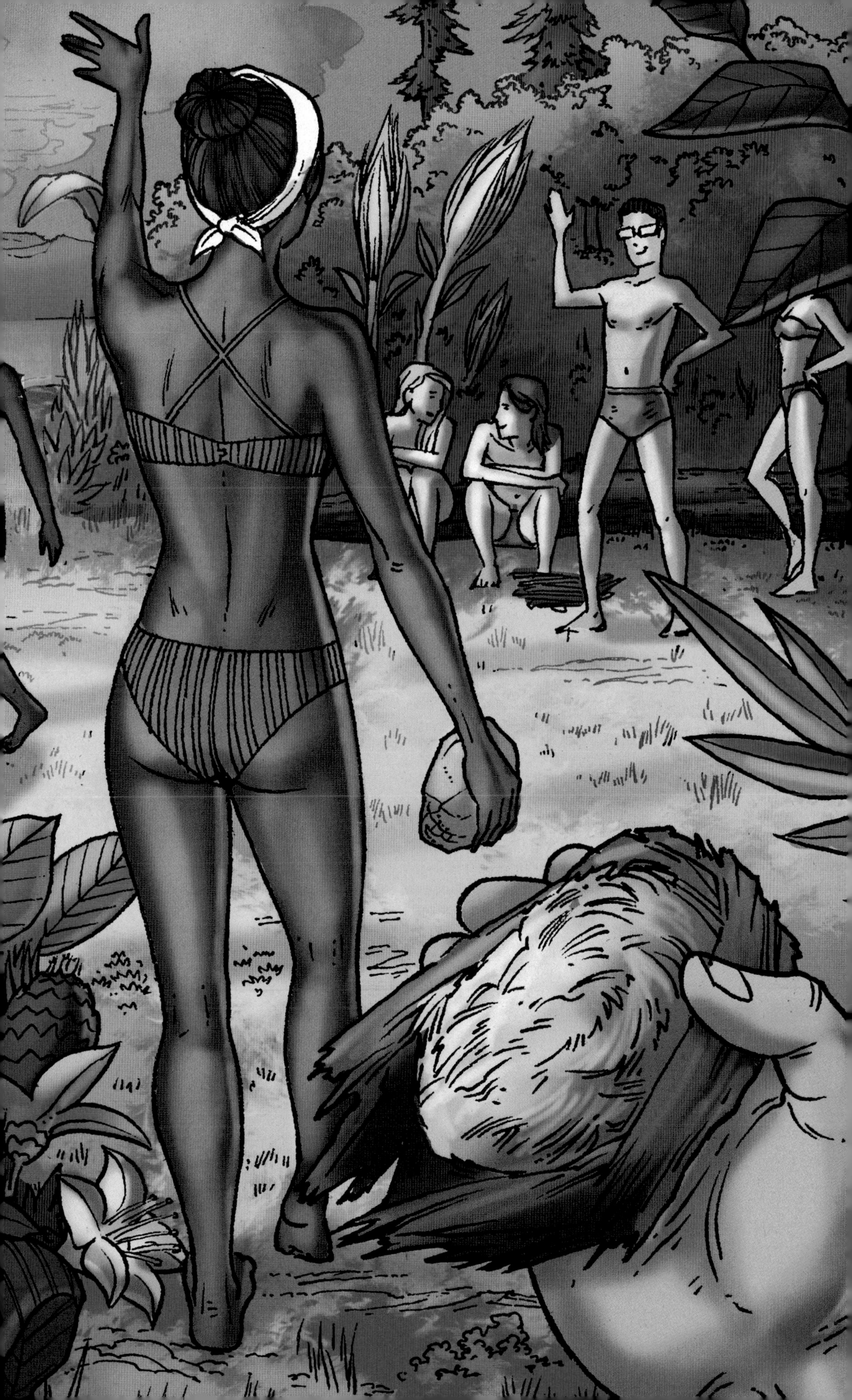

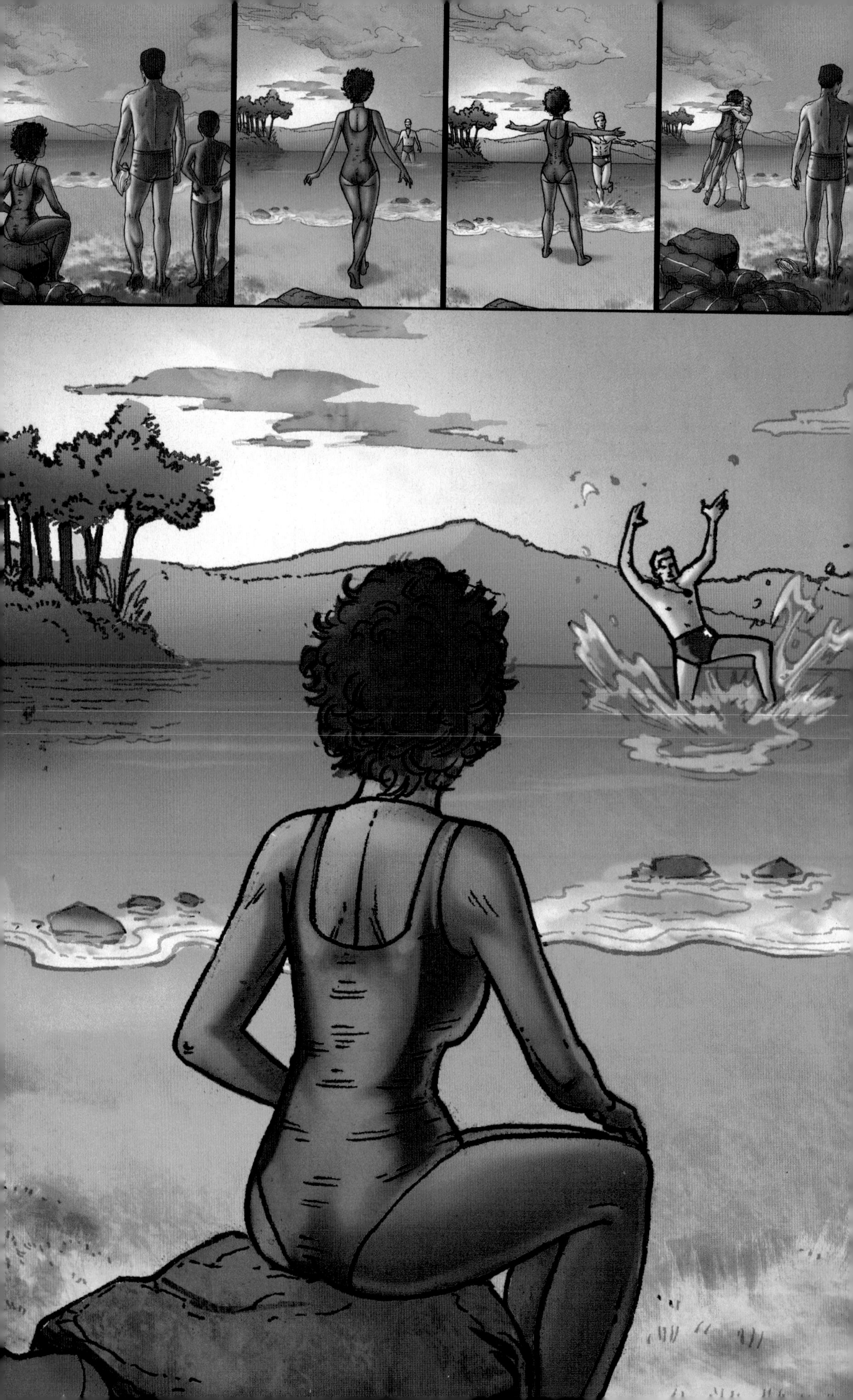

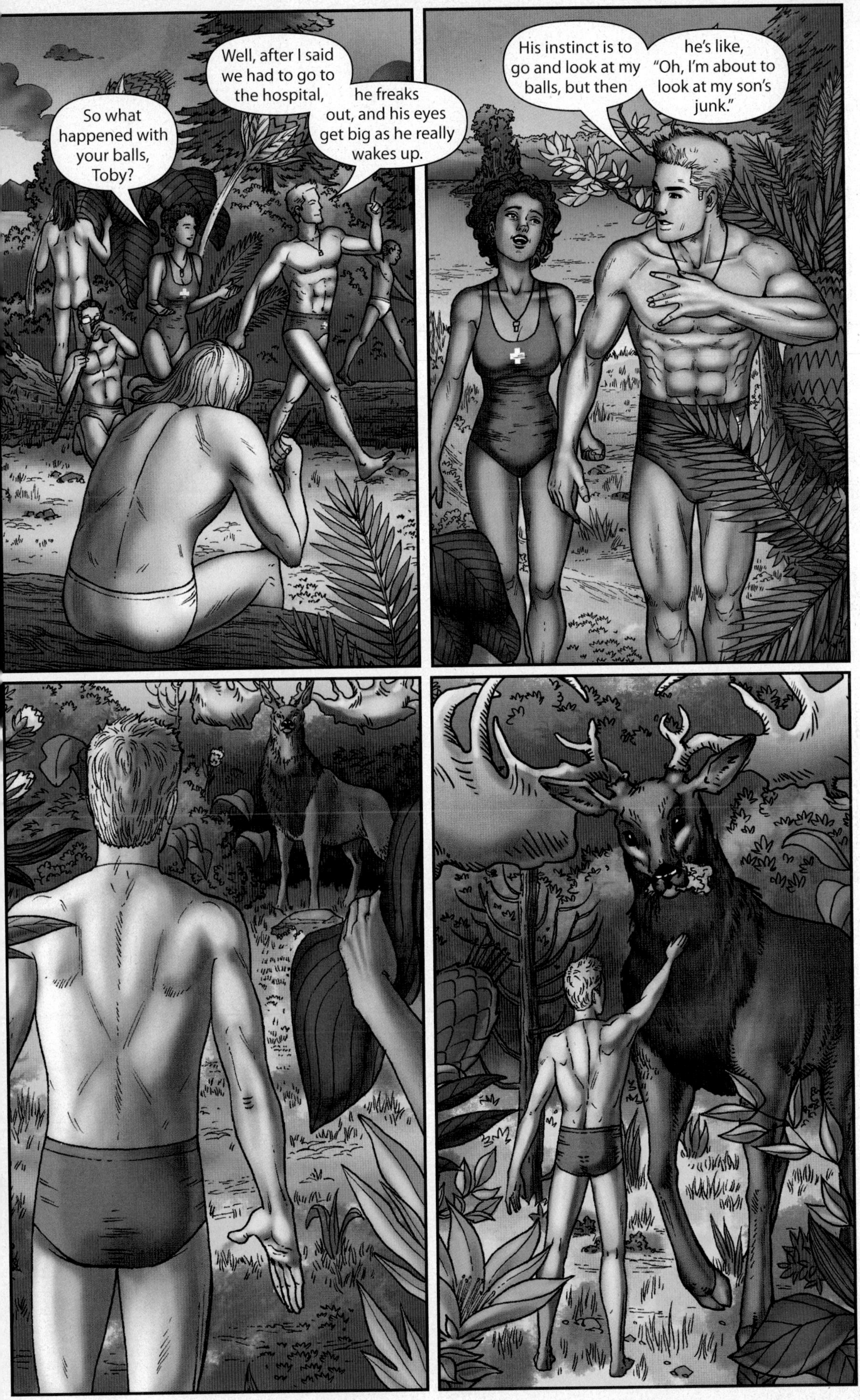
So what happened with your balls, Toby?
Well, after I said we had to go to the hospital,
he freaks out, and his eyes get big as he really wakes up.
His instinct is to go and look at my balls, but then
he's like, "Oh, I'm about to look at my son's junk."

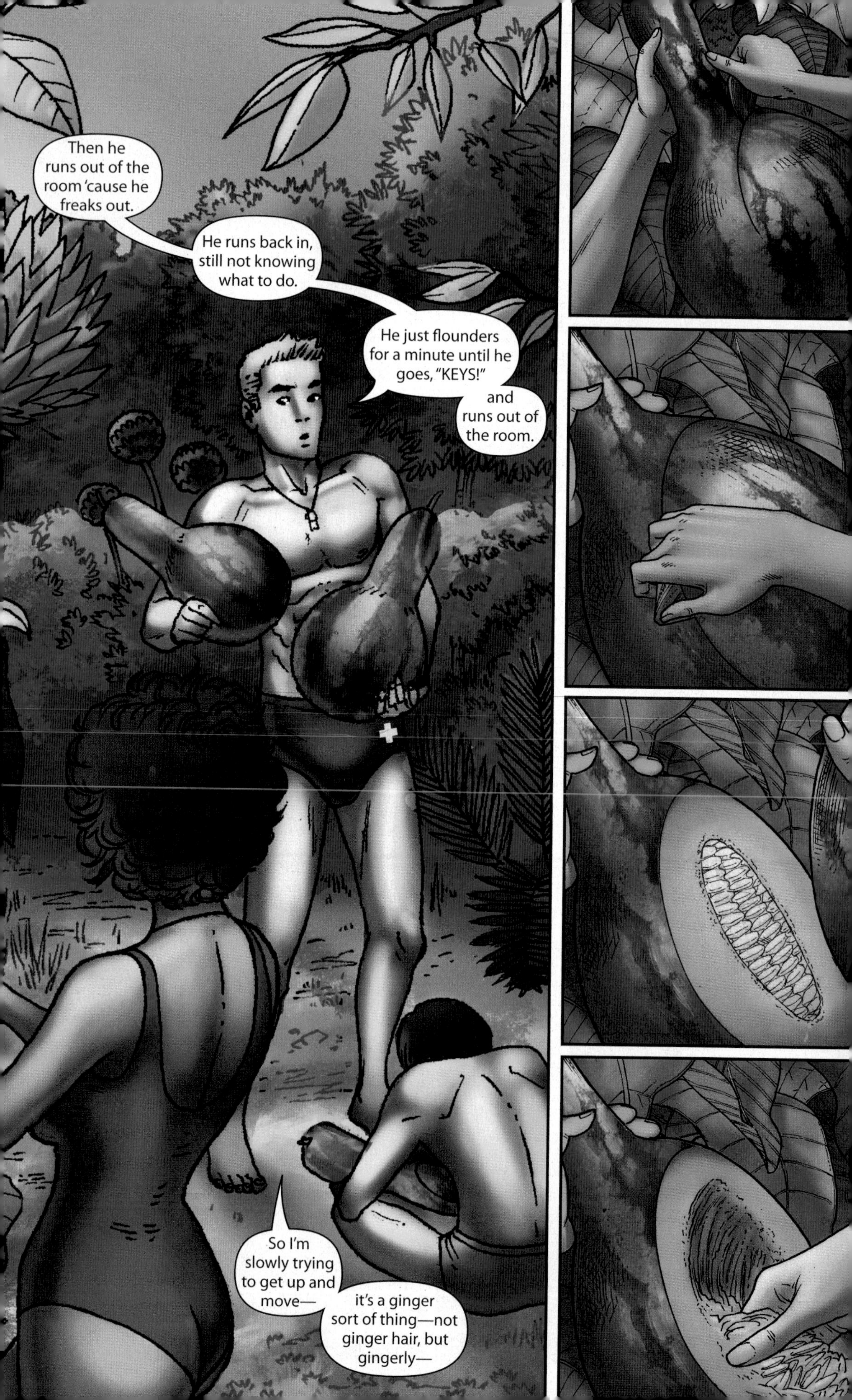
Then he runs out of the room 'cause he freaks out.
He runs back in, still not knowing what to do.
He just flounders for a minute until he goes, "KEYS!"
and runs out of the room.
So I'm slowly trying to get up and move—
it's a ginger sort of thing—not ginger hair, but gingerly—

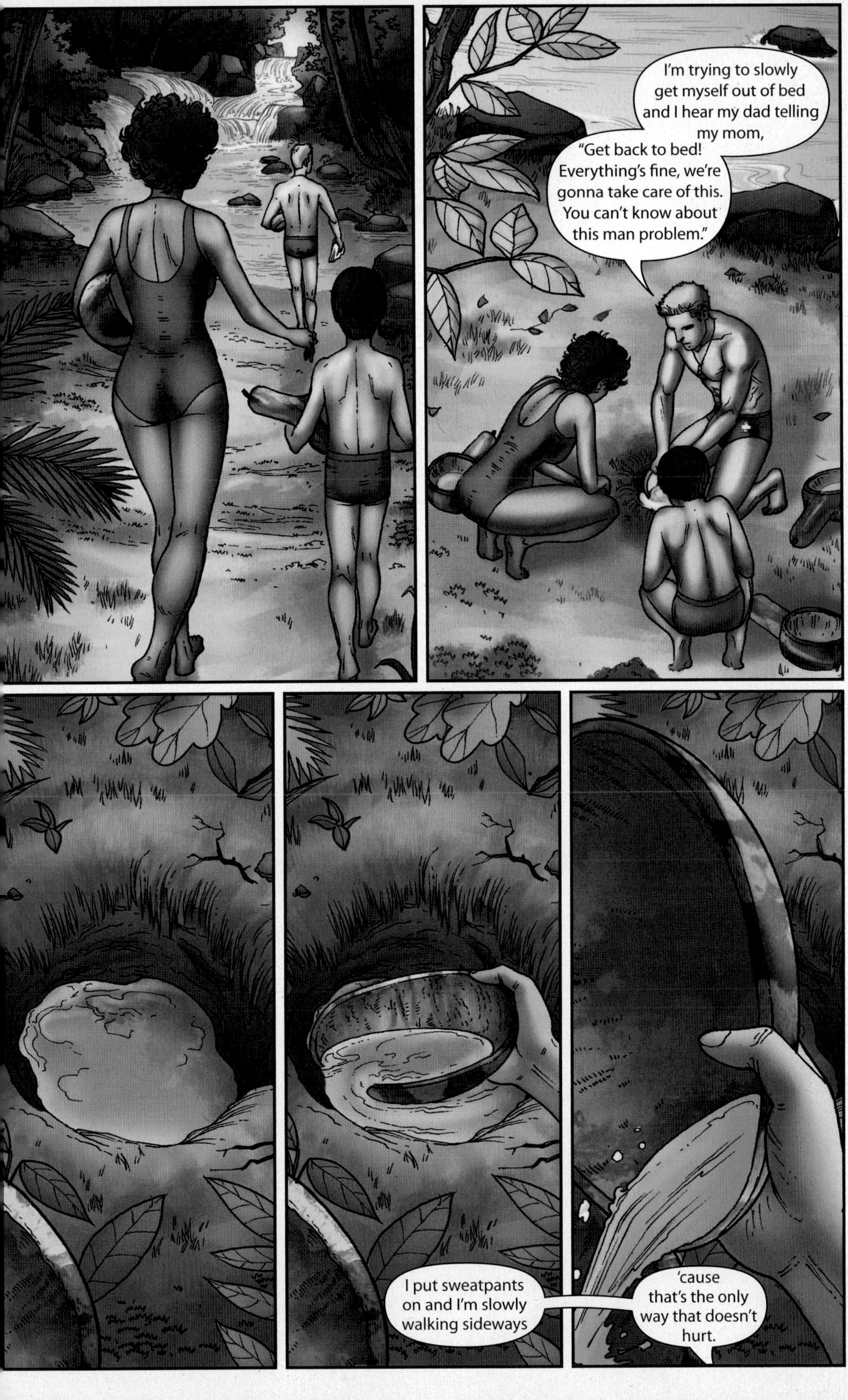
I'm trying to slowly get myself out of bed and I hear my dad telling my mom,
"Get back to bed! Everything's fine, we're gonna take care of this. You can't know about this man problem."
I put sweatpants on and I'm slowly walking sideways
'cause that's the only way that doesn't hurt.

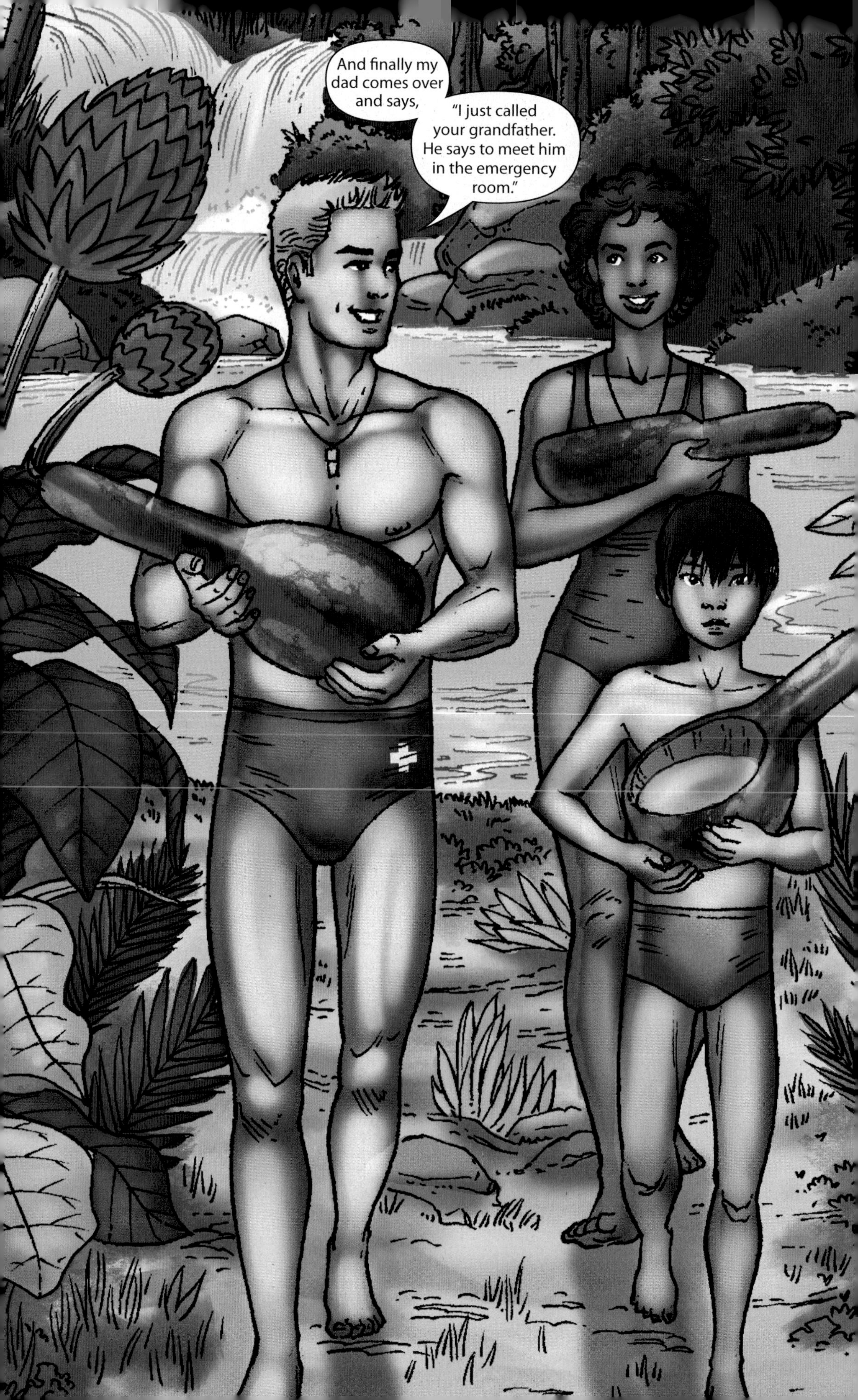
And finally my dad comes over and says,
"I just called your grandfather. He says to meet him in the emergency room."

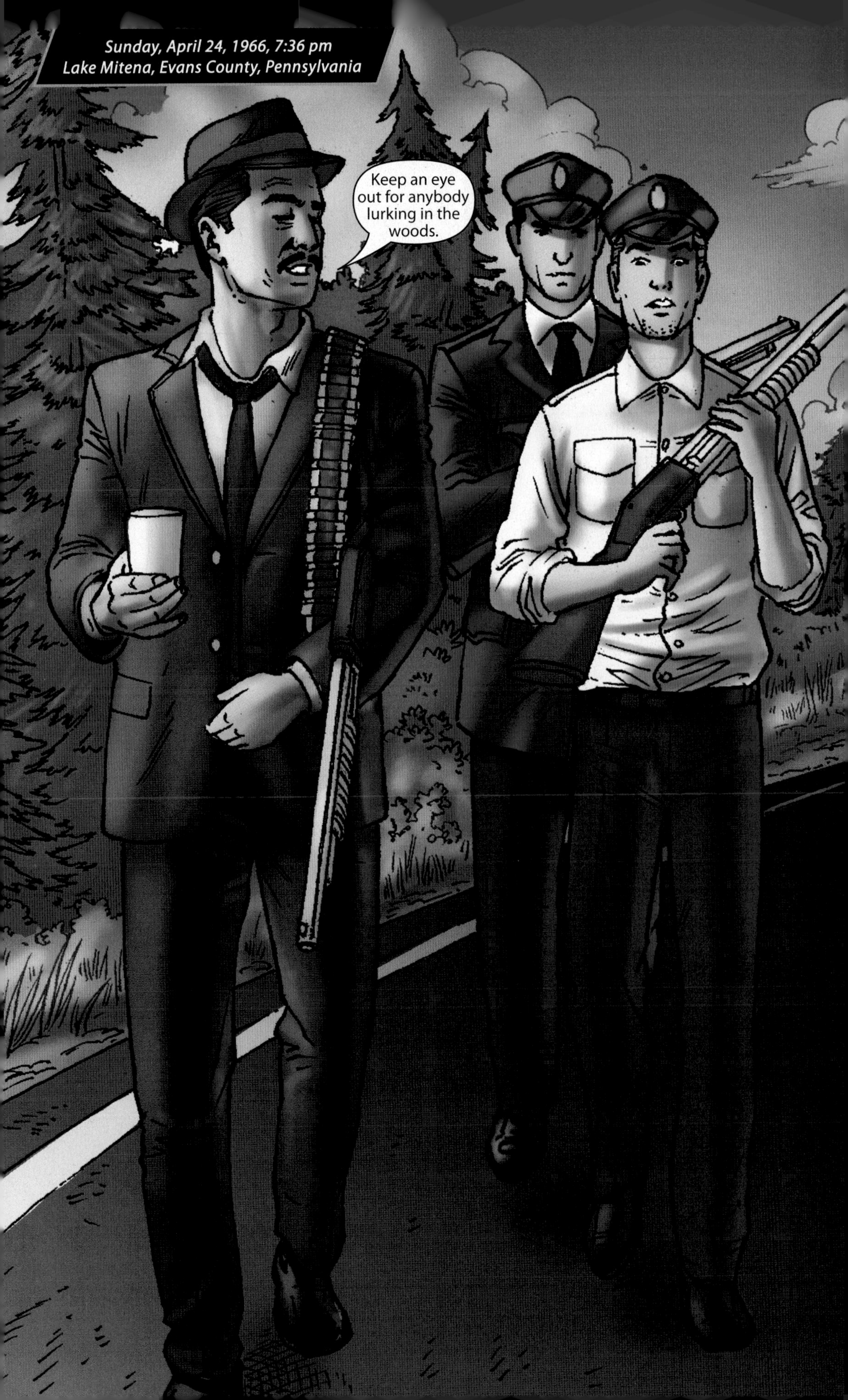
Sunday, April 24, 1966, 7:36 pm
Lake Mitena, Evans County, Pennsylvania
Keep an eye out for anybody lurking in the woods.

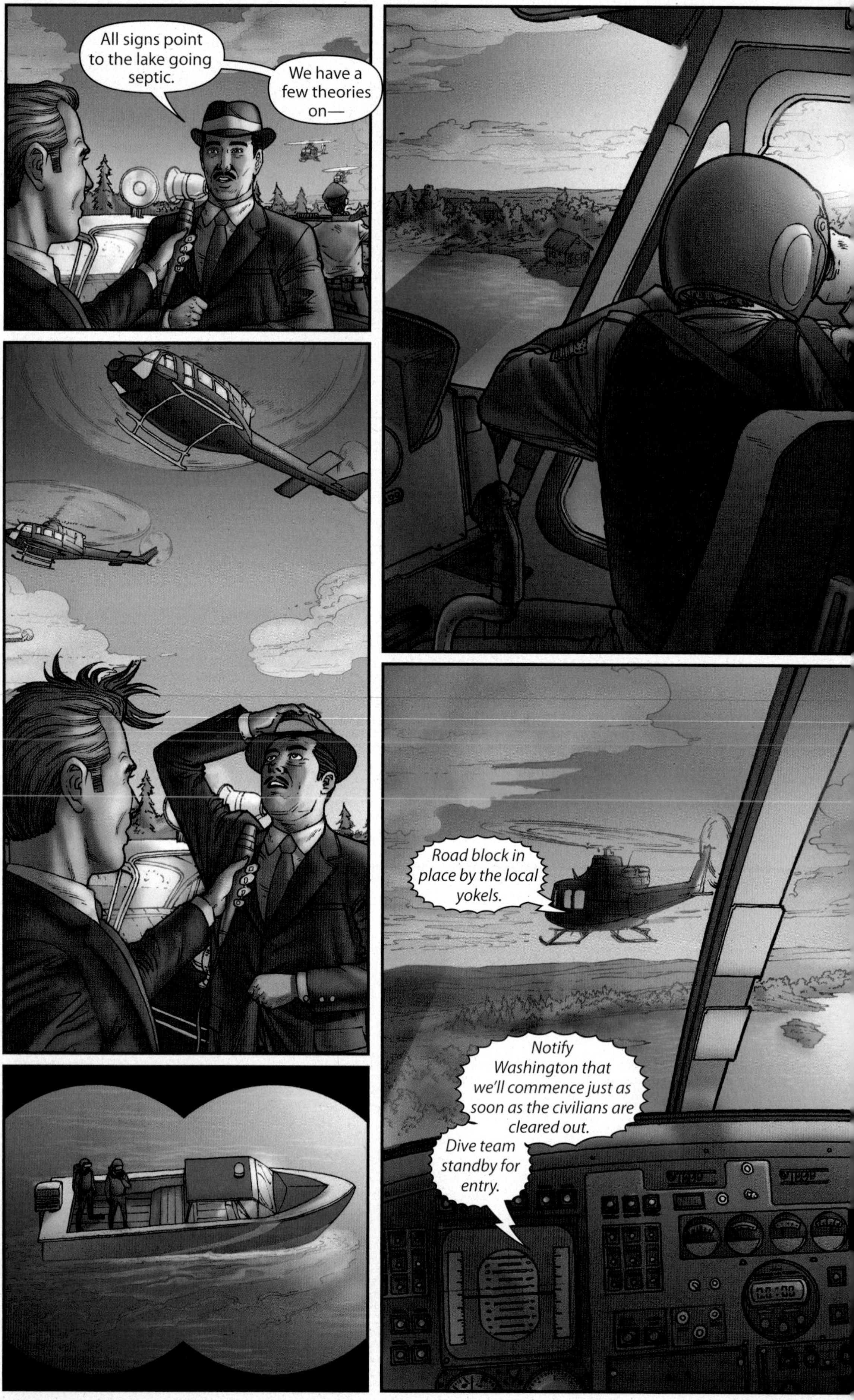
All signs point to the lake going septic.
We have a few theories on—
Road block in place by the local yokels.
Notify Washington that we'll commence just as soon as the civilians are cleared out.
Dive team standby for entry.

THEN NOW

USA

Health & Nutrition	1960s	2010s	Increase
Average female adult	140.2 lbs	166.3 lbs	18.6%
Average male adult	166.3 lbs	195.5 lbs	17.6%
Adult obesity	10.7%	35.9%	235.5%
Childhood obesity	9.0%	39.9%	333.3%
US population with diabetes	2,770,000	29,100,000	950.5%
Estimated daily caloric intake	2,200	3,300	50.0%
Pounds per person per year			
All sugars	114.0	152.0	33.3%
Corn sweeteners	15.0	85.0	467.0%
High fructose corn syrup	0.2	43.7	2175.0%
Meat	161.7	252.7	56.3%
Cheese	9.5	33.2	249.0%
Added fats	47.8	83.9	75.5%
Grains	142.5	175.2	23.0%
Soft drinks	18.3	46.5	154.0%

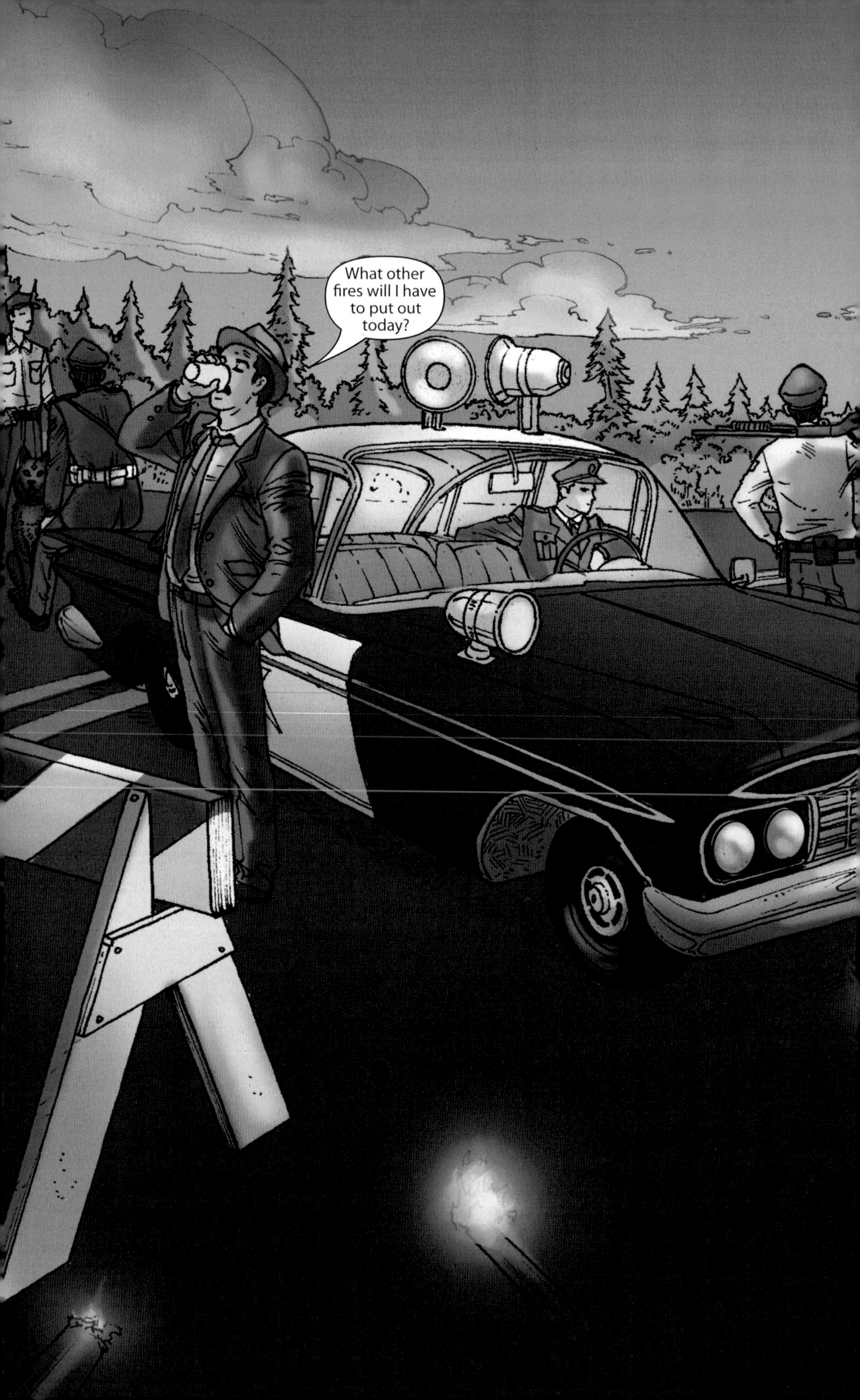
What other fires will I have to put out today?

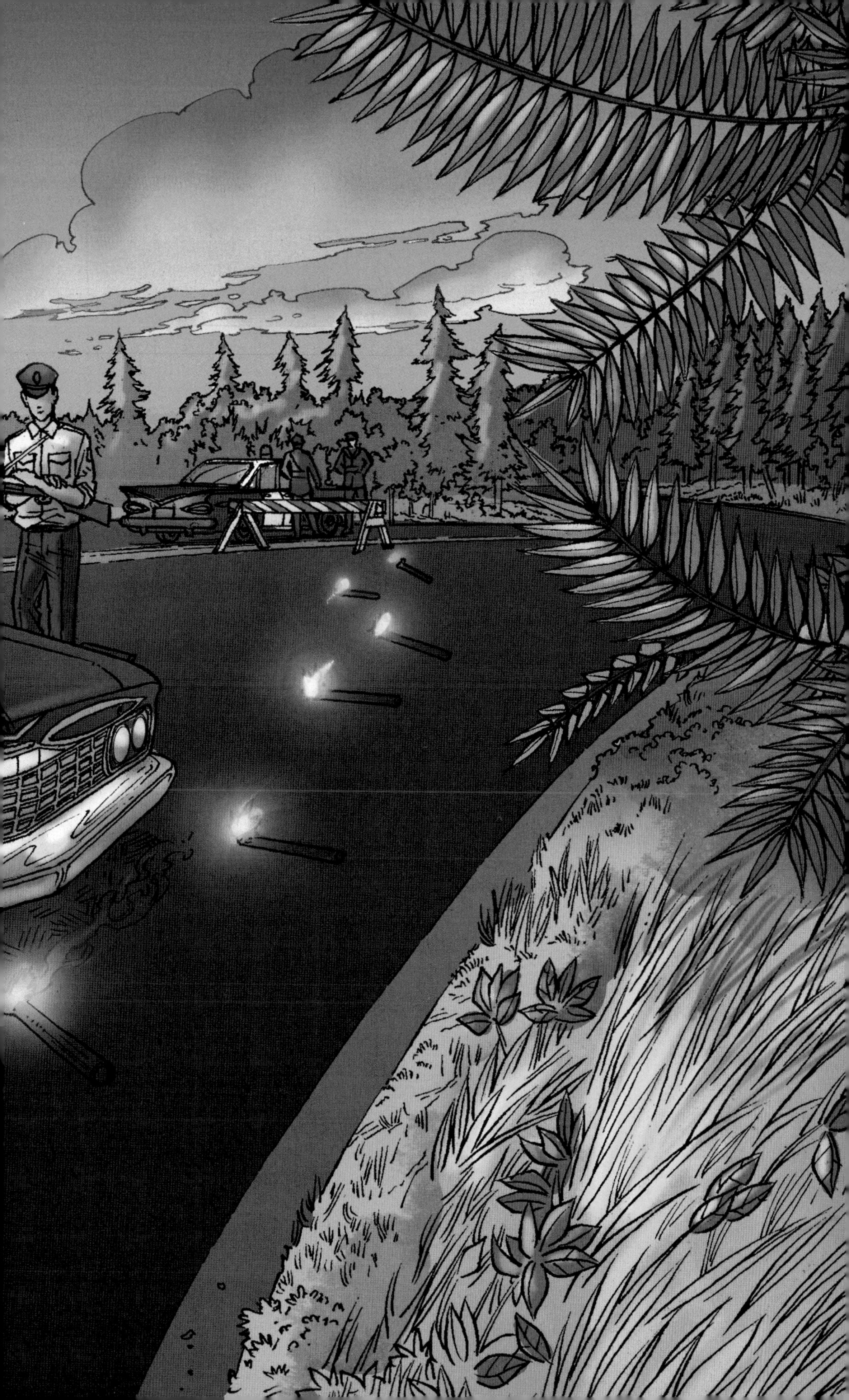

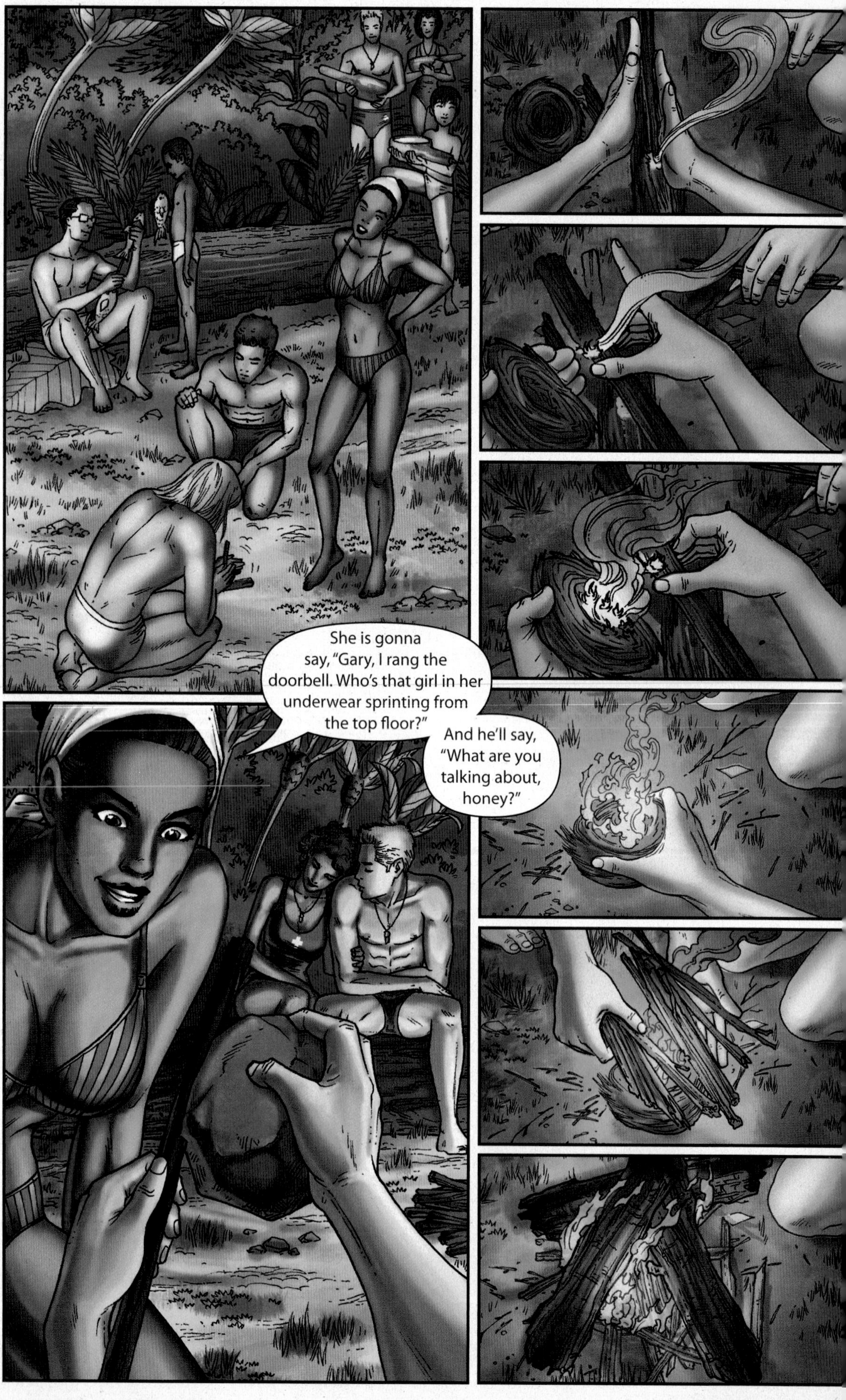
She is gonna say, "Gary, I rang the doorbell. Who's that girl in her underwear sprinting from the top floor?"
And he'll say, "What are you talking about, honey?"

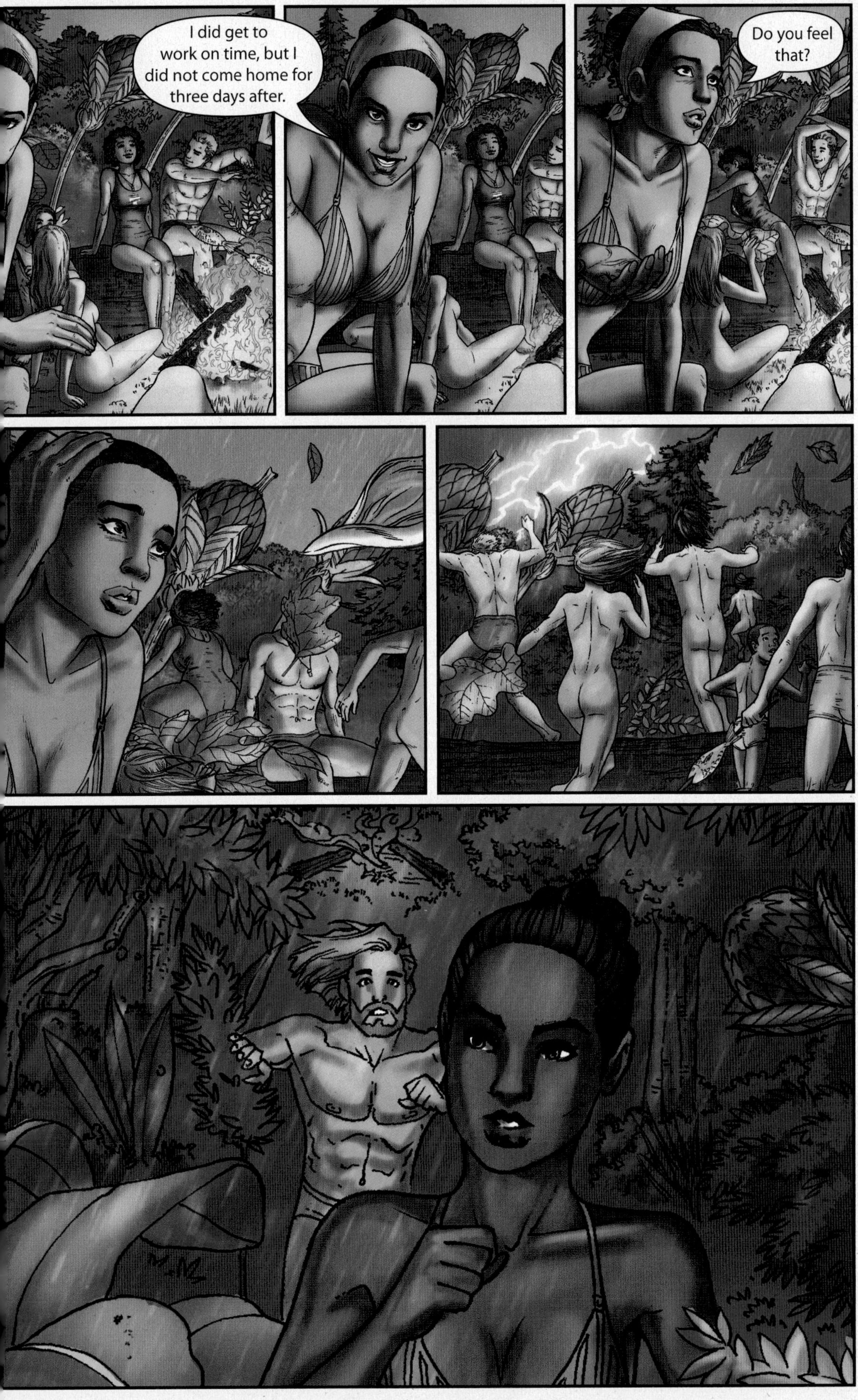

I did get to work on time, but I did not come home for three days after.
Do you feel that?

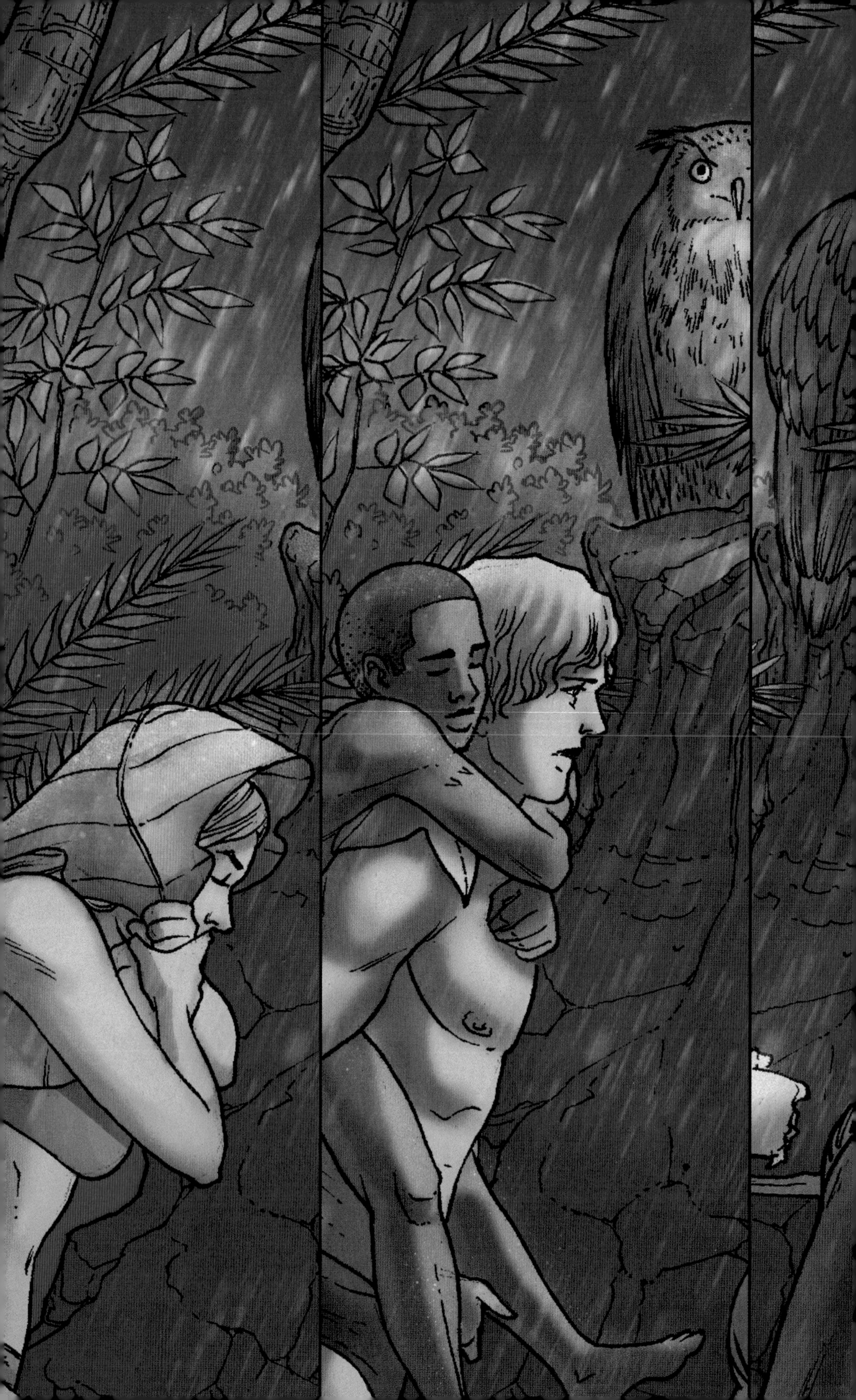

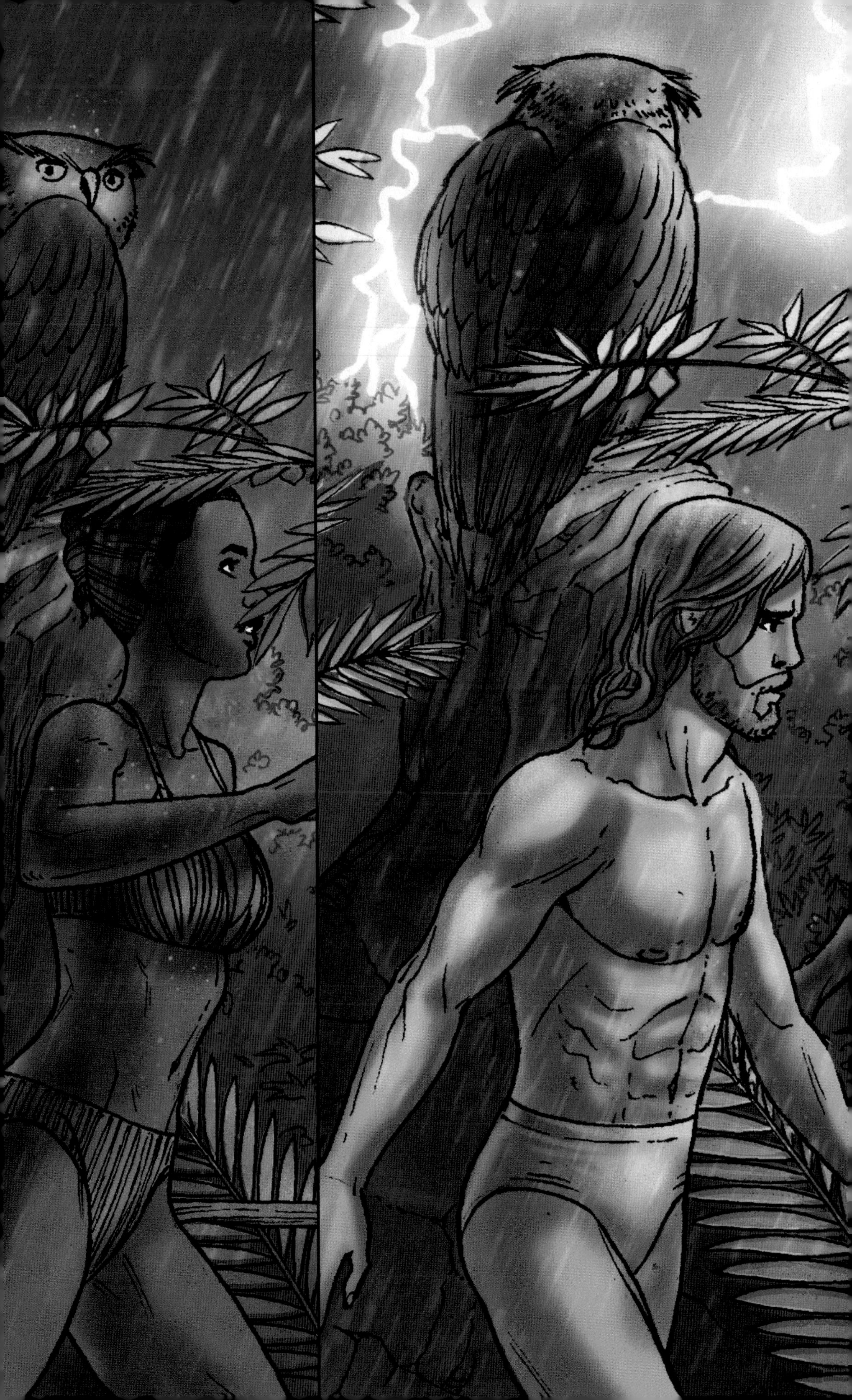

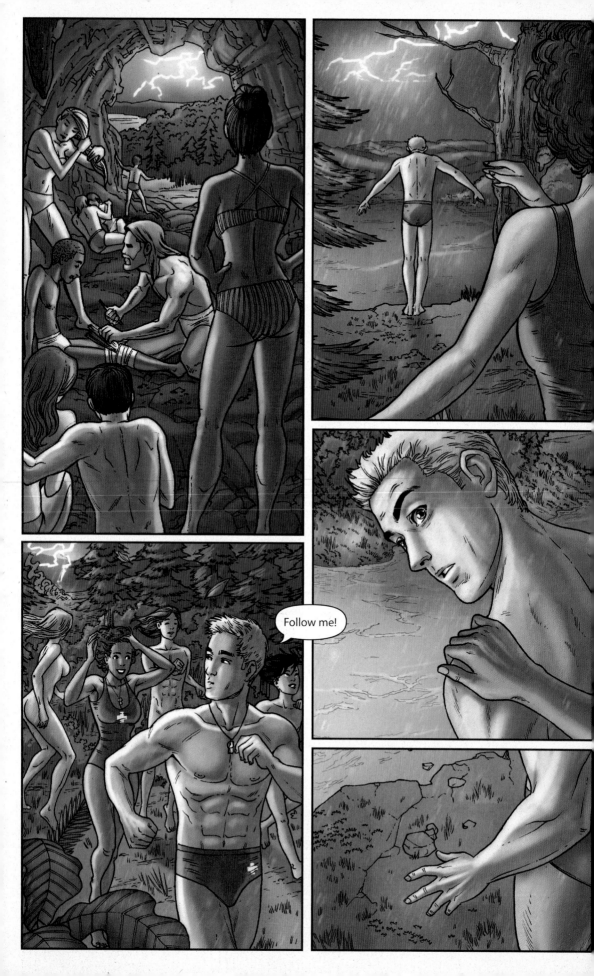

Follow me!

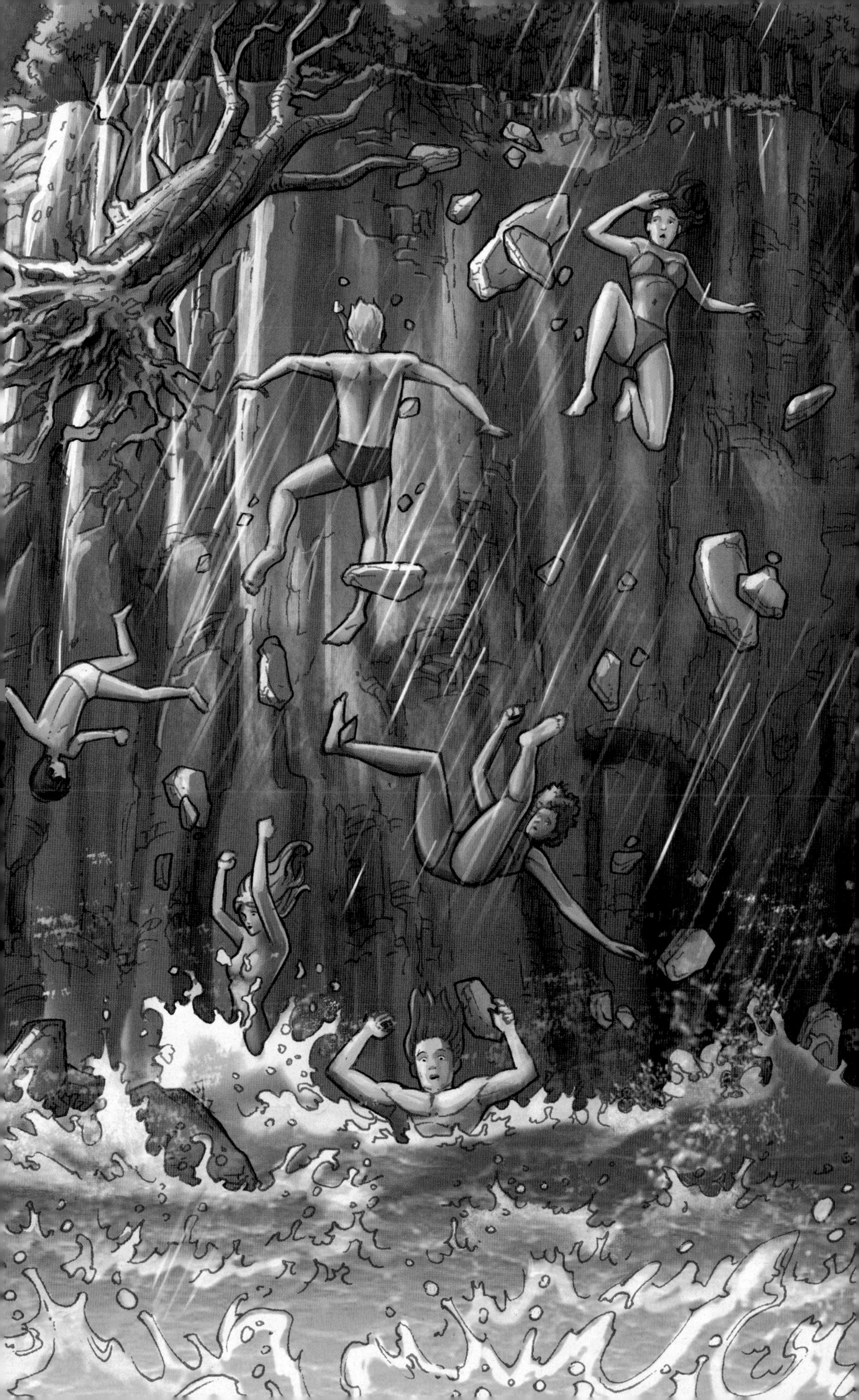

NATURAL RESOURCES

CUMULATIVE DEFORESTATION

WORLD FOREST COVER (in billion hectares)			
Pre-Industrial	1966	2016	2066*
5.9	4.3	4.0	3.7

Between the 1960s and today, humans have destroyed over 300 million hectares of forest. This is roughly the size of the contiguous western United States.

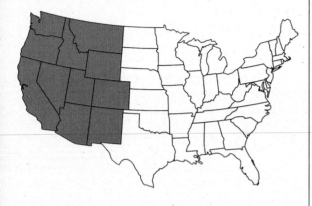

SOIL DEGRADATION

WORLD POPULATION		
1966	2016	2060*
3.1 billion	6.3 billion	9.6 billion
HECTARES OF ARABLE LAND PER CAPITA		
0.42	0.23	0.18

Forty percent of the soil used for agricuture around the world is degraded or seriously degraded from our modern farming practices. Soil is now being lost at between 10 and 40 times the rate at which it can be naturally replenished. Today, the world has a rough estimate of 60 years of topsoil left.

FRESH WATER DEPLETION

Aquifers around the world cannot keep up with our consumption either. Today, 21 out of the 37 largest aquifers in the world are being tapped at unsustainable rates. In the US, the High Plains (HP) Aquifer system is one of the world's largest, spanning portions of 8 states (approximately 174,000 square miles).

DEPLETION OF SUPPLY IN THE HP AQUIFER		
1966	2016	2066*
3%	30%	69%

Once depleted, the HP Aquifer will take 500 to 1,300 years to completely refill.

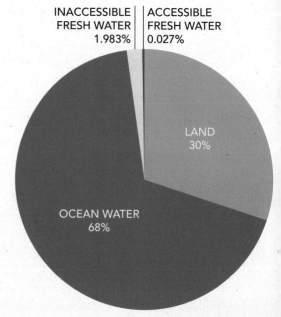

INACCESSIBLE FRESH WATER 1.983%

ACCESSIBLE FRESH WATER 0.027%

LAND 30%

OCEAN WATER 68%

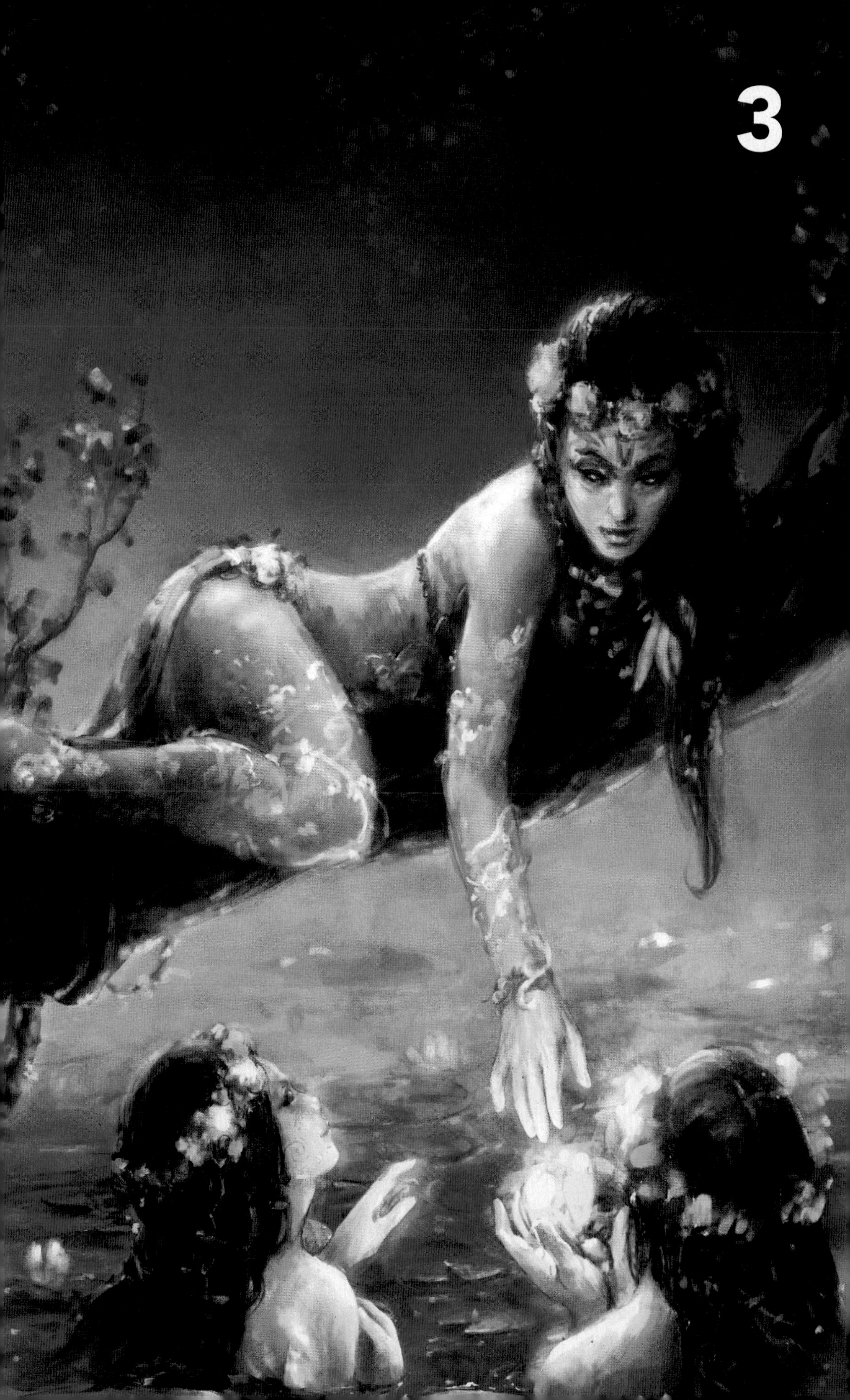
3

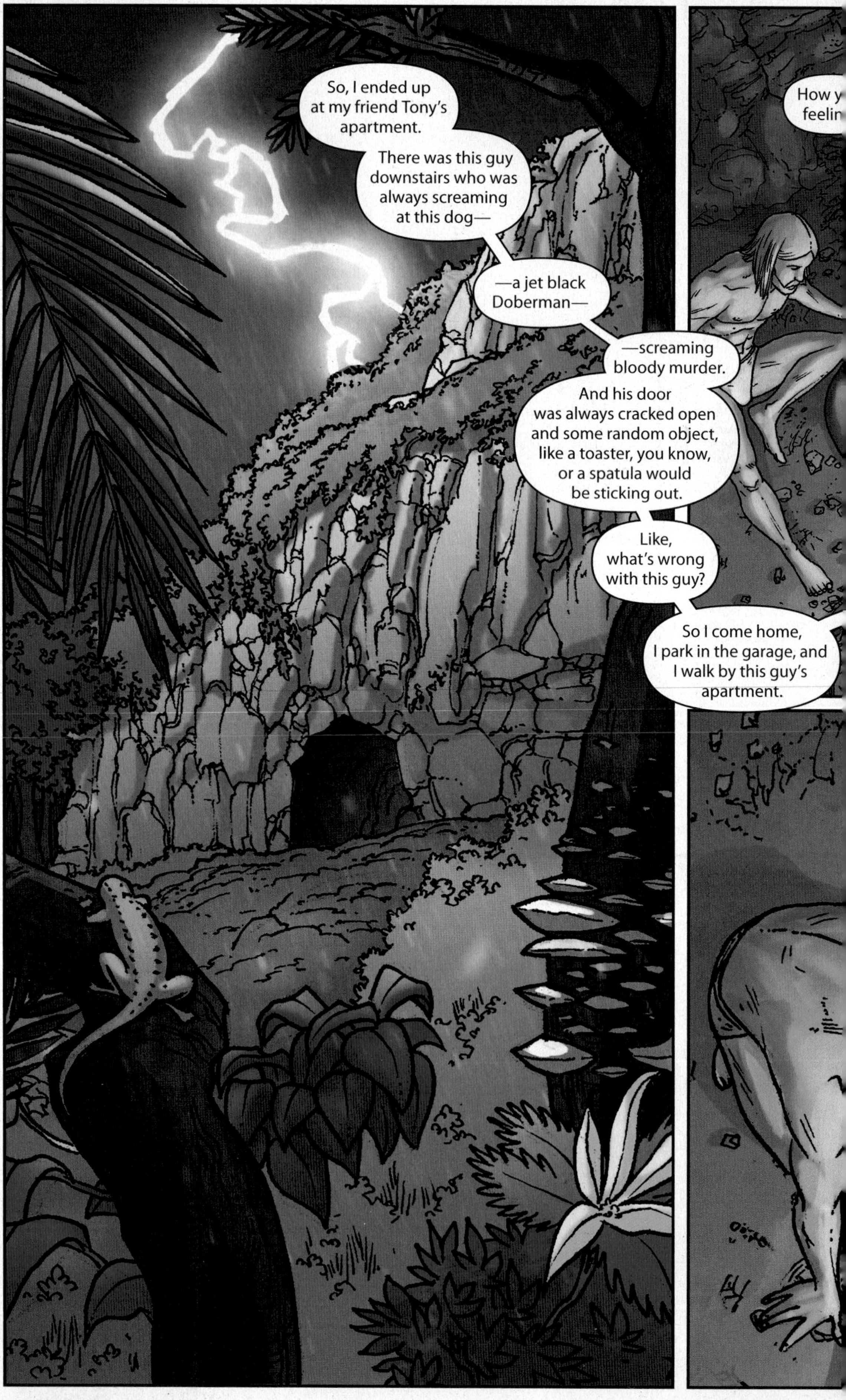

So, I ended up at my friend Tony's apartment.
There was this guy downstairs who was always screaming at this dog—
—a jet black Doberman—
—screaming bloody murder.
And his door was always cracked open and some random object, like a toaster, you know, or a spatula would be sticking out.
Like, what's wrong with this guy?
So I come home, I park in the garage, and I walk by this guy's apartment.

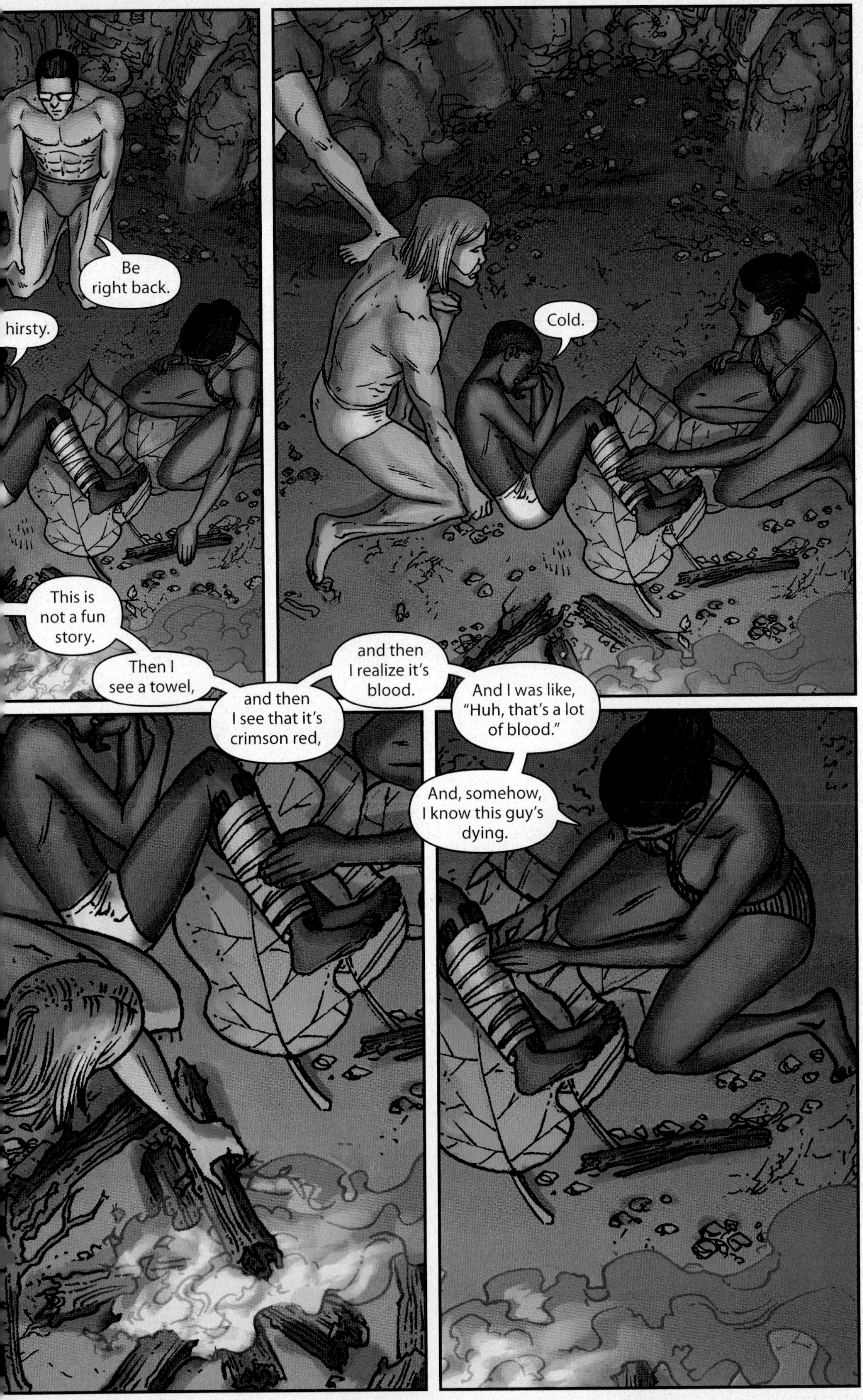
Be right back.
hirsty.
Cold.
This is not a fun story.
Then I see a towel,
and then I see that it's crimson red,
and then I realize it's blood.
And I was like, "Huh, that's a lot of blood."
And, somehow, I know this guy's dying.

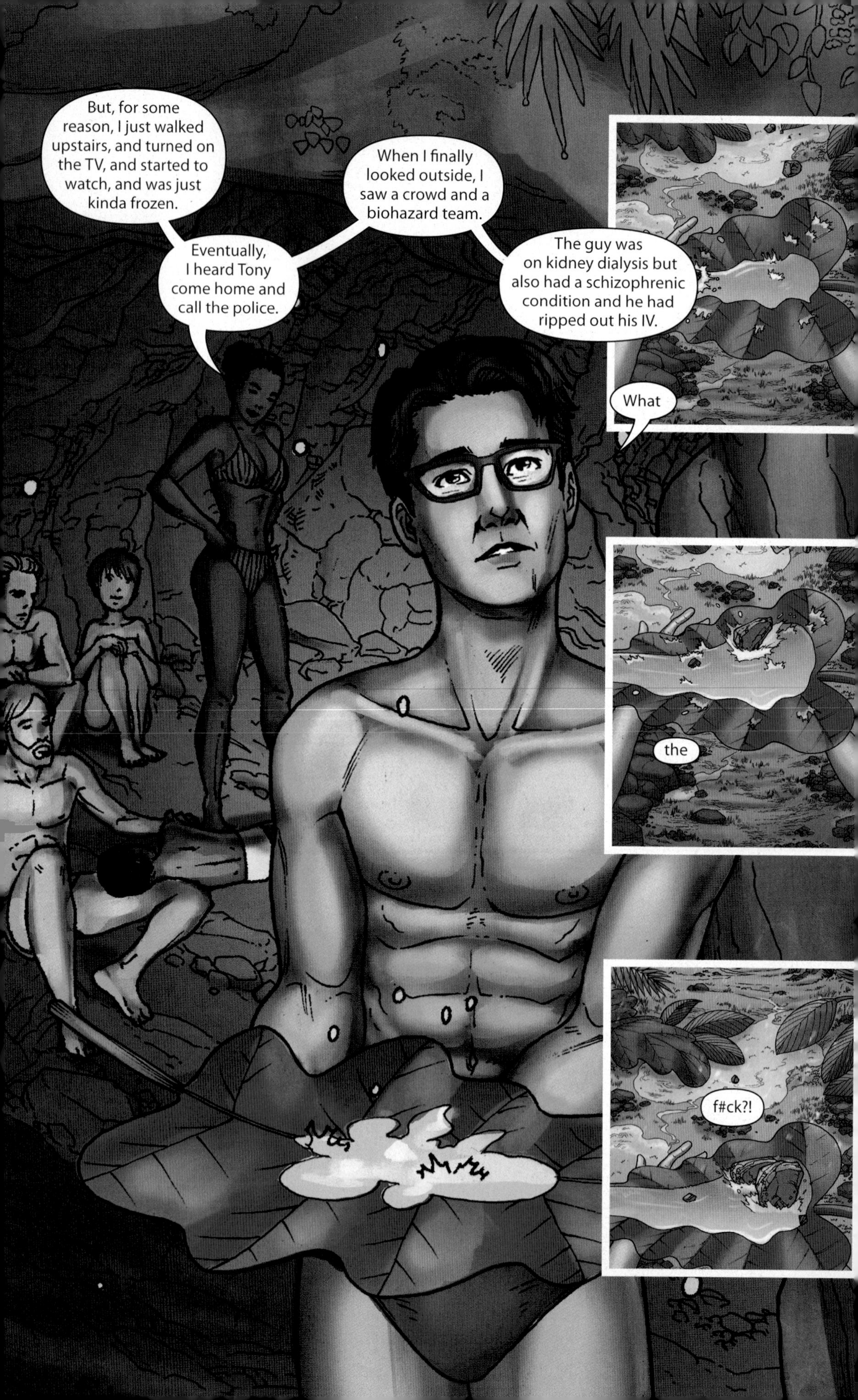
But, for some reason, I just walked upstairs, and turned on the TV, and started to watch, and was just kinda frozen.
Eventually, I heard Tony come home and call the police.
When I finally looked outside, I saw a crowd and a biohazard team.
The guy was on kidney dialysis but also had a schizophrenic condition and he had ripped out his IV.
What
the
f#ck?!

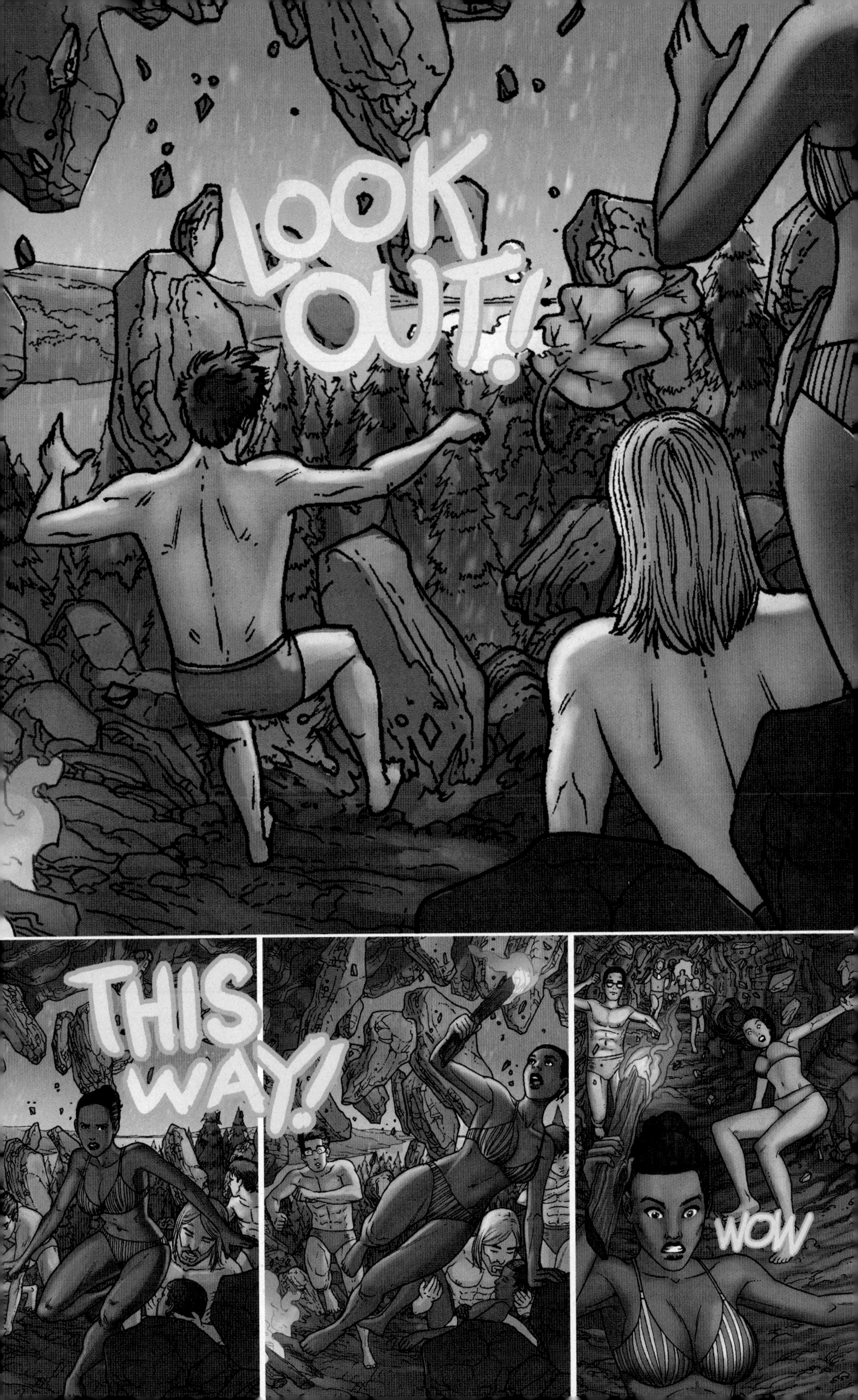
LOOK OUT!
THIS WAY!
WOW

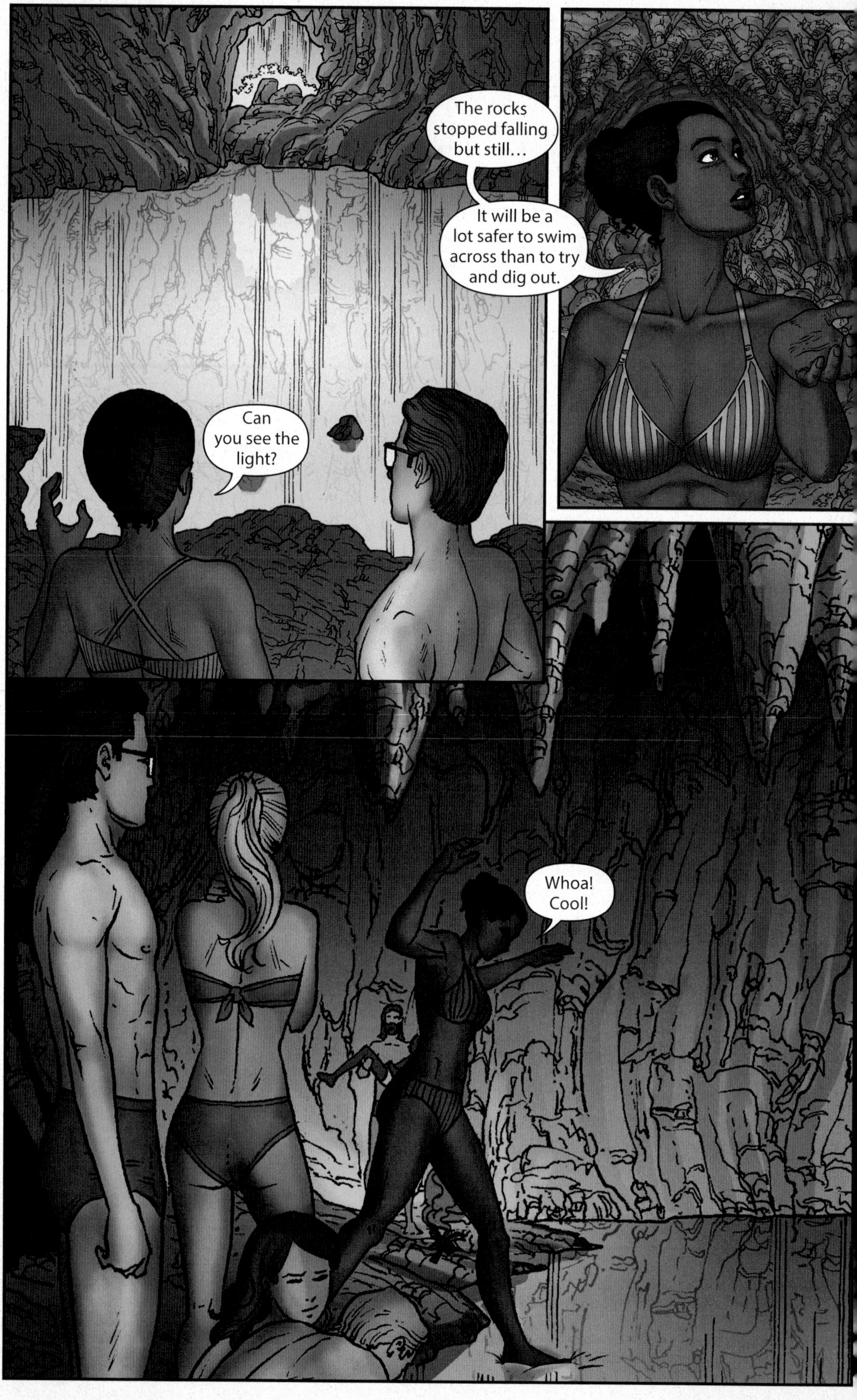
The rocks stopped falling but still…
It will be a lot safer to swim across than to try and dig out.
Can you see the light?
Whoa! Cool!

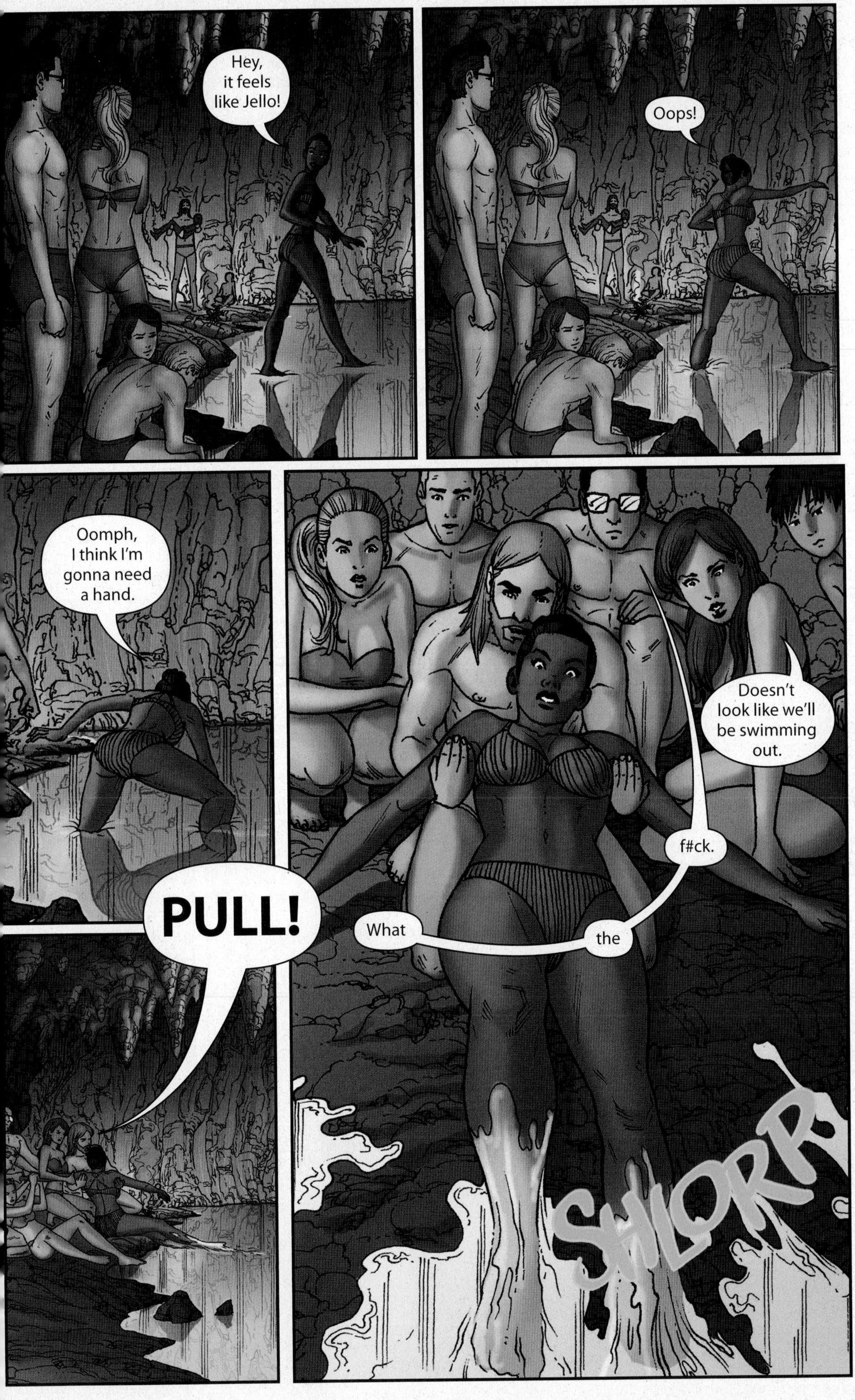
Hey, it feels like Jello!
Oops!
Oomph, I think I'm gonna need a hand.
PULL!
Doesn't look like we'll be swimming out.
What the f#ck.
SHLORP!

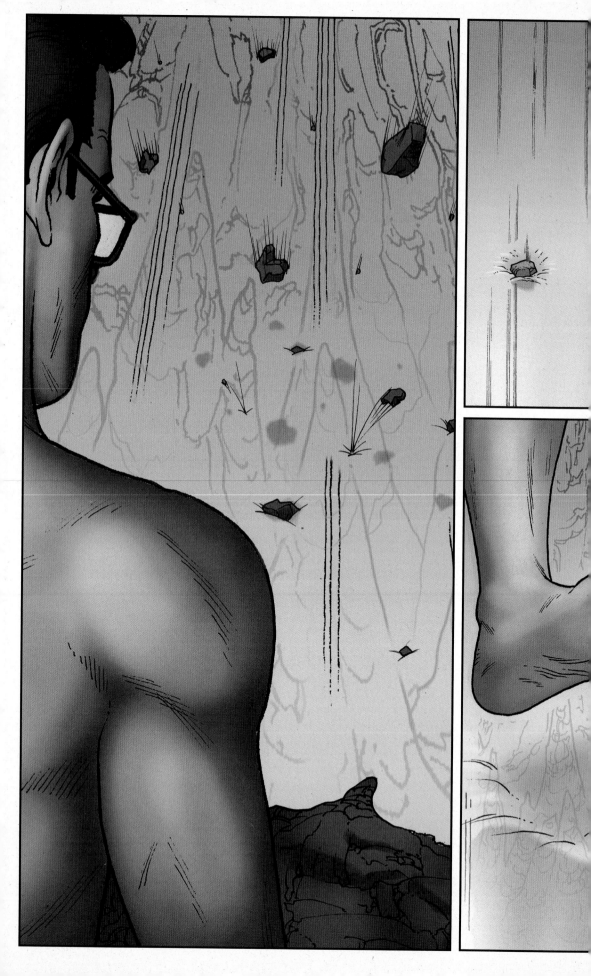

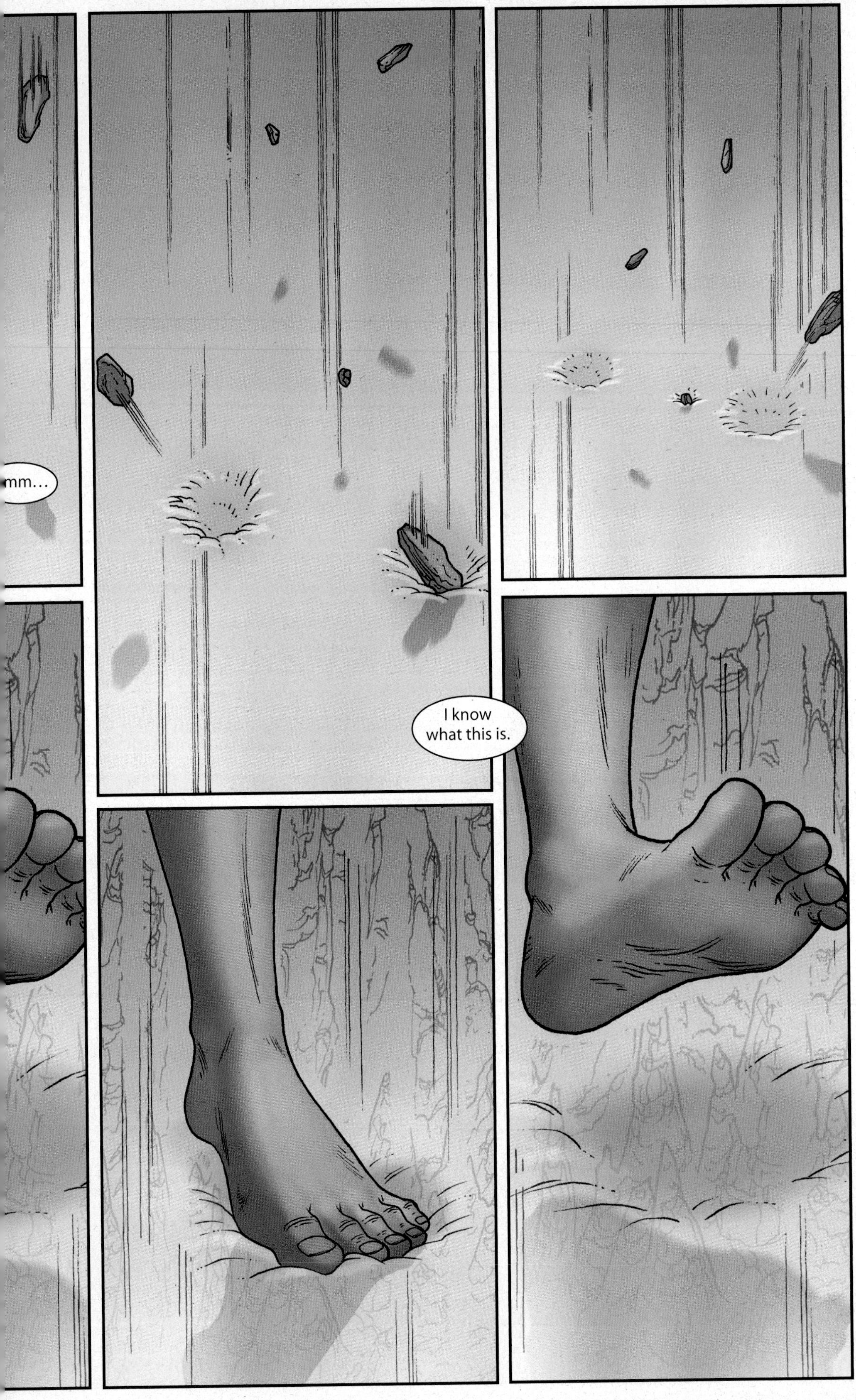
mm…
I know
what this is.

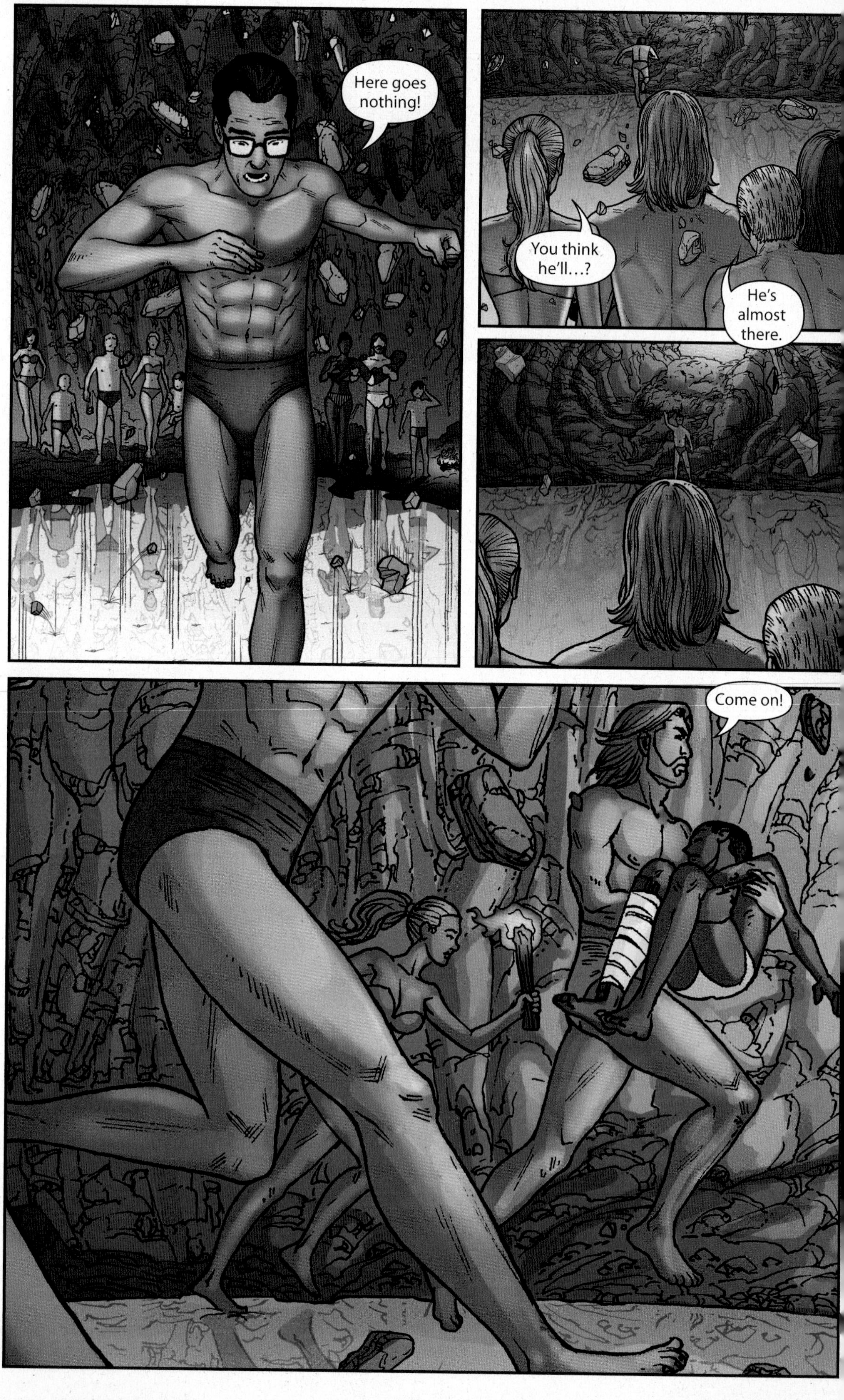
Here goes nothing!
You think he'll…?
He's almost there.
Come on!

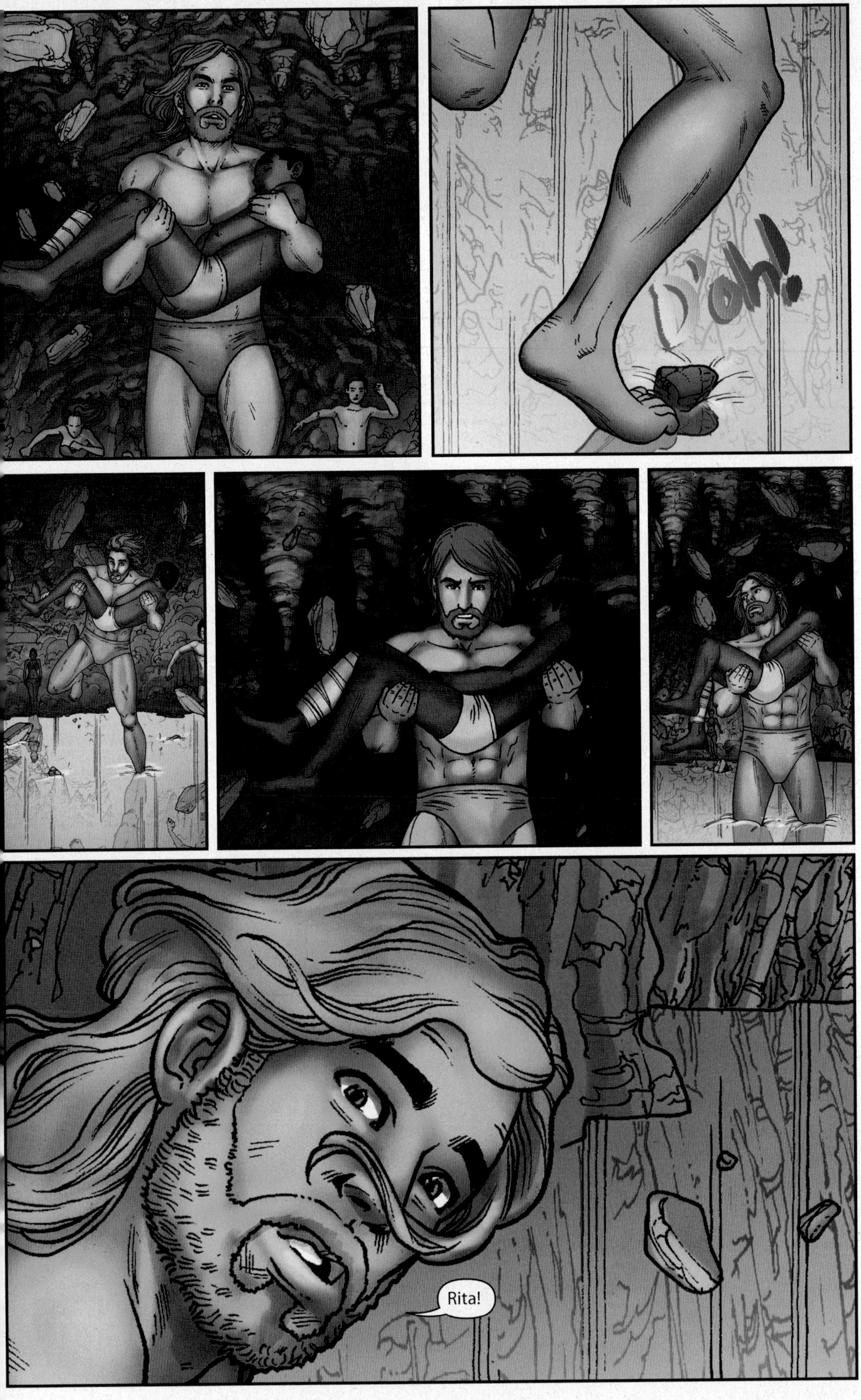
D'oh!
Rita!

HOME ECONOMICS

In the Workplace (Full-Time)	1960	2013*	% Increase
Women	14,800,000	43,200,000	192%
Men	36,600,000	56,100,000	53%
Average Earnings (2013 Dollars)			
Women	$25,633	$39,157	53%
Men	$42,247	$50,033	18%

Ratio of Earnings Women : Men

1967	$0.60 : $1.00
2013	$0.77 : $1.00

Median age of first marriage	1960	2013
Women	20.3	27
Men	22.8	29
% of US children living with two parents in their first marriage	73%	46%
% of unmarried couples living together	1.1%	12%
Average cost to raise a child to 18 (not adjusted for inflation)	$27,000	$245,000
Median sales price of a new home (not adjusted for inflation)	$14,100	$281,800

1960	2013
Median annual family income	
$5,600	$51,939
Total cost over 18 years of a home and of raising a child	
$41,000	$526,000

*ESTIMATED DATA

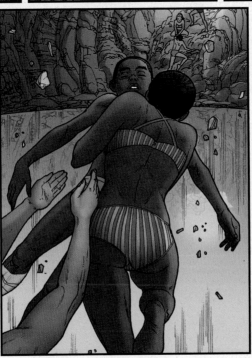

Quick, someone take him.

Austin! Hold on!

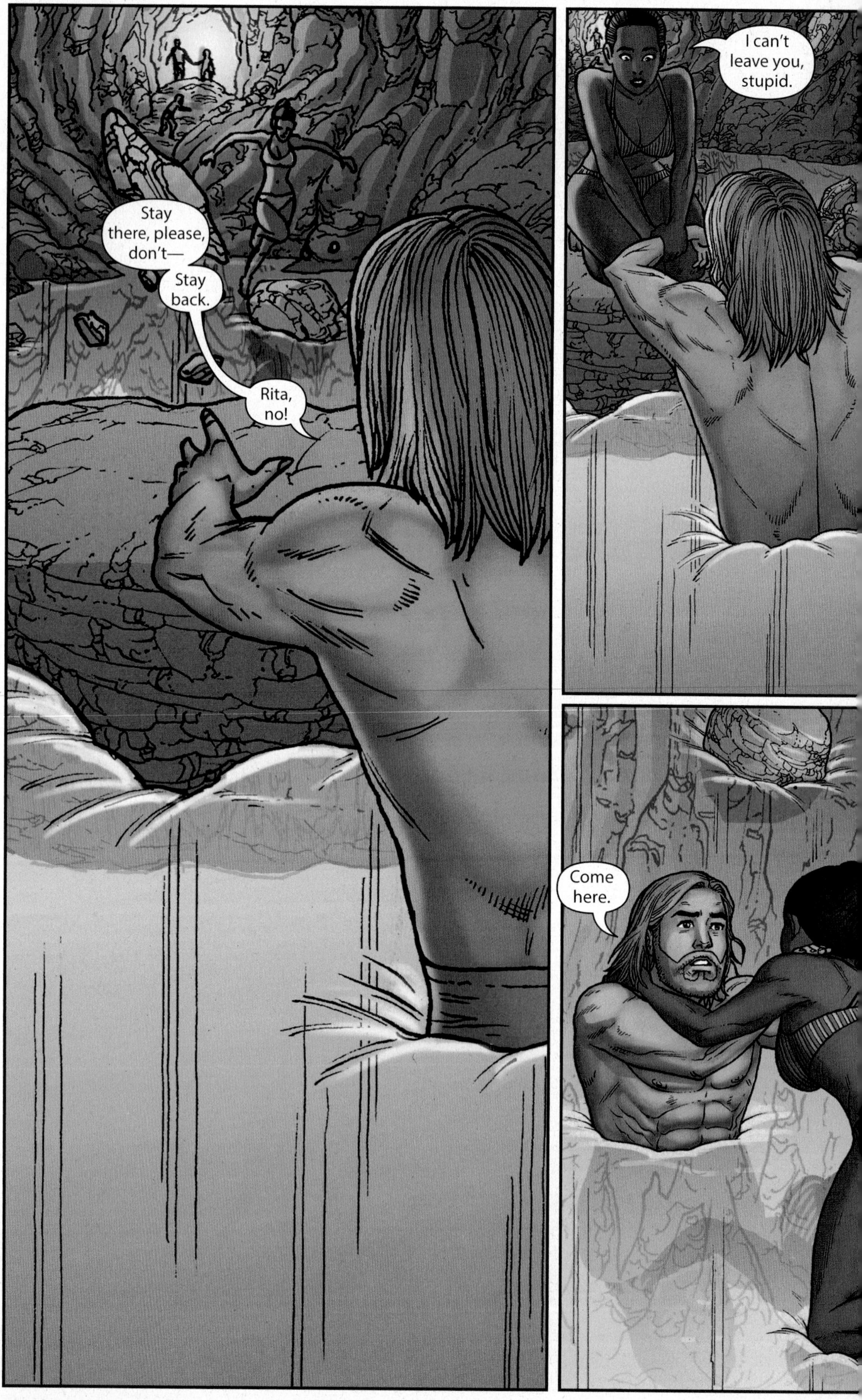
Stay there, please, don't—
Stay back.
Rita, no!
I can't leave you, stupid.
Come here.

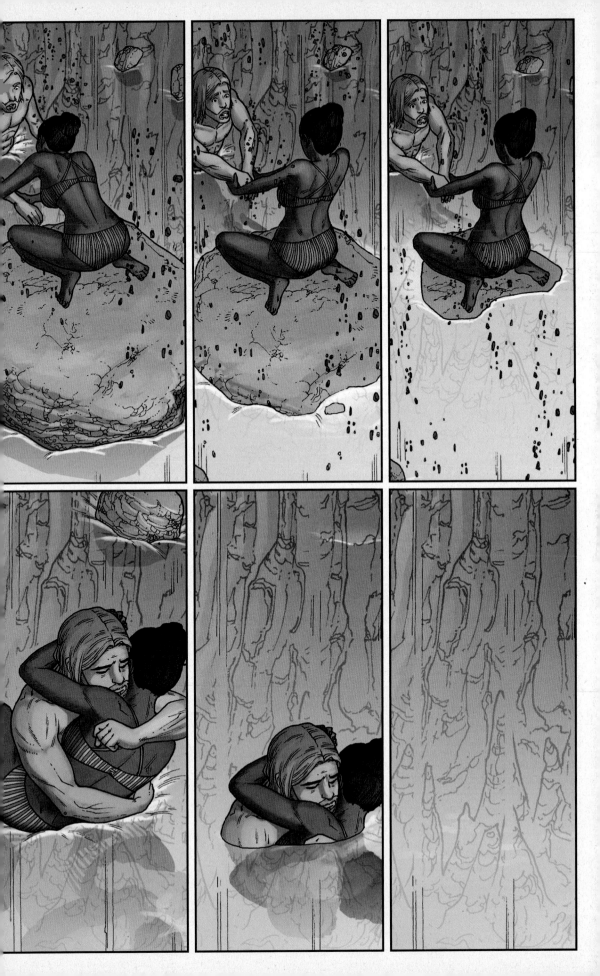

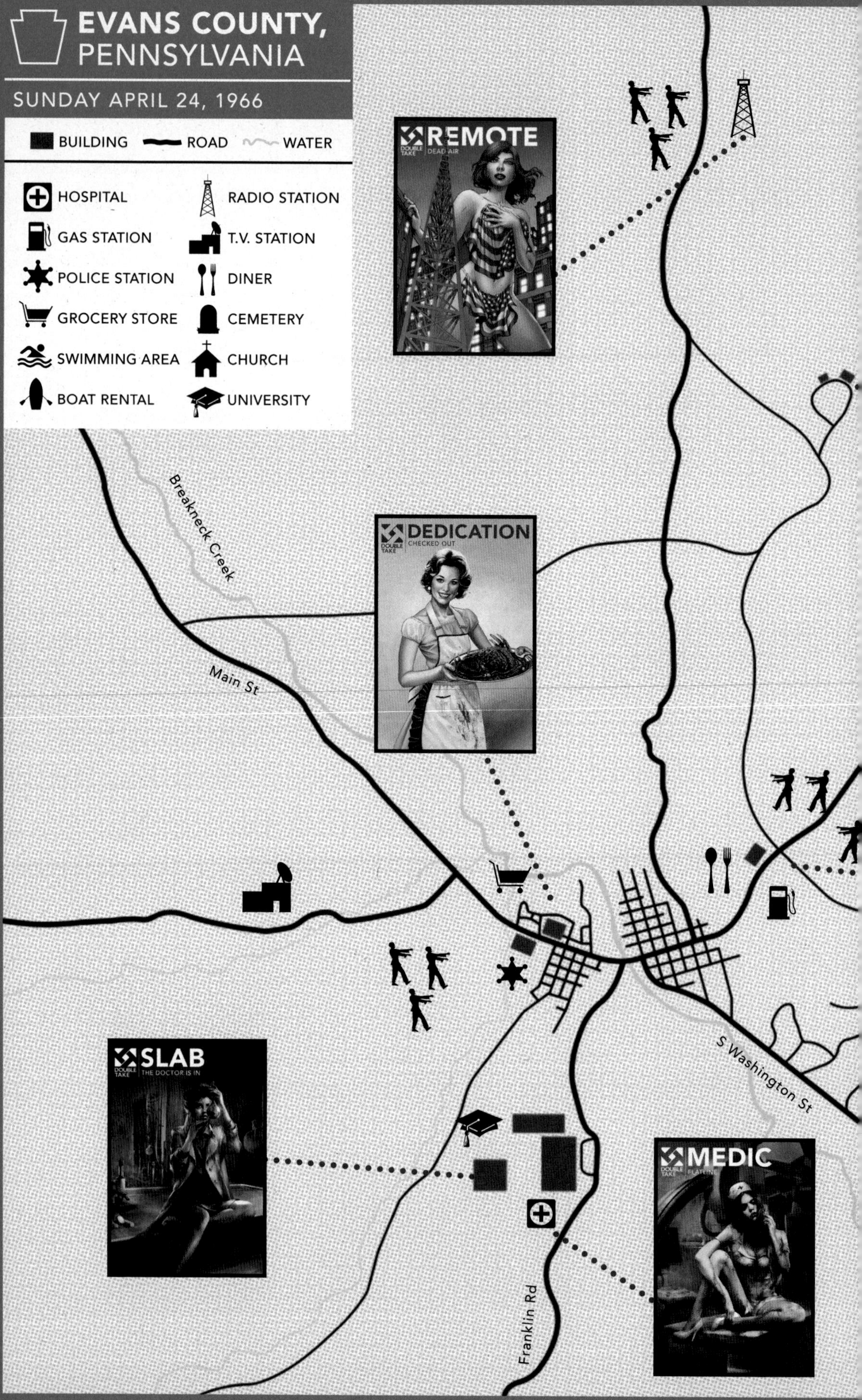
EVANS COUNTY, PENNSYLVANIA
SUNDAY APRIL 24, 1966
BUILDING
ROAD
WATER
HOSPITAL
RADIO STATION
GAS STATION
T.V. STATION
POLICE STATION
DINER
GROCERY STORE
CEMETERY
SWIMMING AREA
CHURCH
BOAT RENTAL
UNIVERSITY
DOUBLE TAKE
REMOTE
DEAD AIR
DOUBLE TAKE
DEDICATION
CHECKED OUT
Breakneck Creek
Main St
DOUBLE TAKE
SLAB
THE DOCTOR IS IN
S Washington St
DOUBLE TAKE
MEDIC
Franklin Rd

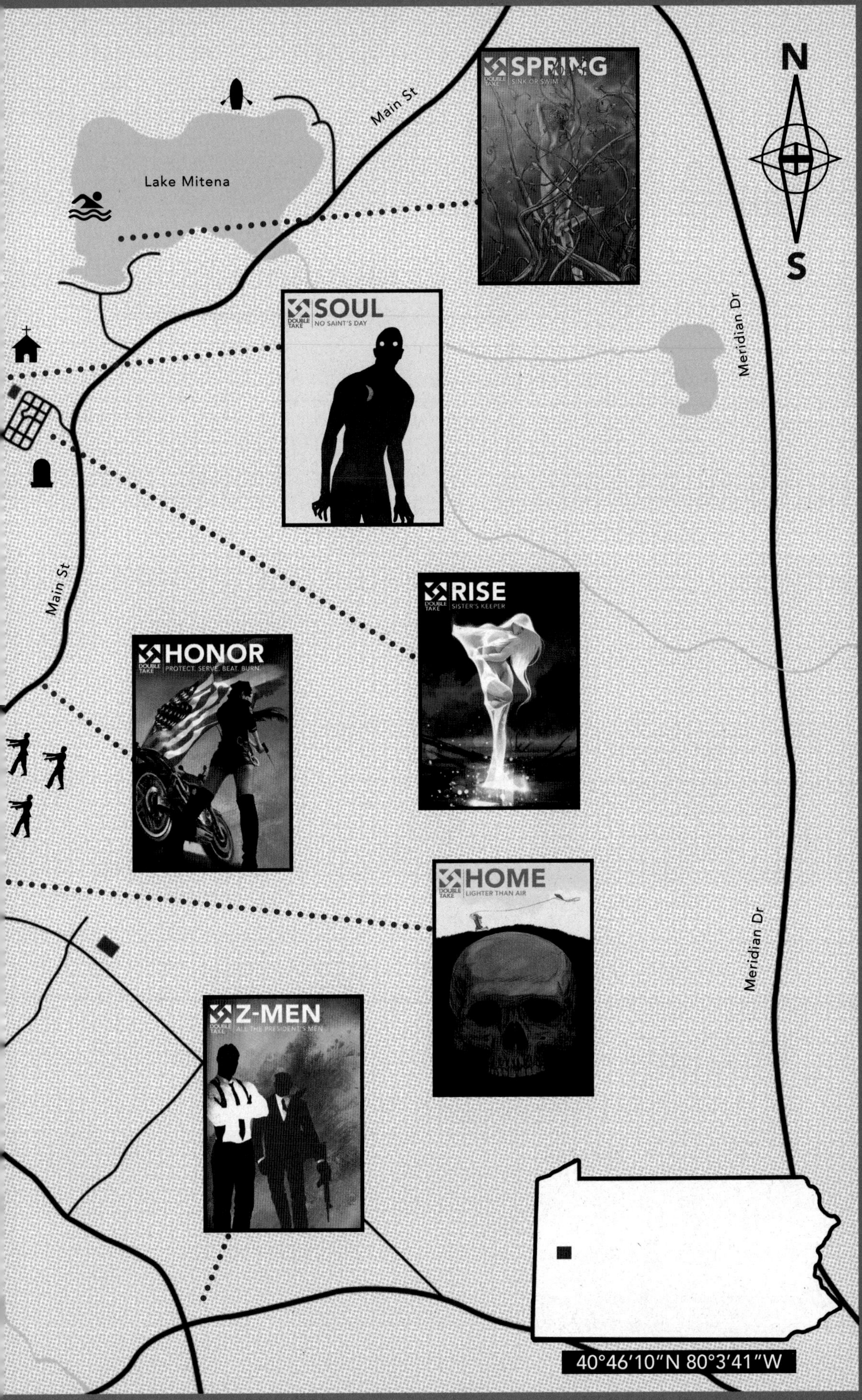

N
S
Main St
Lake Mitena
SPRING
DOUBLE TAKE
SINK OR SWIM
SOUL
DOUBLE TAKE
NO SAINT'S DAY
Meridian Dr
Main St
RISE
DOUBLE TAKE
SISTER'S KEEPER
HONOR
DOUBLE TAKE
PROTECT. SERVE. BEAT. BURN.
HOME
DOUBLE TAKE
LIGHTER THAN AIR
Meridian Dr
Z-MEN
DOUBLE TAKE
ALL THE PRESIDENT'S MEN
40°46′10″N 80°3′41″W

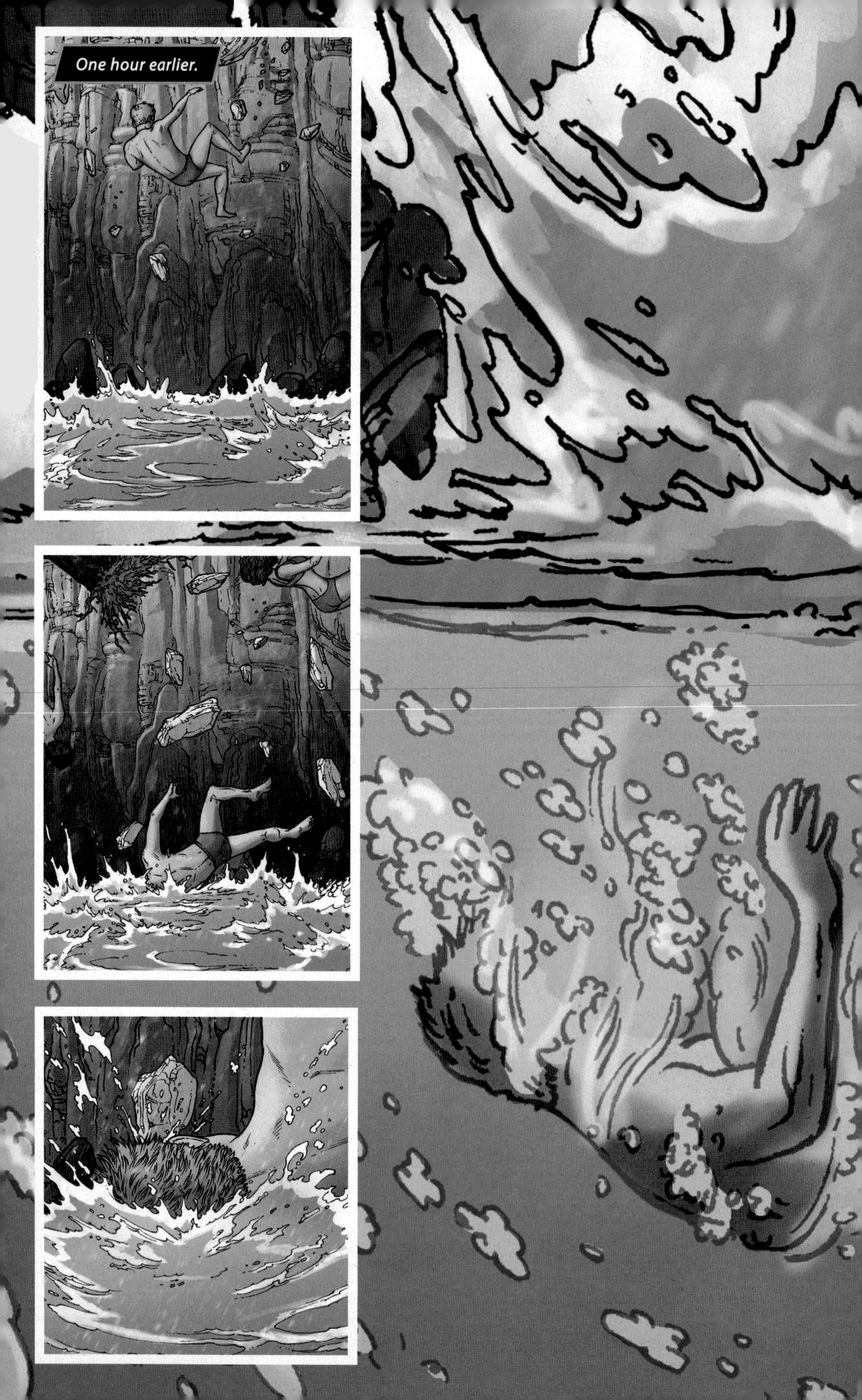
One hour earlier.

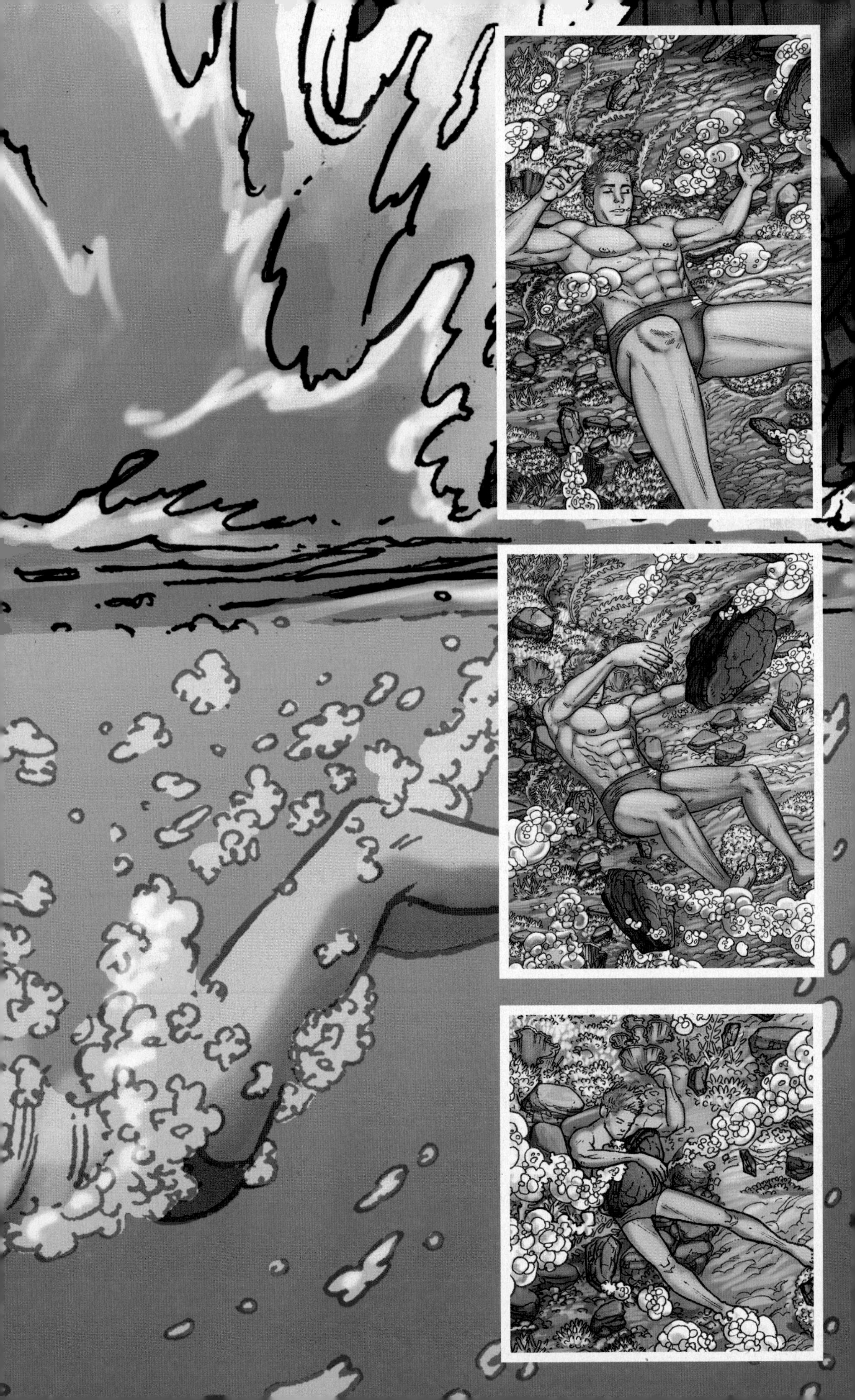

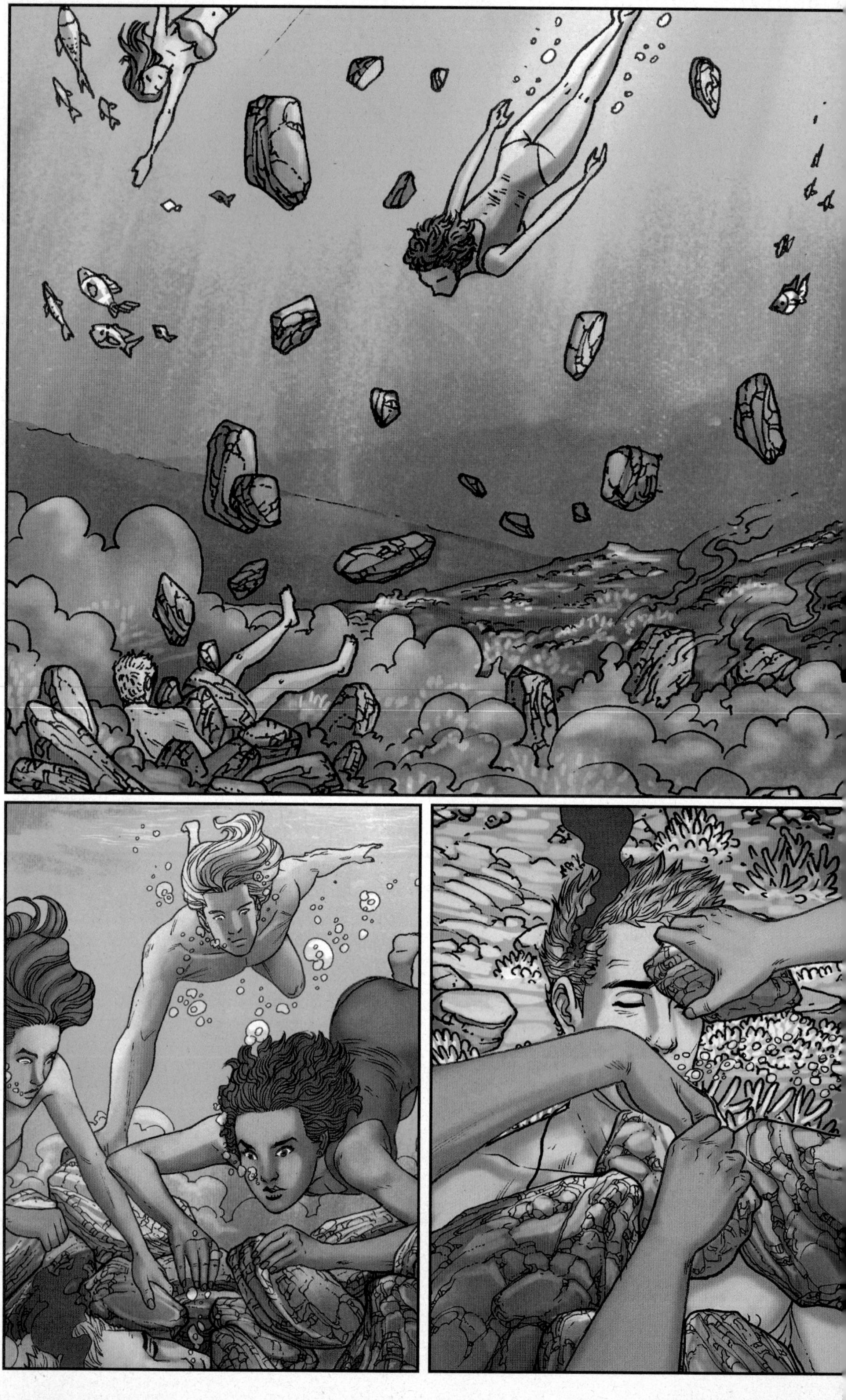

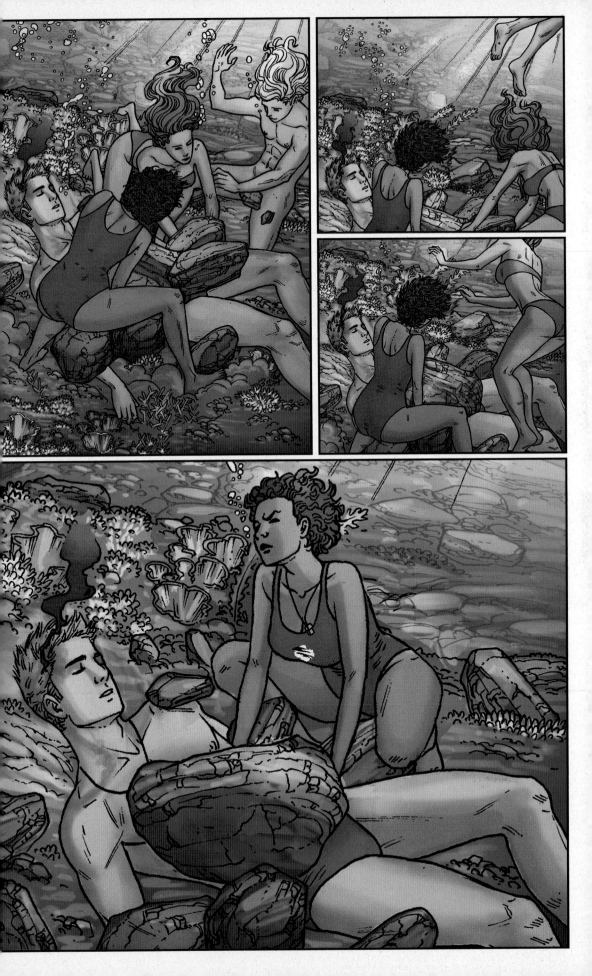

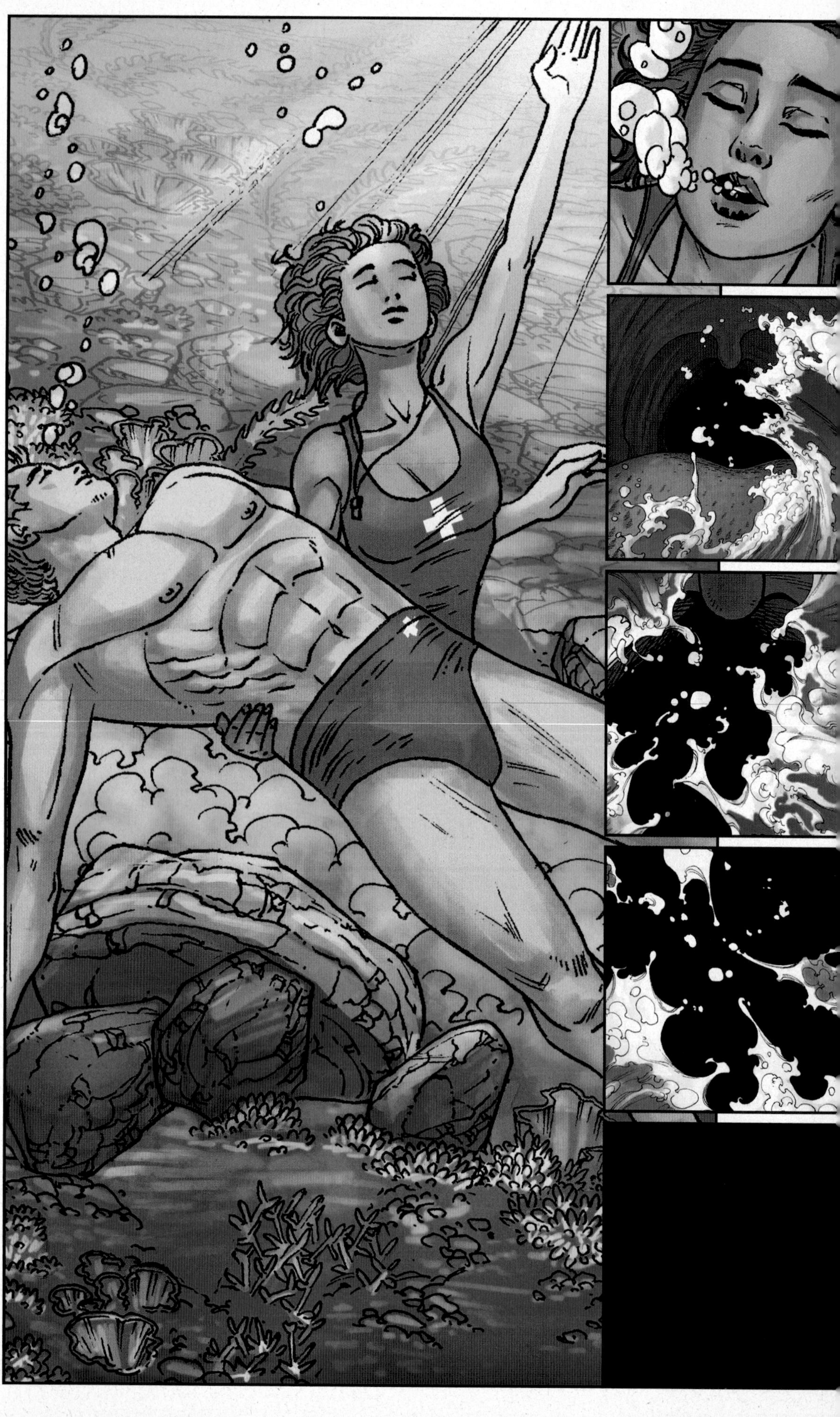

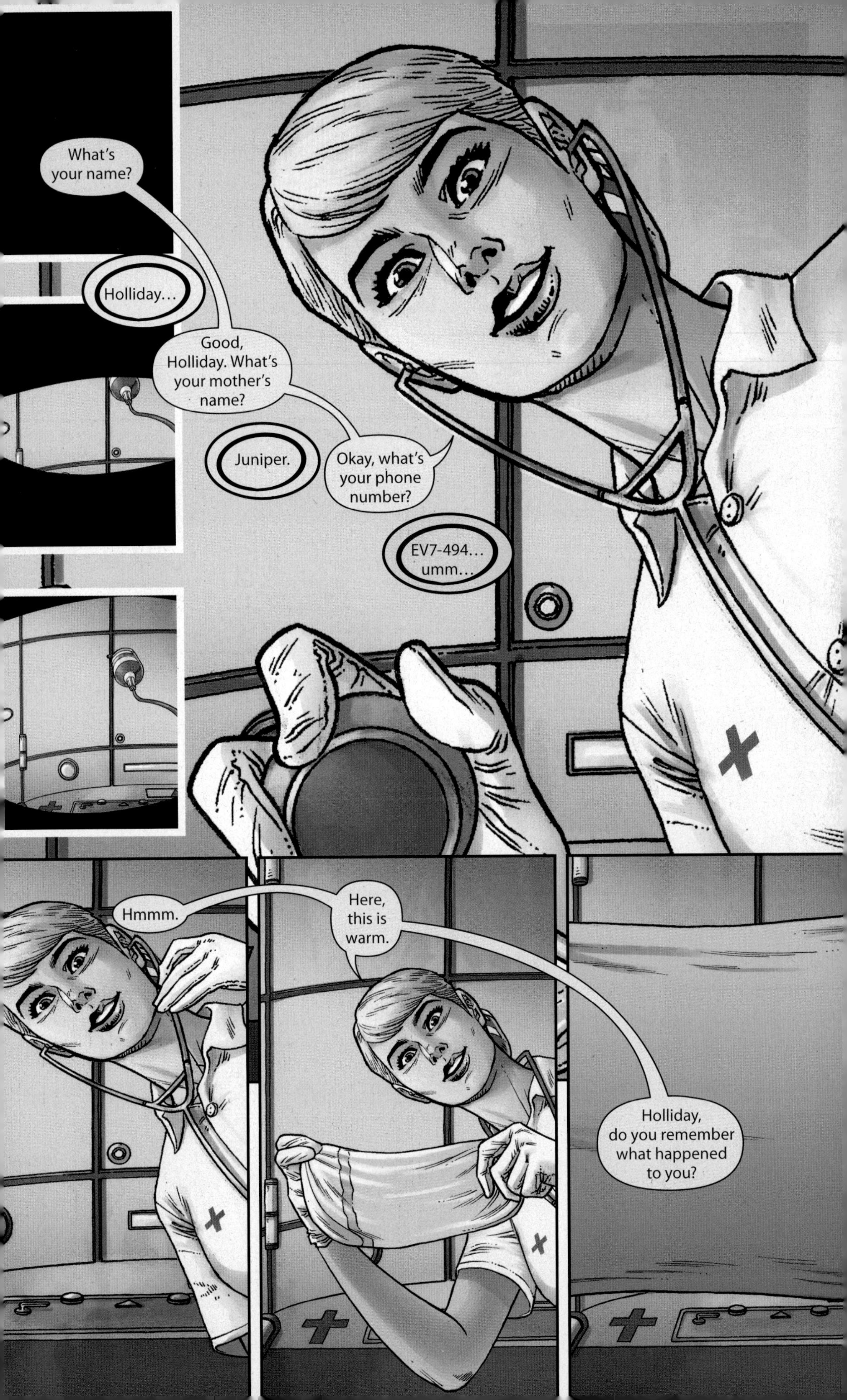

What's your name?
Holliday...
Good, Holliday. What's your mother's name?
Juniper.
Okay, what's your phone number?
EV7-494... umm...
Hmmm.
Here, this is warm.
Holliday, do you remember what happened to you?

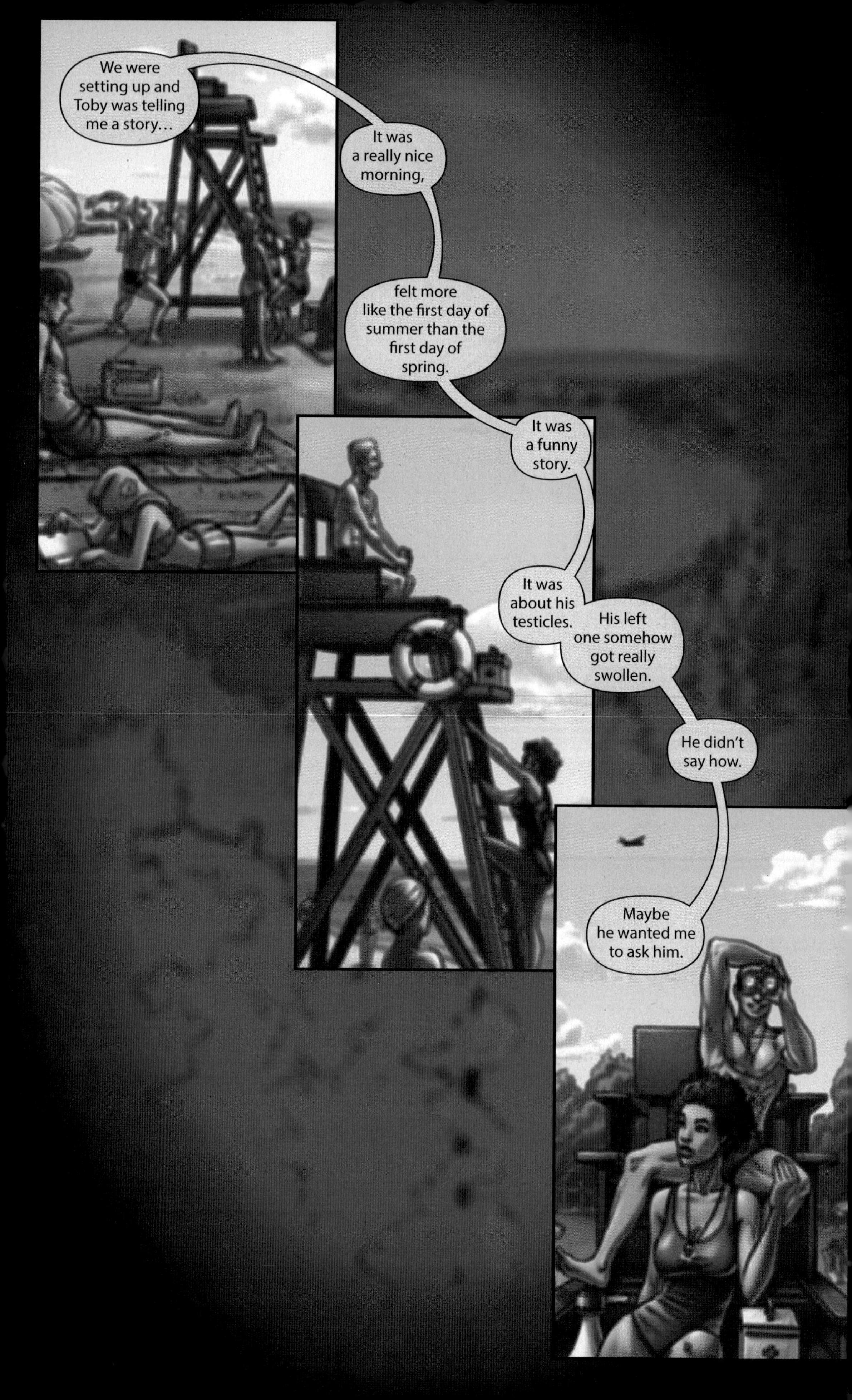
We were setting up and Toby was telling me a story…
It was a really nice morning,
felt more like the first day of summer than the first day of spring.
It was a funny story.
It was about his testicles.
His left one somehow got really swollen.
He didn't say how.
Maybe he wanted me to ask him.

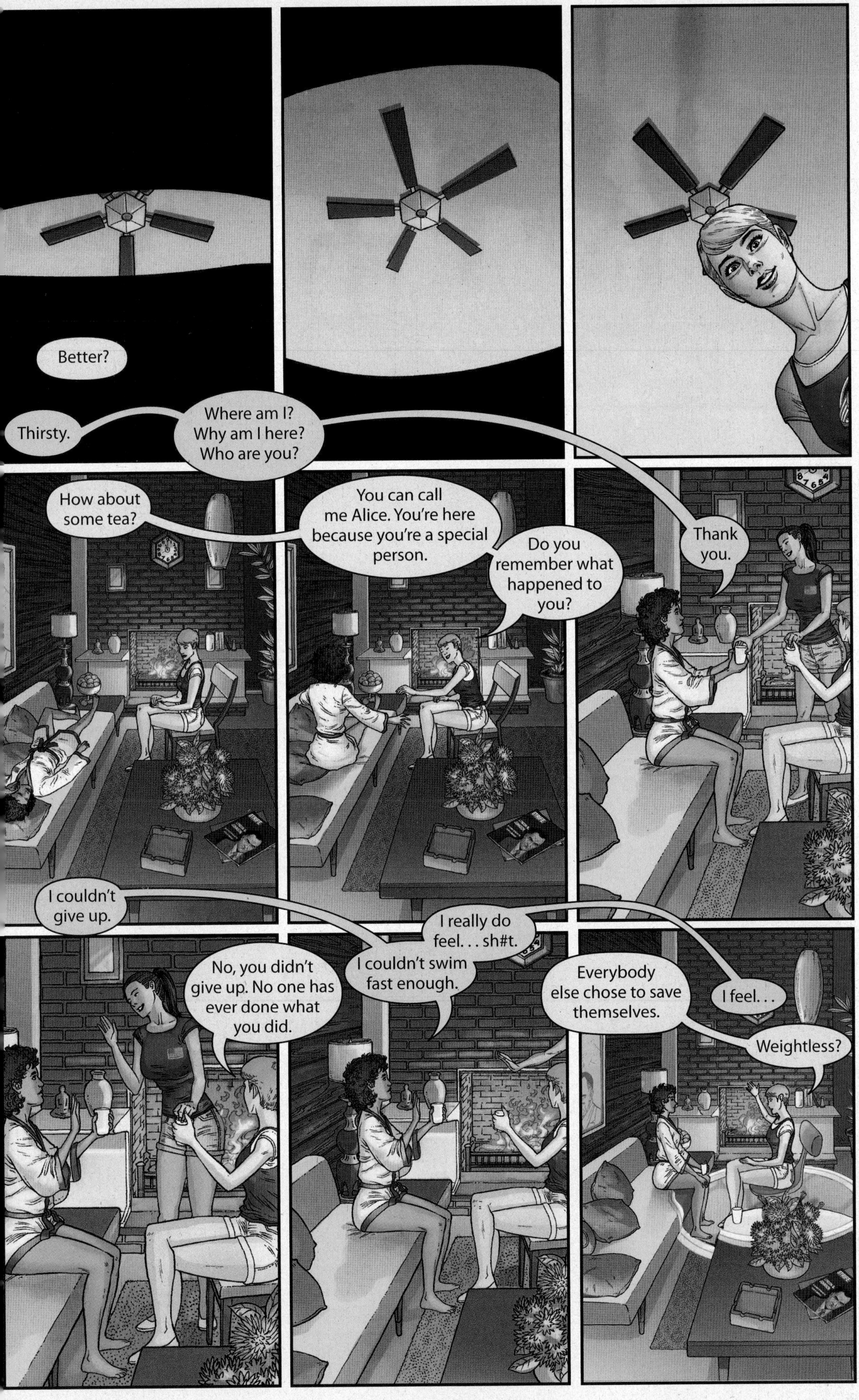
Better?
Thirsty.
Where am I? Why am I here? Who are you?
How about some tea?
You can call me Alice. You're here because you're a special person.
Do you remember what happened to you?
Thank you.
I couldn't give up.
No, you didn't give up. No one has ever done what you did.
I couldn't swim fast enough.
I really do feel. . . sh#t.
Everybody else chose to save themselves.
I feel. . .
Weightless?

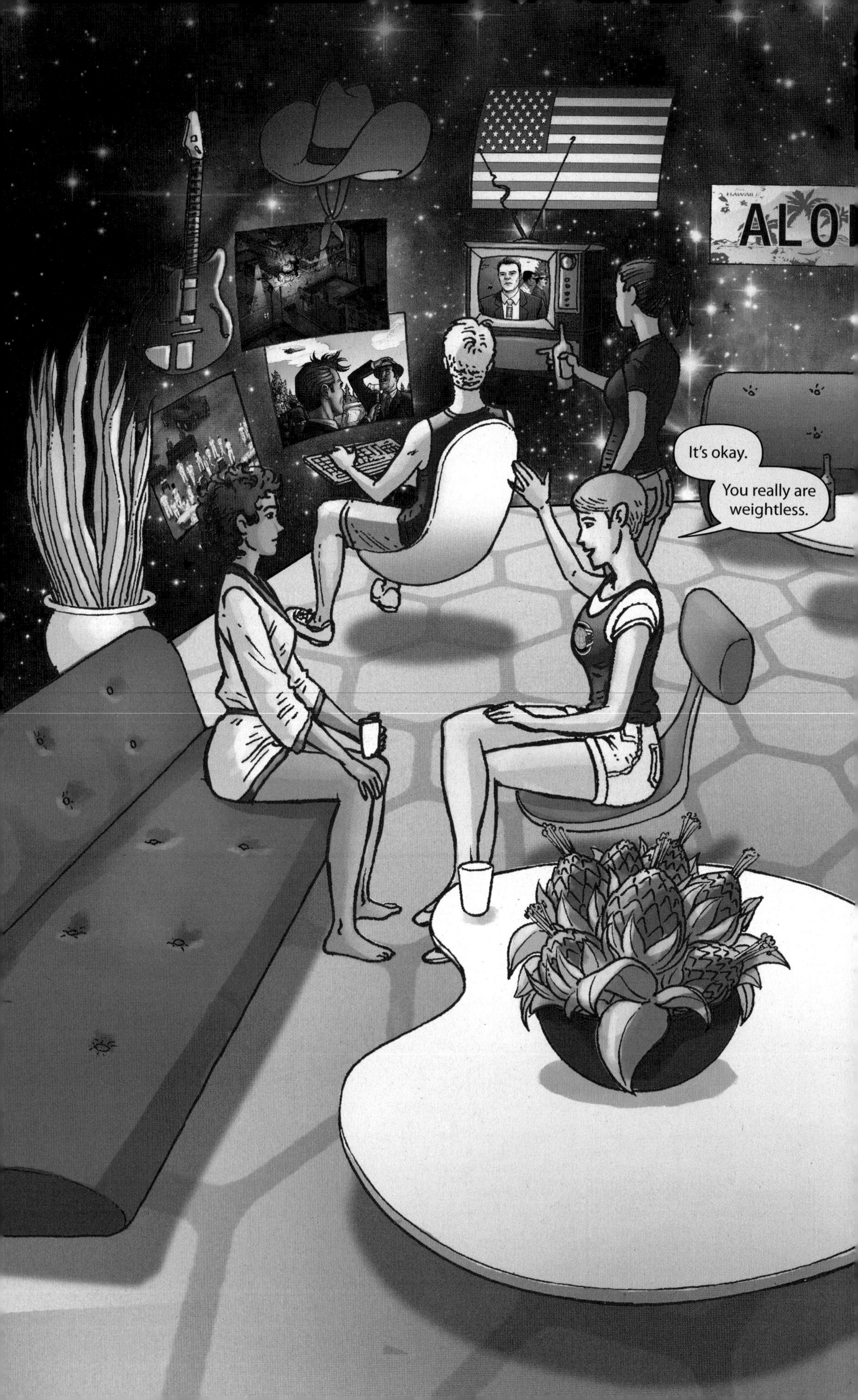
It's okay.
You really are weightless.

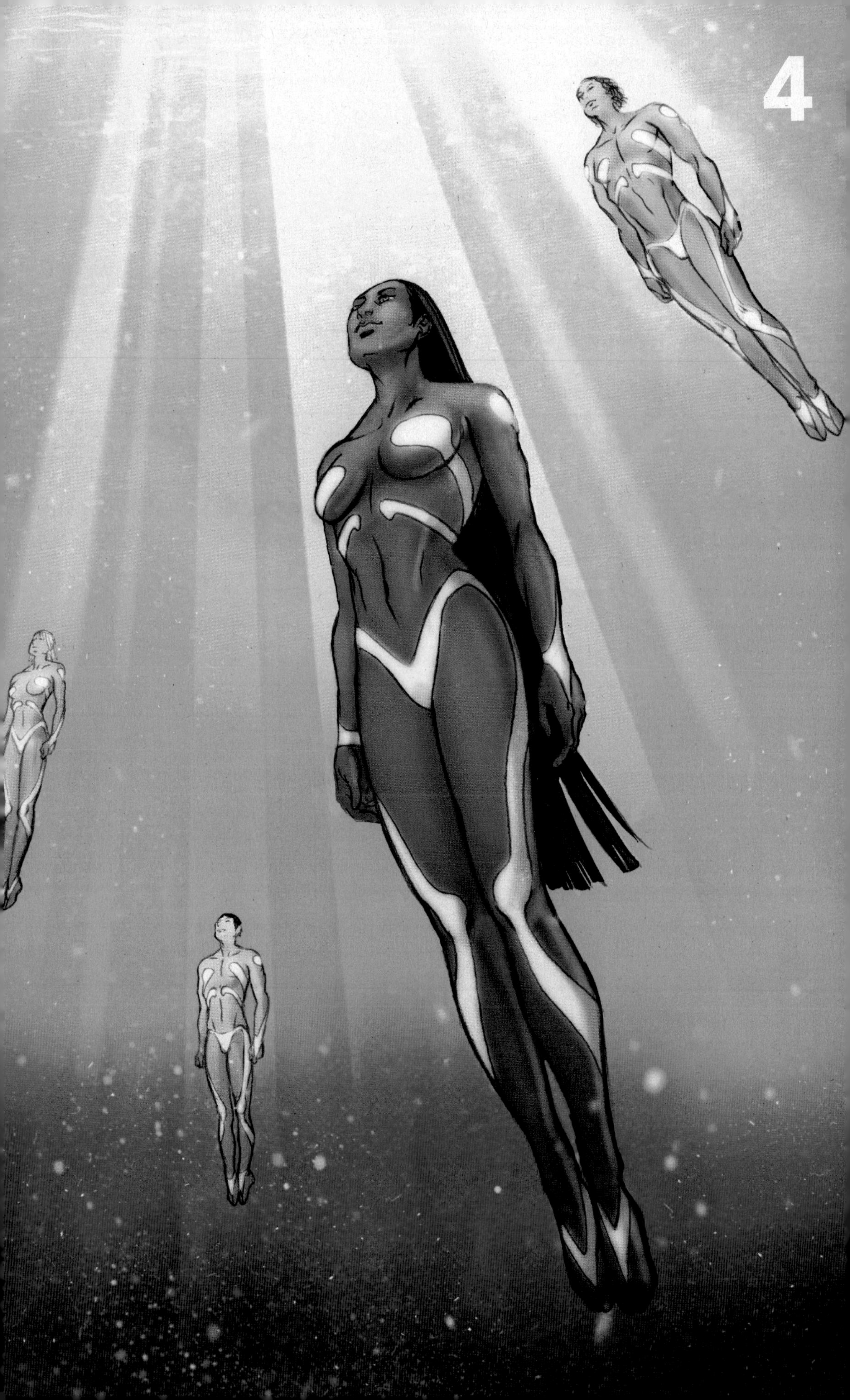
4

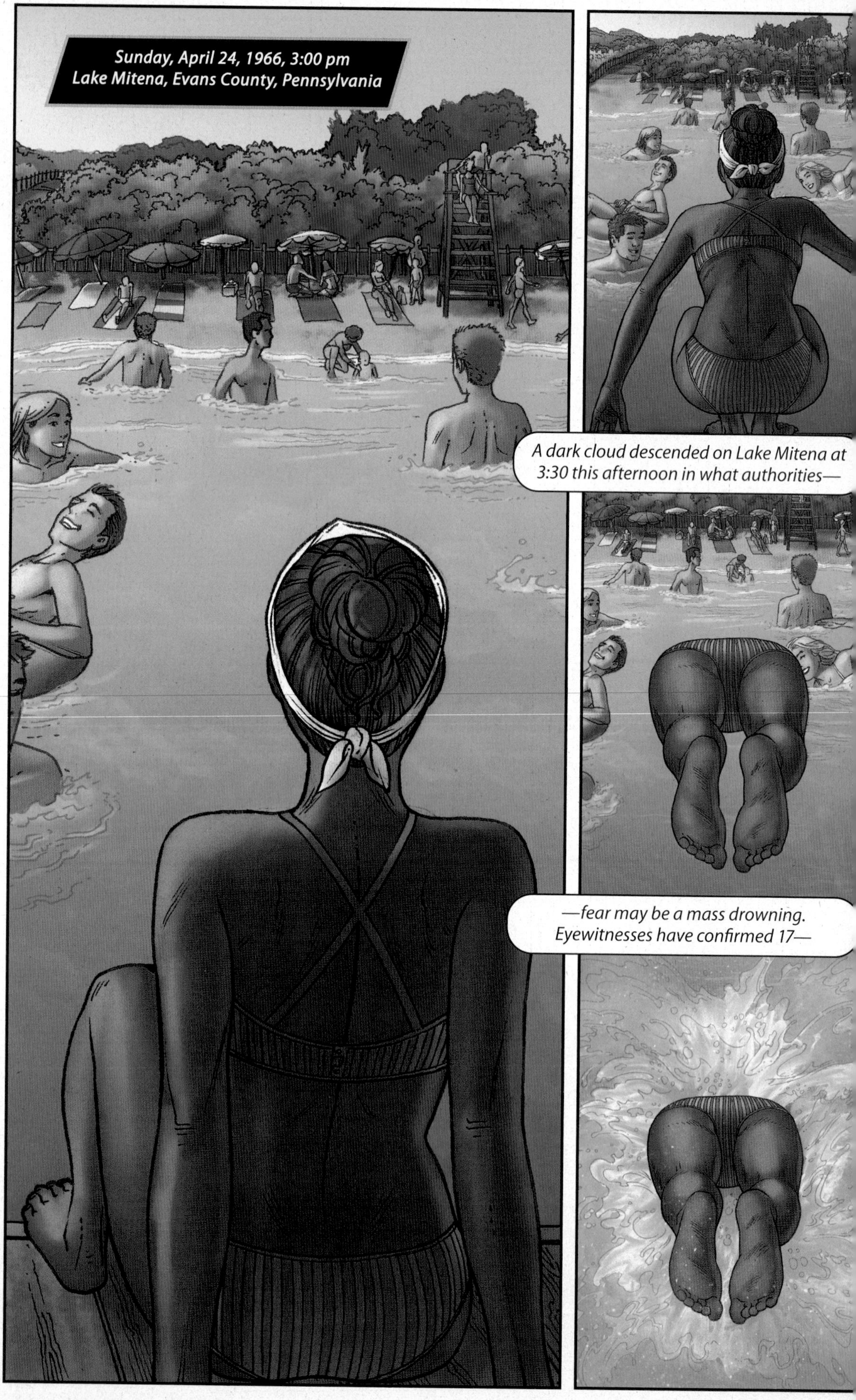
Sunday, April 24, 1966, 3:00 pm
Lake Mitena, Evans County, Pennsylvania
A dark cloud descended on Lake Mitena at 3:30 this afternoon in what authorities—
—fear may be a mass drowning. Eyewitnesses have confirmed 17—

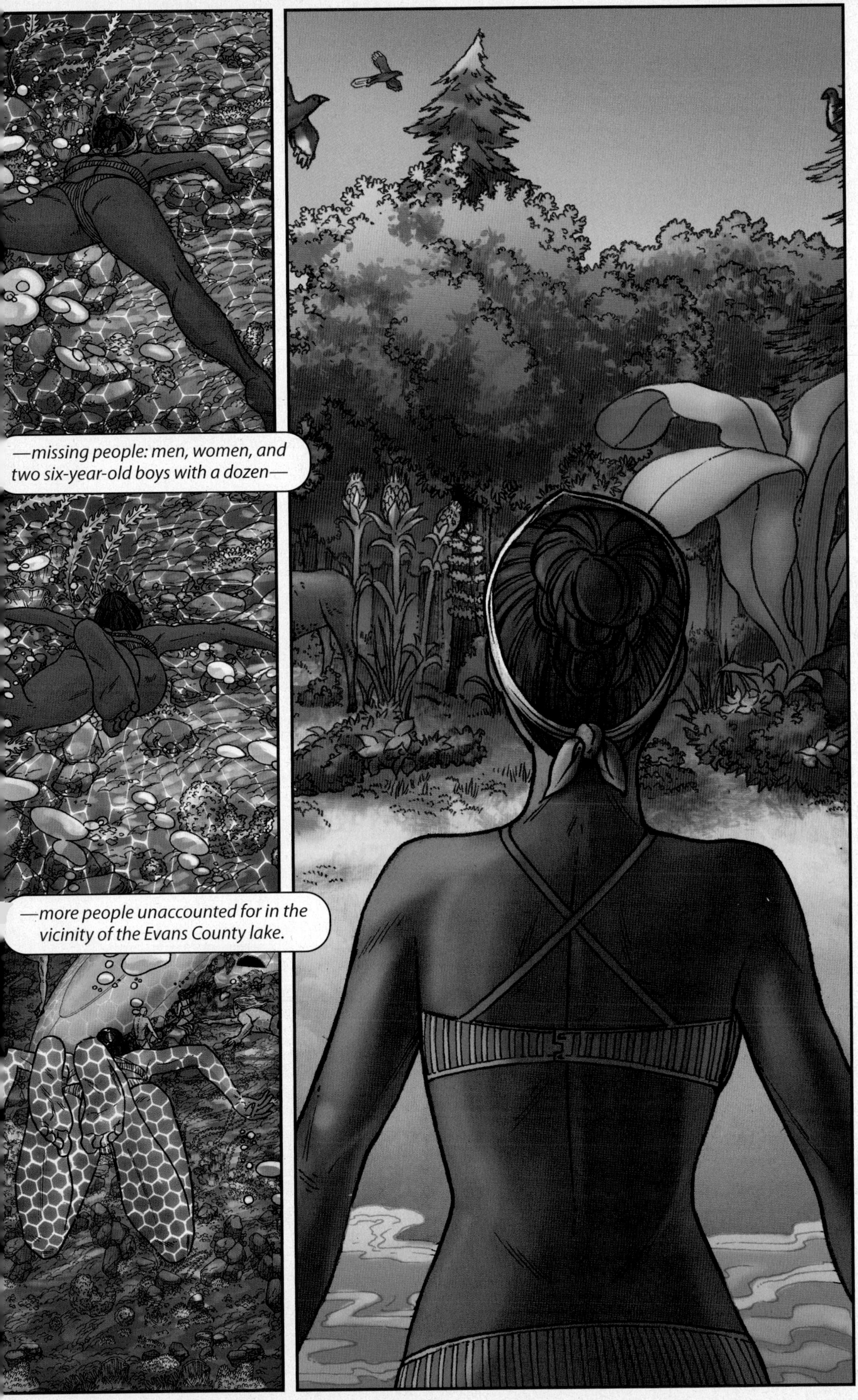
—missing people: men, women, and two six-year-old boys with a dozen—
—more people unaccounted for in the vicinity of the Evans County lake.

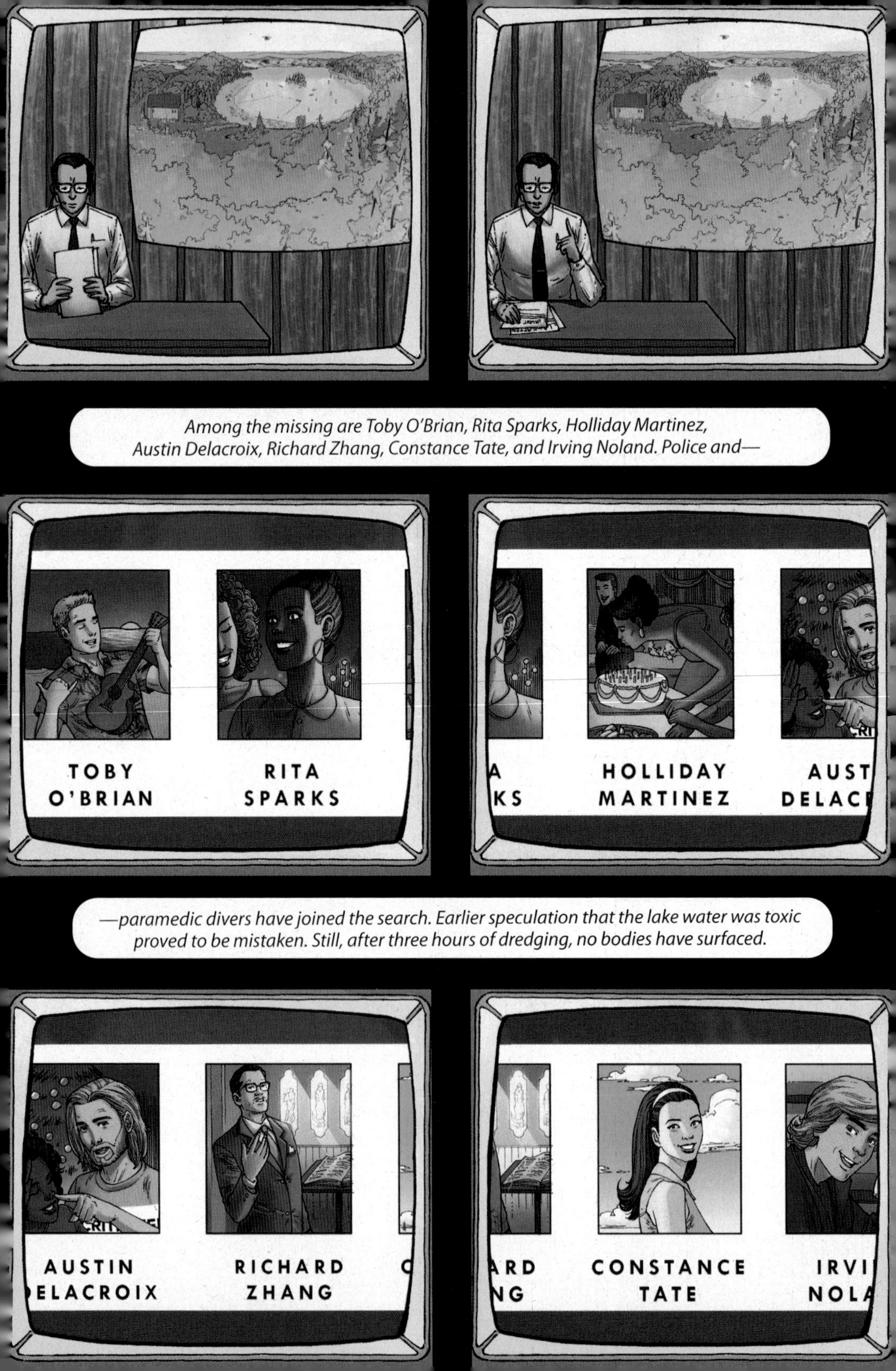
Among the missing are Toby O'Brian, Rita Sparks, Holliday Martinez, Austin Delacroix, Richard Zhang, Constance Tate, and Irving Noland. Police and—
TOBY O'BRIAN
RITA SPARKS
HOLLIDAY MARTINEZ
—paramedic divers have joined the search. Earlier speculation that the lake water was toxic proved to be mistaken. Still, after three hours of dredging, no bodies have surfaced.
AUSTIN DELACROIX
RICHARD ZHANG
CONSTANCE TATE

PRIME TIME GUIDE

APRIL 24TH–30TH, 1966

		ABC	CBS	NBC	WJAC-TV DuBOIS
	6:30	Local	Local	Bell Telephone Hour/NBC News Specials	Walter Kronkite
	7:00	Voyage to the Bottom of the Sea	Lassie		Rifleman
	7:30		It's About Time	Walt Disney's Wonderful World of Color	To Tell the Truth
	8:00	The FBI	Ed Sullivan Show		I've Got a Secret
	8:30			Hey Landlord!	Lucy Show
	9:00		Garry Moore Show	Bonanza	Andy Griffith Show
	9:30	The Sunday Night Movie			Hazel
	10:00		Candid Camera	Andy Williams Show	Strollin' 20's
	10:30		What's My Line?		
	7:30	Iron Horse	Gilligan's Island	The Monkees	Gunsmoke
	8:00		Run, Buddy, Run	I Dream of Jeannie	Pirate Fever 66
	8:30	The Rat Patrol	The Lucy Show	Roger Miller Show	Lucy Show
	9:00	The Felony Squad	Andy Griffith Show	The Road West	Andy Griffith Show
	9:30	Peyton Place	Family Affair		Family Affair
	10:00	The Big Valley	Jess Arthur Show	Run for Your Life	Run for Your Life
	10:30		I've Got a Secret		
	7:30	Combat!	Daktari	The Girl from U.N.C.L.E.	12 O'Clock High
	8:00				
	8:30	The Rounders	Red Skelton Hour	Occasional Wife	Legend of Jesse James
	9:00	The Pruitts of Southampton			Shenandoah
	9:30	Love on a Rooftop	Petticoat Junction	Tuesday Night at the Movies	Peyton Place
	10:00	The Fugitive	CBS News Special		Ben Casey
	10:30				
	7:30	Batman	Lost In Space	The Virginian	Hullabaloo
	8:00	The Monroes			John Forsythe Show
	8:30		The Beverly Hillbillies		Dr. Kildare
	9:00	The Man Who Never Was	Green Acres	Bob Hope Show and Specials	Andy Williams Show
	9:30	Peyton Place	Gomer Pyle, USMC		
	10:00	ABC Stage 67	Danny Kaye Show	I Spy	Run for Your Life
	10:30				
	7:30	Batman	Jericho	Daniel Boone	Batman
	8:00	F Troop			Hullabaloo
	8:30	Tammy Grimes Show	My Three Sons	Star Trek	Lucy Show
	9:00	Bewitched			Family Affair
	9:30	That Girl	The CBS Thursday Night Movies	The Hero	My Three Sons
	10:00	Hawk		Dean Martin Show	Big Valley
	10:30				
	7:30	The Green Hornet	The Wild, Wild West	Tarzan	World Today
	8:00	The Time Tunnel			12 O'Clock High
	8:30		Hogan's Heroes	The Man from U.N.C.L.E.	Hazel
	9:00	Milton Barie Show			Peyton Place
	9:30		The CBS Friday Night Movies	T.H.E. Cat	Lucy Show
	10:00	12 O'Clock High		Laredo	Merv Griffin Show
	10:30				
	7:30	Shane	Jackie Gleason Show	Flipper	Pitt at Johnstown Quiz
	8:00			Please Don't Eat the Daisies	John Forsythe Show
	8:30	The Lawrence Welk Show	Pistols 'N' Petticoats	Get Smart	Dr. Kildare
	9:00		Mission: Impossible		Andy Williams Show
	9:30	The Hollywood Palace		Saturday Night at the Movies	
	10:00		Gunsmoke		Run for Your Life
	10:30	ABC Scope			

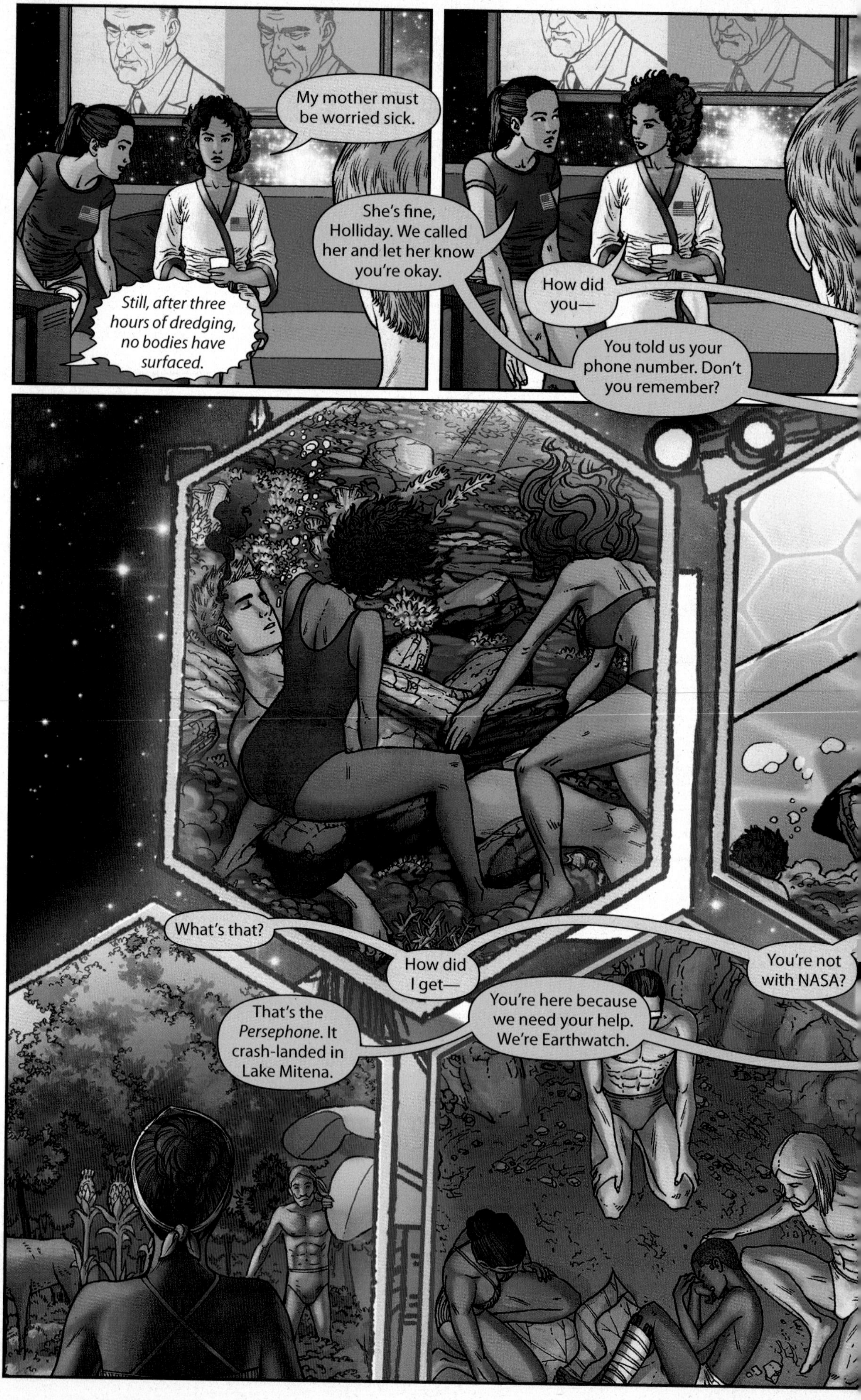
My mother must be worried sick.
Still, after three hours of dredging, no bodies have surfaced.
She's fine, Holliday. We called her and let her know you're okay.
How did you—
You told us your phone number. Don't you remember?
What's that?
How did I get—
You're not with NASA?
That's the *Persephone*. It crash-landed in Lake Mitena.
You're here because we need your help. We're Earthwatch.

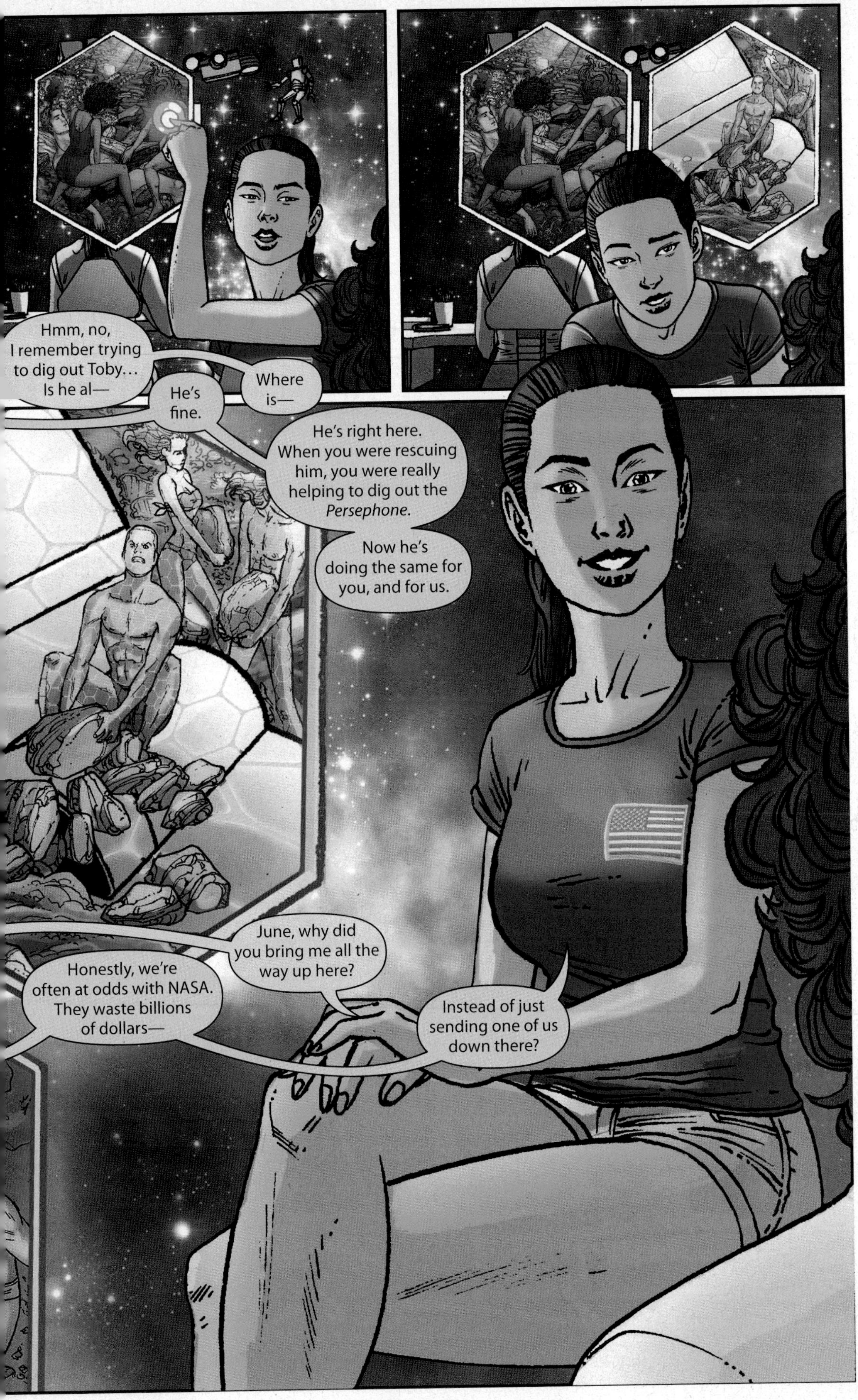
Hmm, no, I remember trying to dig out Toby… Is he al—
Where is—
He's fine.
He's right here. When you were rescuing him, you were really helping to dig out the *Persephone*.
Now he's doing the same for you, and for us.
June, why did you bring me all the way up here?
Instead of just sending one of us down there?
Honestly, we're often at odds with NASA. They waste billions of dollars—

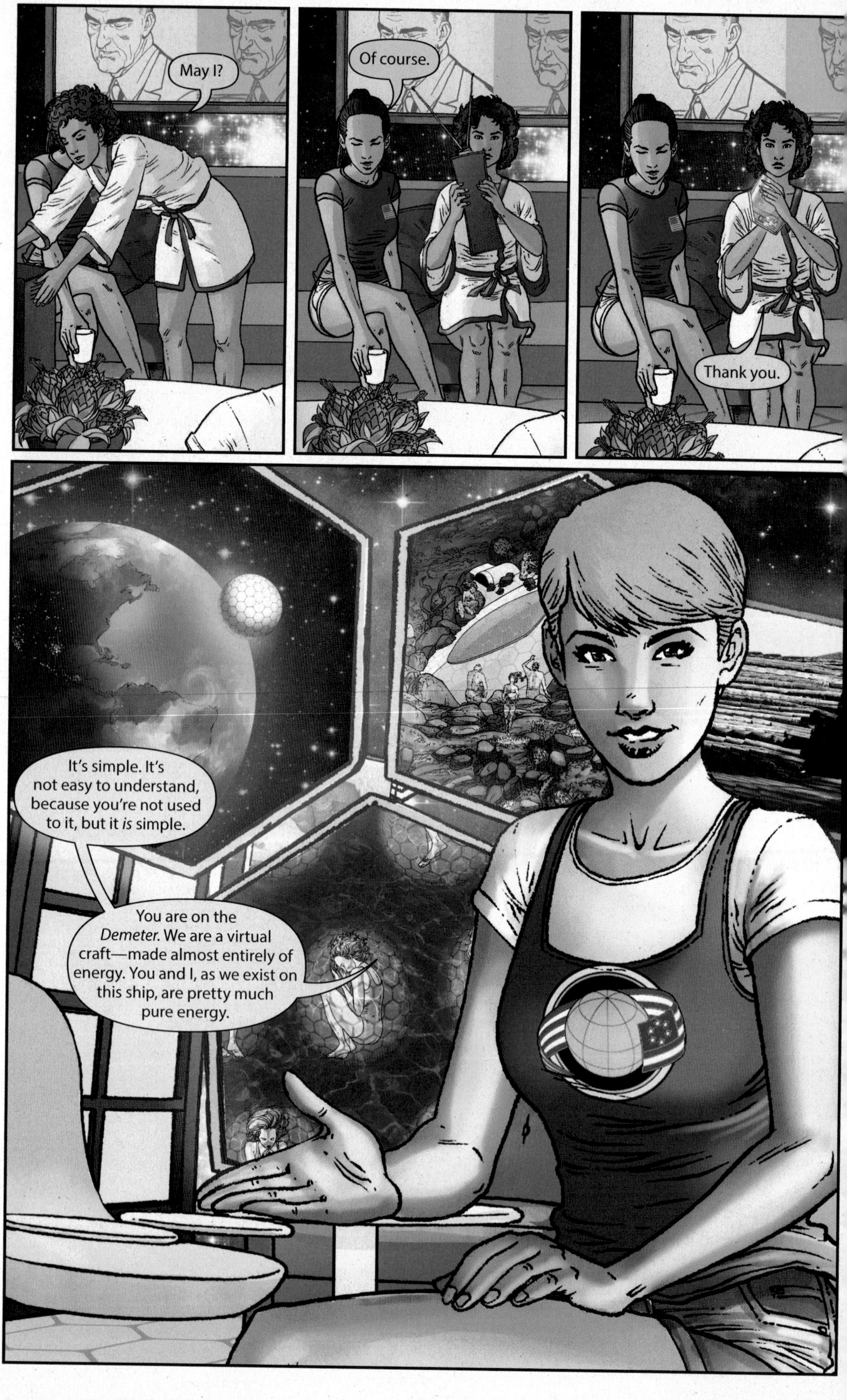
May I?
Of course.
Thank you.
It's simple. It's not easy to understand, because you're not used to it, but it *is* simple.
You are on the *Demeter*. We are a virtual craft—made almost entirely of energy. You and I, as we exist on this ship, are pretty much pure energy.

THE AMERICAN STUDENT
DEBT CRISIS

	1960s*	2010s	DIFFERENCE
Median Family Income	$45,700	$51,939	14%
Total Annual Student Loans	$891.4 million	$260 billion	29,068%
Federal	$891.4 million	$178 billion	19,869%
Non-federal	$0	$81 billion	0%
Average Public College Tuition	$7,432	$14,500	103%
Average Private College Tuition	$15,348	$34,000	130%
Average Income for Male Grad	$91,100	$36,000	-61%
Average Income for Female Grad	$25,000	$36,000	44%
Bachelor Degrees Conferred	5,200,000	19,000,000	265%
Public Law School Tuition	$3,664	$42,000	1,046%
Private Law School Tuition	$1,661	$24,000	1,345%

As of late 2014, federal-owned student loans totaled $850 billion, jumping up 750% from $100 billion in the mid-1990s; student loans now make up almost half of the federal portfolio (not including assets owned by the Federal reserve and land).

*IN 2016 DOLLARS

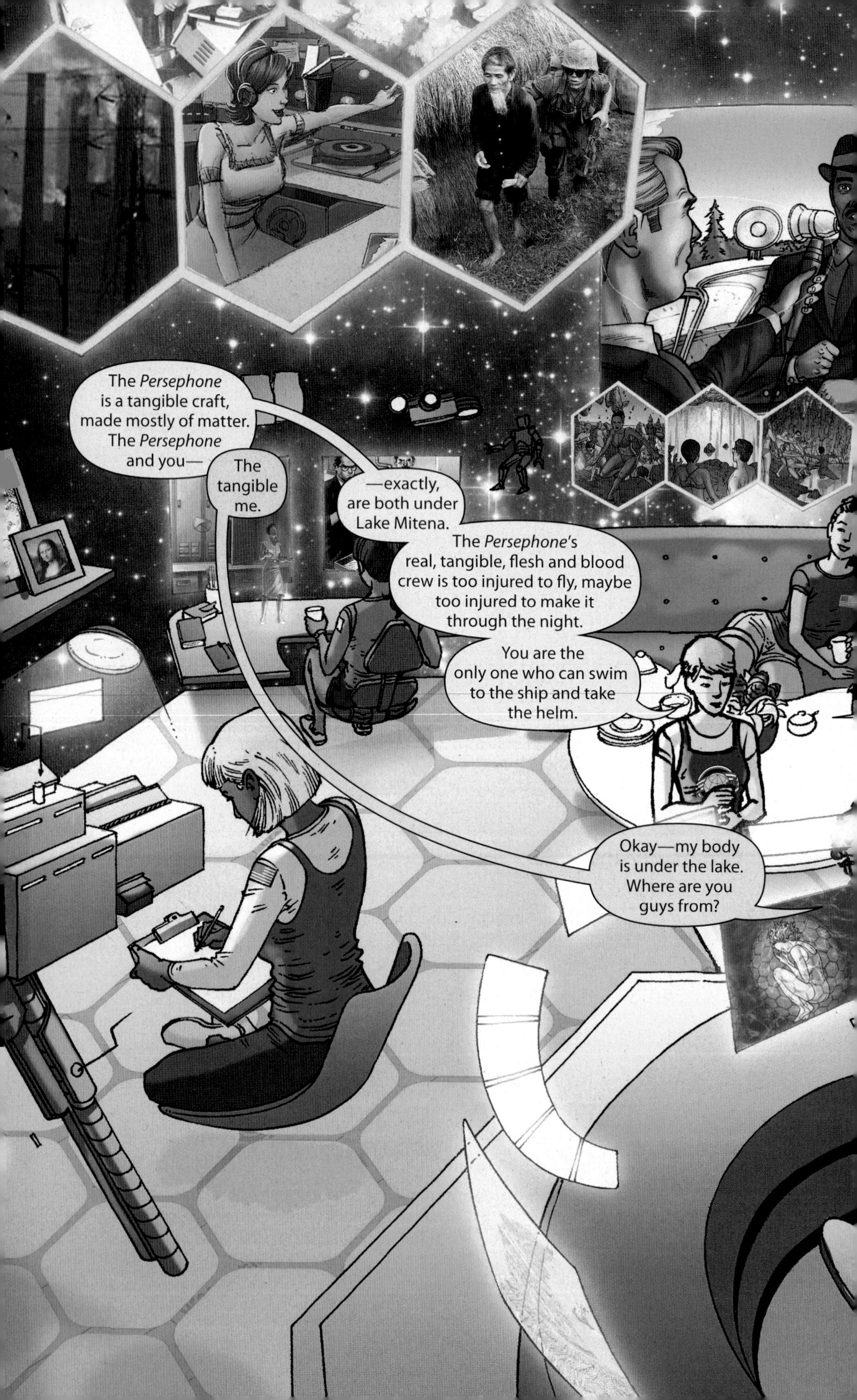
The *Persephone* is a tangible craft, made mostly of matter. The *Persephone* and you—
The tangible me.
—exactly, are both under Lake Mitena.
The *Persephone*'s real, tangible, flesh and blood crew is too injured to fly, maybe too injured to make it through the night.
You are the only one who can swim to the ship and take the helm.
Okay—my body is under the lake. Where are you guys from?

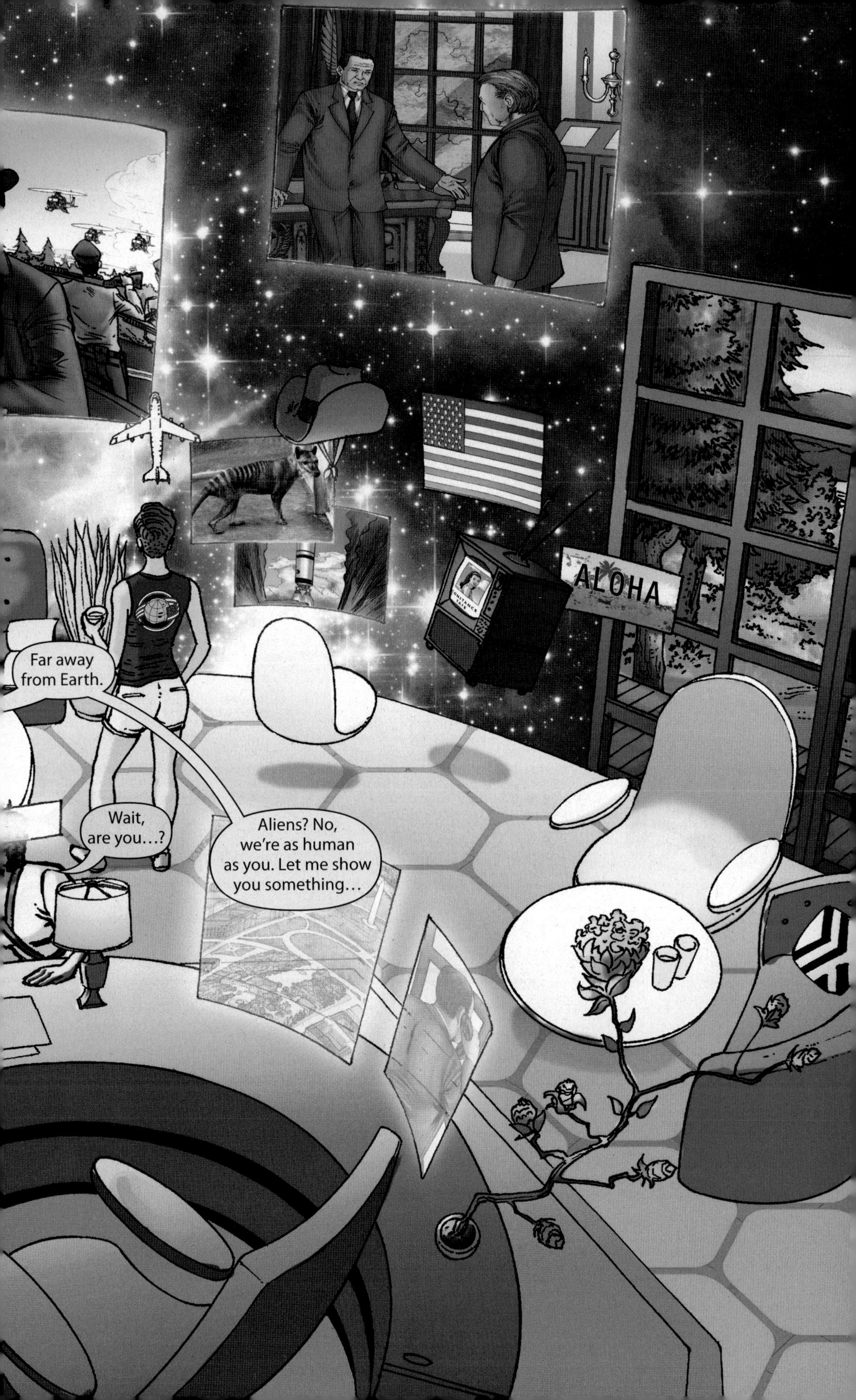
ALOHA
Far away from Earth.
Wait, are you…?
Aliens? No, we're as human as you. Let me show you something…

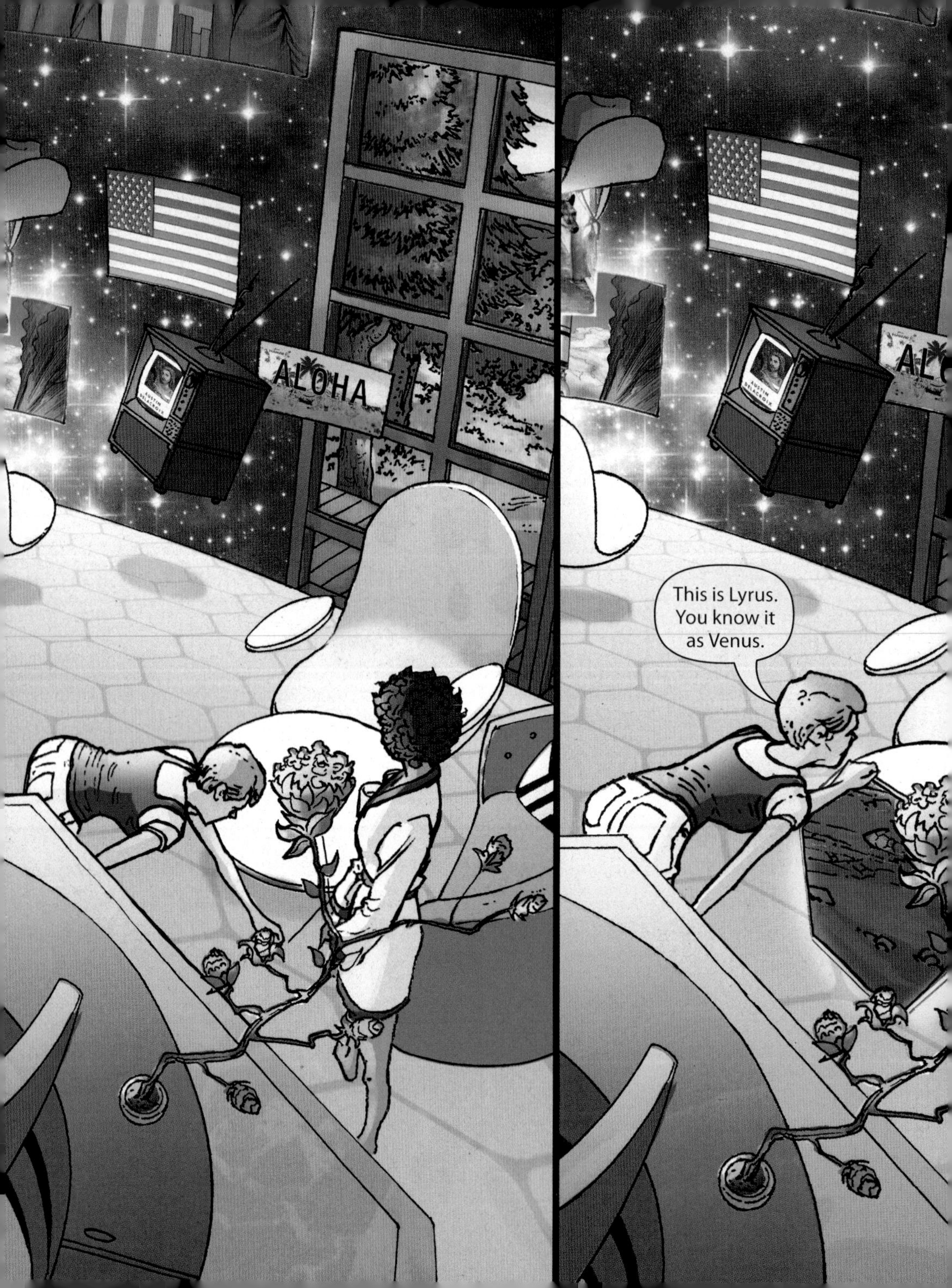
ALOHA
AUSTIN DELACROIX
This is Lyrus. You know it as Venus.

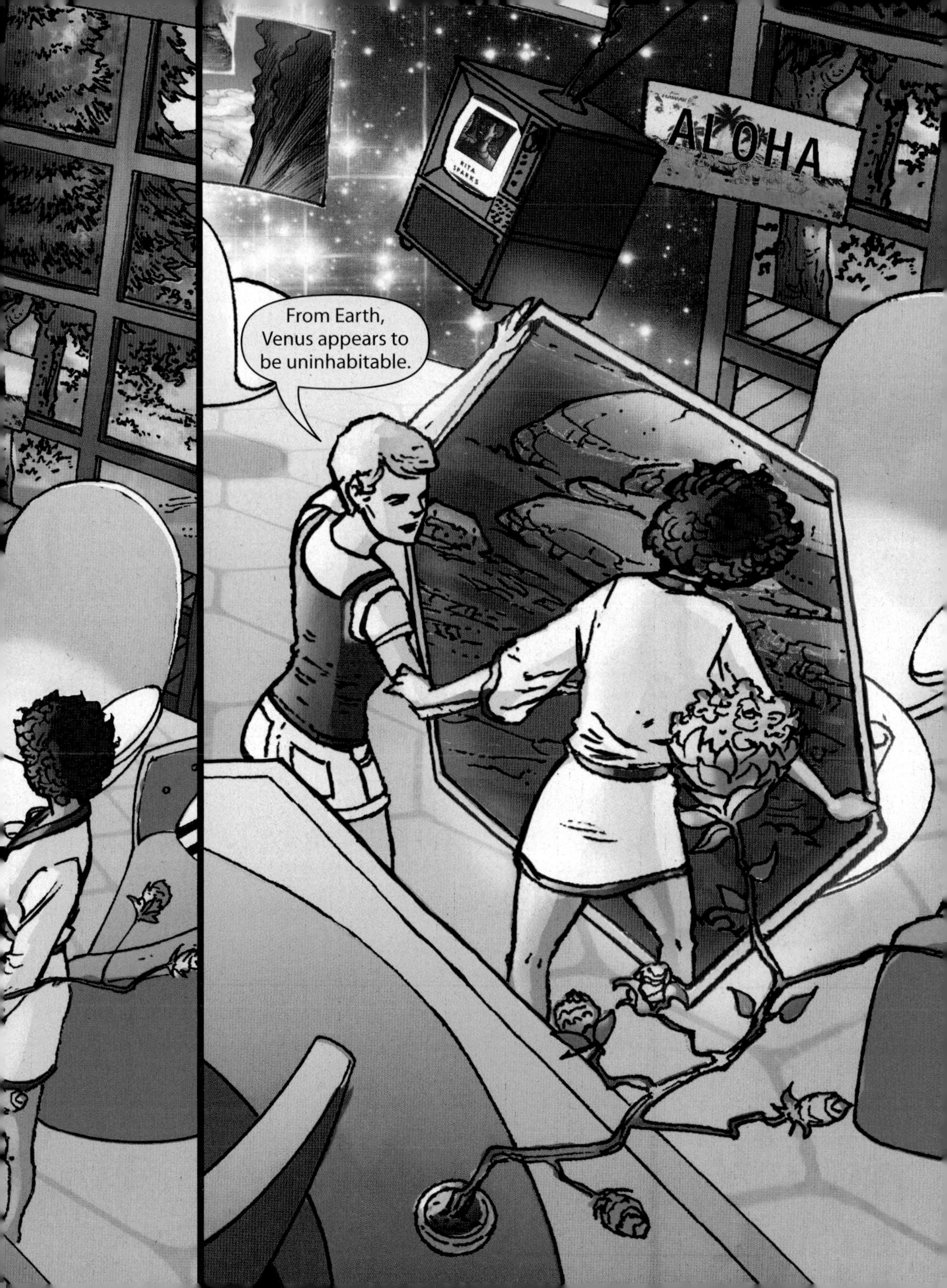
From Earth, Venus appears to be uninhabitable.
ALOHA
RITA SPARKS

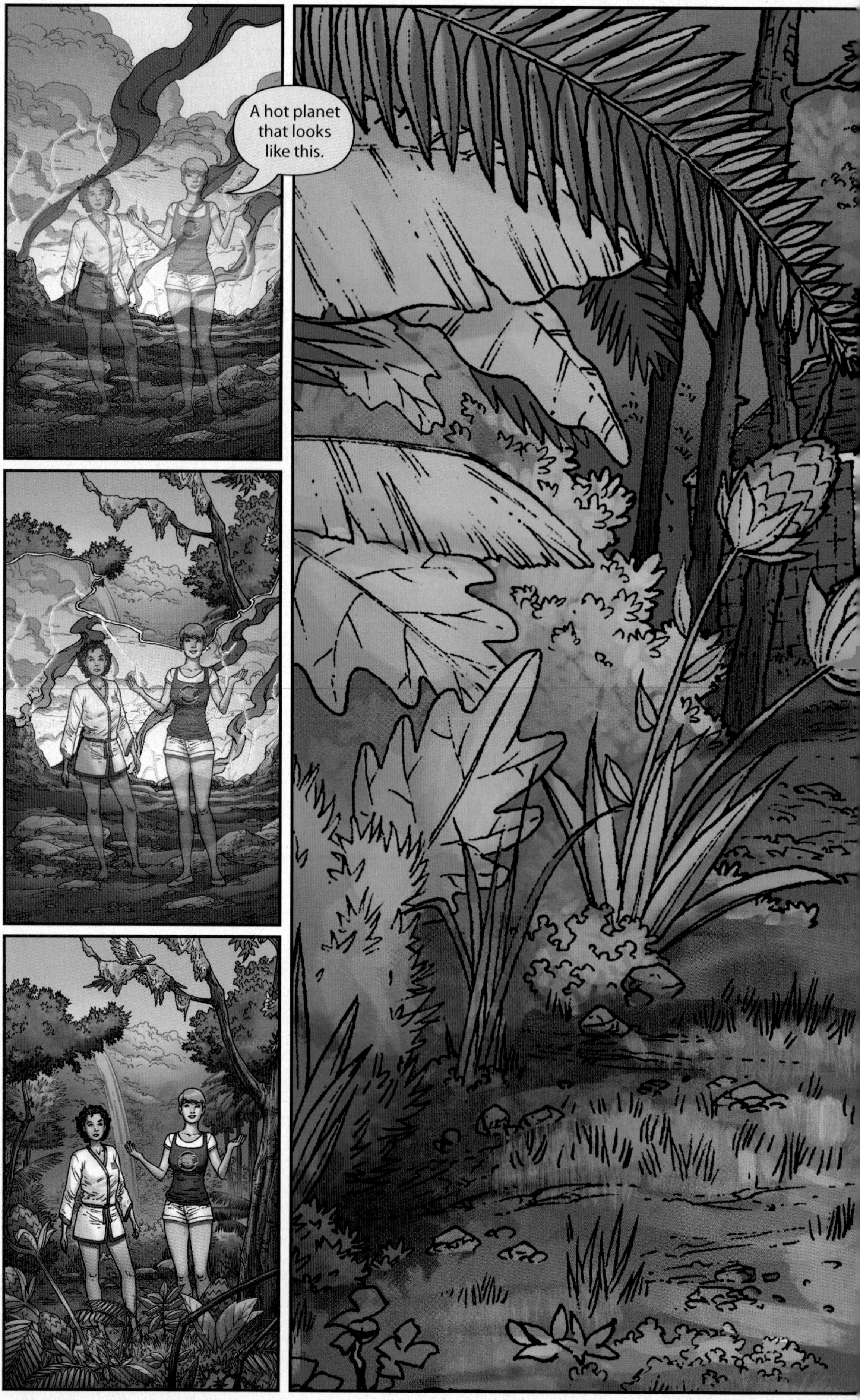
A hot planet that looks like this.

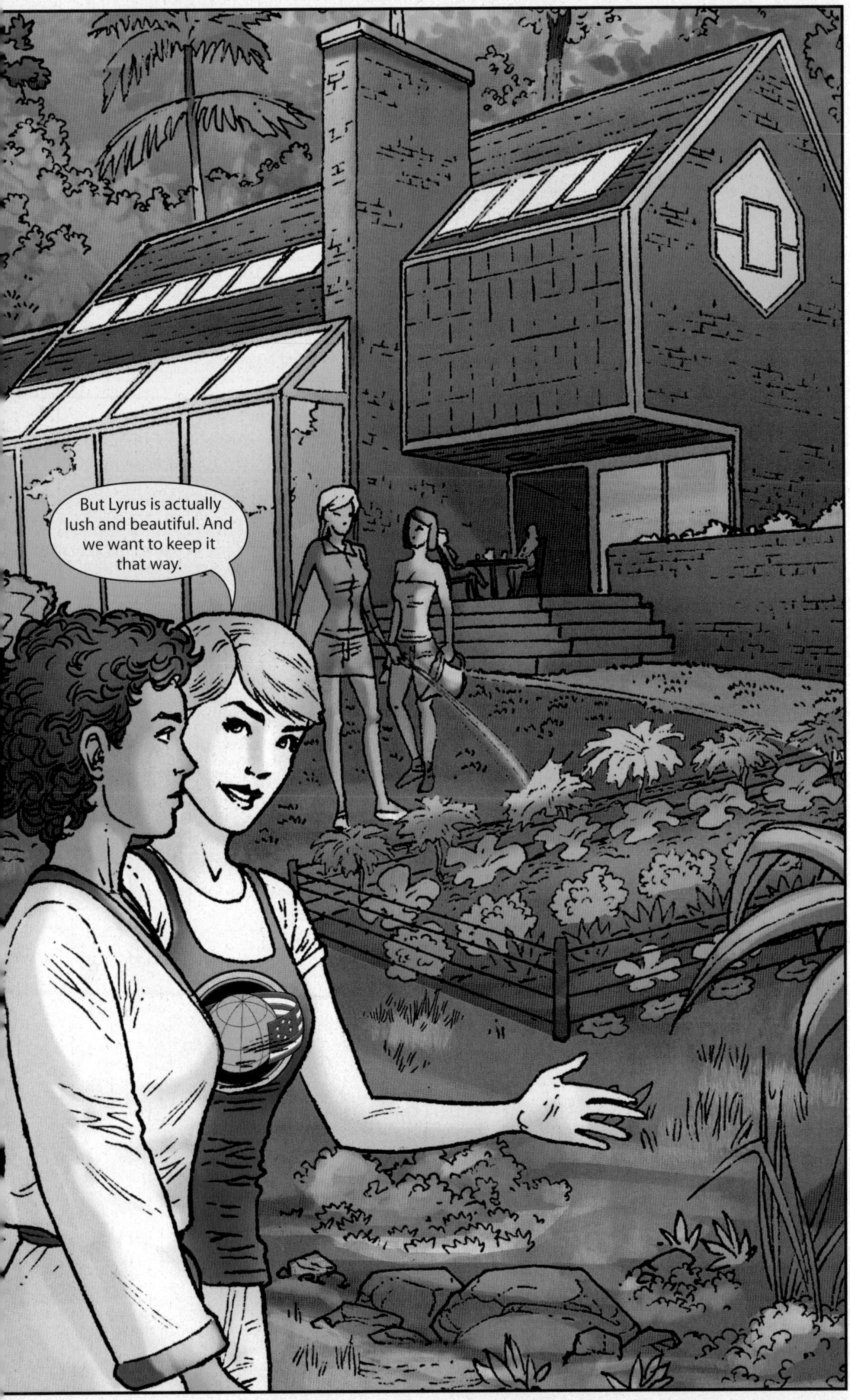
But Lyrus is actually lush and beautiful. And we want to keep it that way.

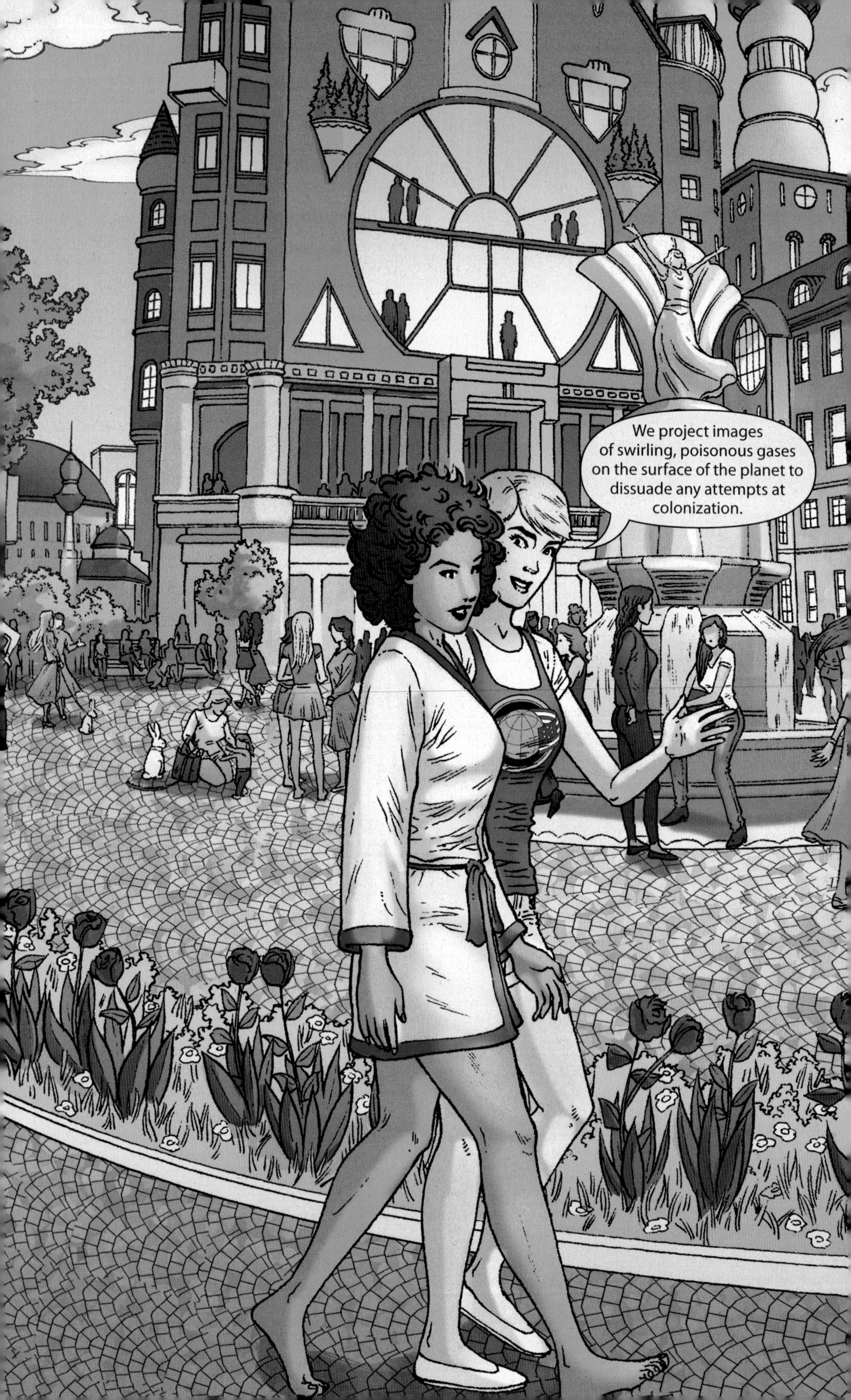
We project images of swirling, poisonous gases on the surface of the planet to dissuade any attempts at colonization.

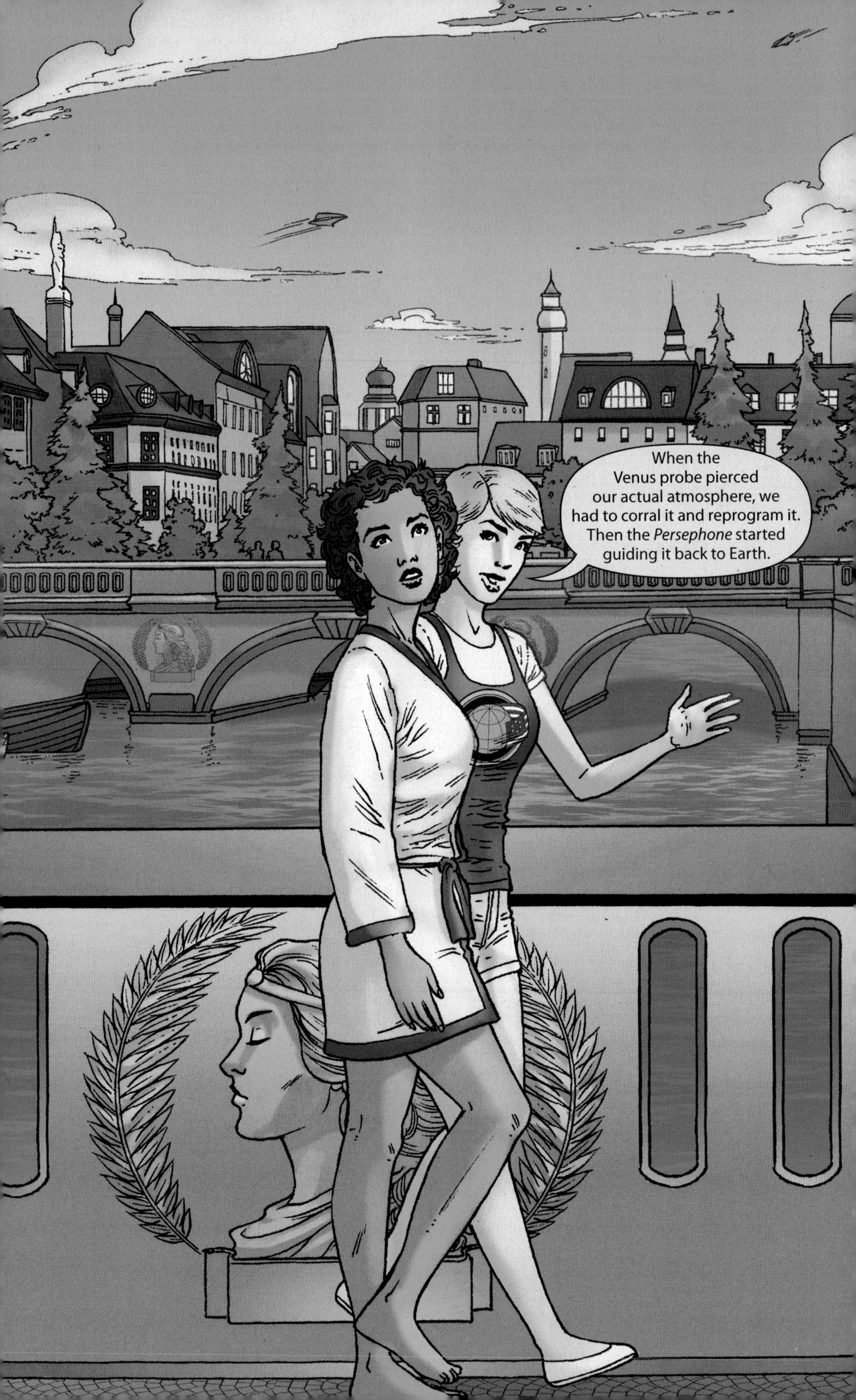
When the Venus probe pierced our actual atmosphere, we had to corral it and reprogram it. Then the *Persephone* started guiding it back to Earth.

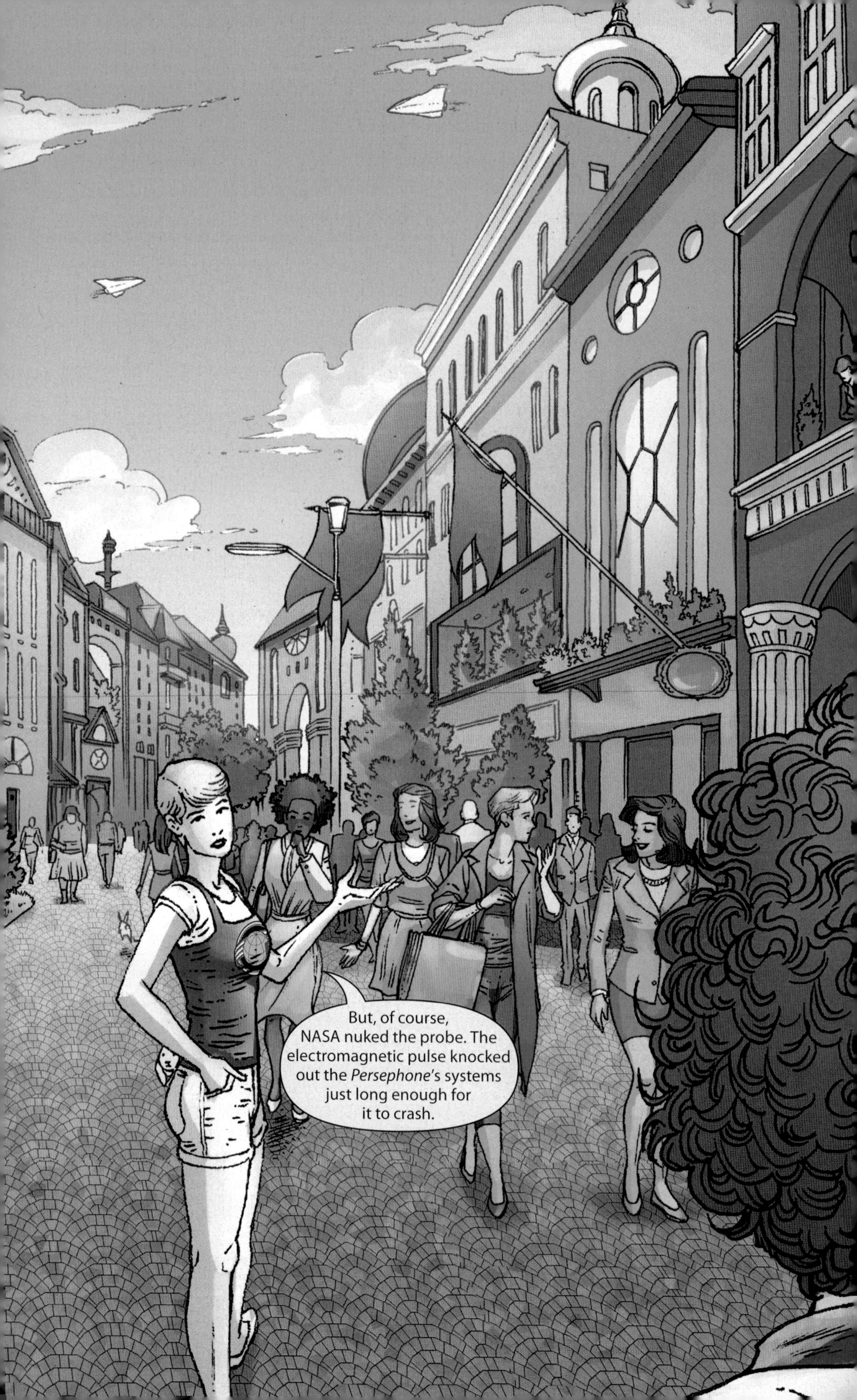
But, of course, NASA nuked the probe. The electromagnetic pulse knocked out the *Persephone*'s systems just long enough for it to crash.

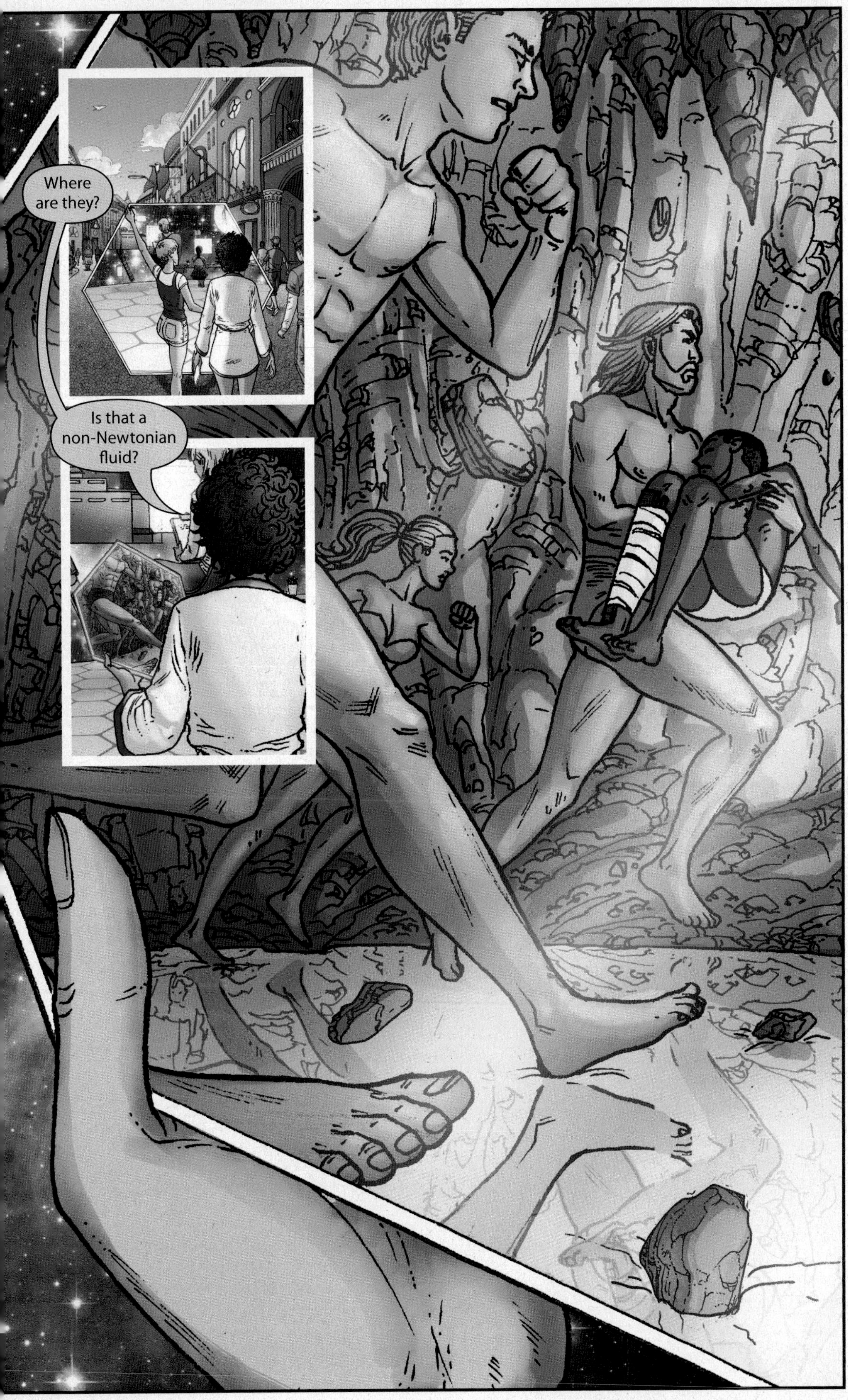
Where are they?
Is that a non-Newtonian fluid?

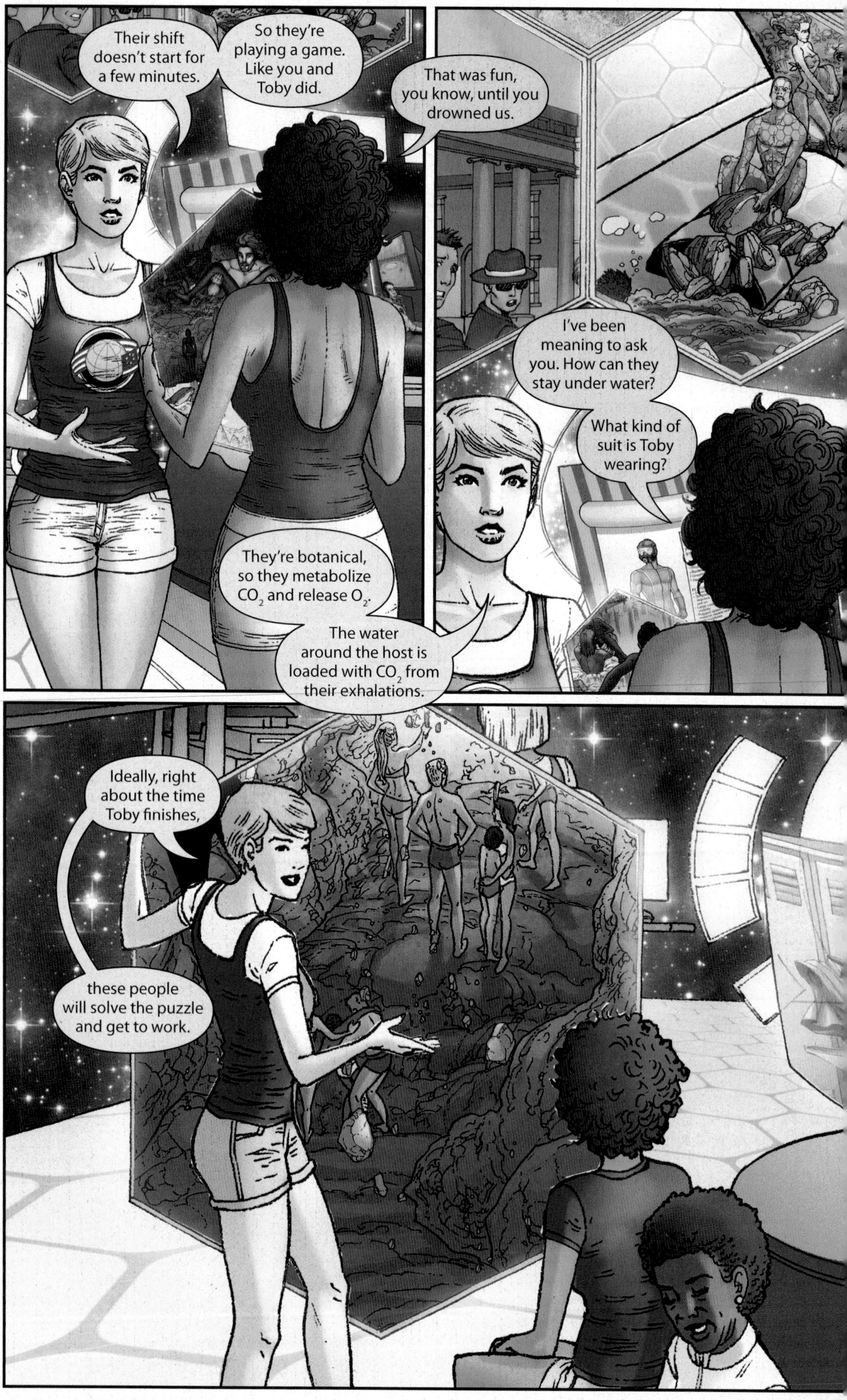
Their shift doesn't start for a few minutes.
So they're playing a game. Like you and Toby did.
That was fun, you know, until you drowned us.
I've been meaning to ask you. How can they stay under water?
What kind of suit is Toby wearing?
They're botanical, so they metabolize CO_2 and release O_2.
The water around the host is loaded with CO_2 from their exhalations.
Ideally, right about the time Toby finishes,
these people will solve the puzzle and get to work.

LETTER FROM THE EDITOR

Charlotte Greenbaum | April 26, 2016

Here's a riddle: What do you do with a BFA in Printmaking when you don't really want to be an artist? Answer: take an unpaid internship in New York.

Move to Williamsburg and sublet your sister's friend's room. Regret this immediately. Work at food website where you spend most of your time selecting photogenic avocados. Iron many, many linens. Go to your boss's house in Park Slope to pick up a cut crystal punch bowl for a photo shoot. Your sister has an emergency and you need to pick her miniature dachshund. Carry the punch bowl and dachshund around while you look for the G train and rain pours from the sky. Realize that the G train is a myth. Realize that you do not belong at this job. Realize you cannot afford to live in Williamsburg.

Move to Bushwick and sublet a room in your sister's friend's apartment. Apply for an internship at a comic book publisher. Somehow become a social media, marketing, and publishing intern because you are a millennial and obviously understand the internet. Begin to give unsolicited opinions on cover art (you did go to art school, after all). Offer to work on editorial assignments, assured that you have a good grasp of Microsoft Office. You are wrong. Live in fear of PowerPoint. Realize that even though you're a millennial, you're not that good at social media. Realize that living in Bushwick kind of sucks. Realize you want to to be on the creative team instead.

Move to Crown Heights and sublet a room in the apartment of some girl your sister knows via Tumblr. Show your boss how great you are at art corrections. Become an intern for the production team. Buy an air conditioner and subsequently eat a lot of rice and beans. Try to organize freelancers. Become adept at giving notes and art direction. Get an opportunity to join the creative team, but only if you completely rewrite and redraw one of the books. You have three weeks to get it done. Work with writers recruited from The Moth Radio Hour for dialogue. Collaborate with an insanely talented artist who suffers all your first-time editor fumblings. Go to the office on the weekends. Teach yourself InDesign on the fly. Illustrator is trickier. The direct selection tool is your friend. Realize you have no idea when and where to use semi-colons. Realize the book will be published on time. Realize you've gotten the job. Sleep.

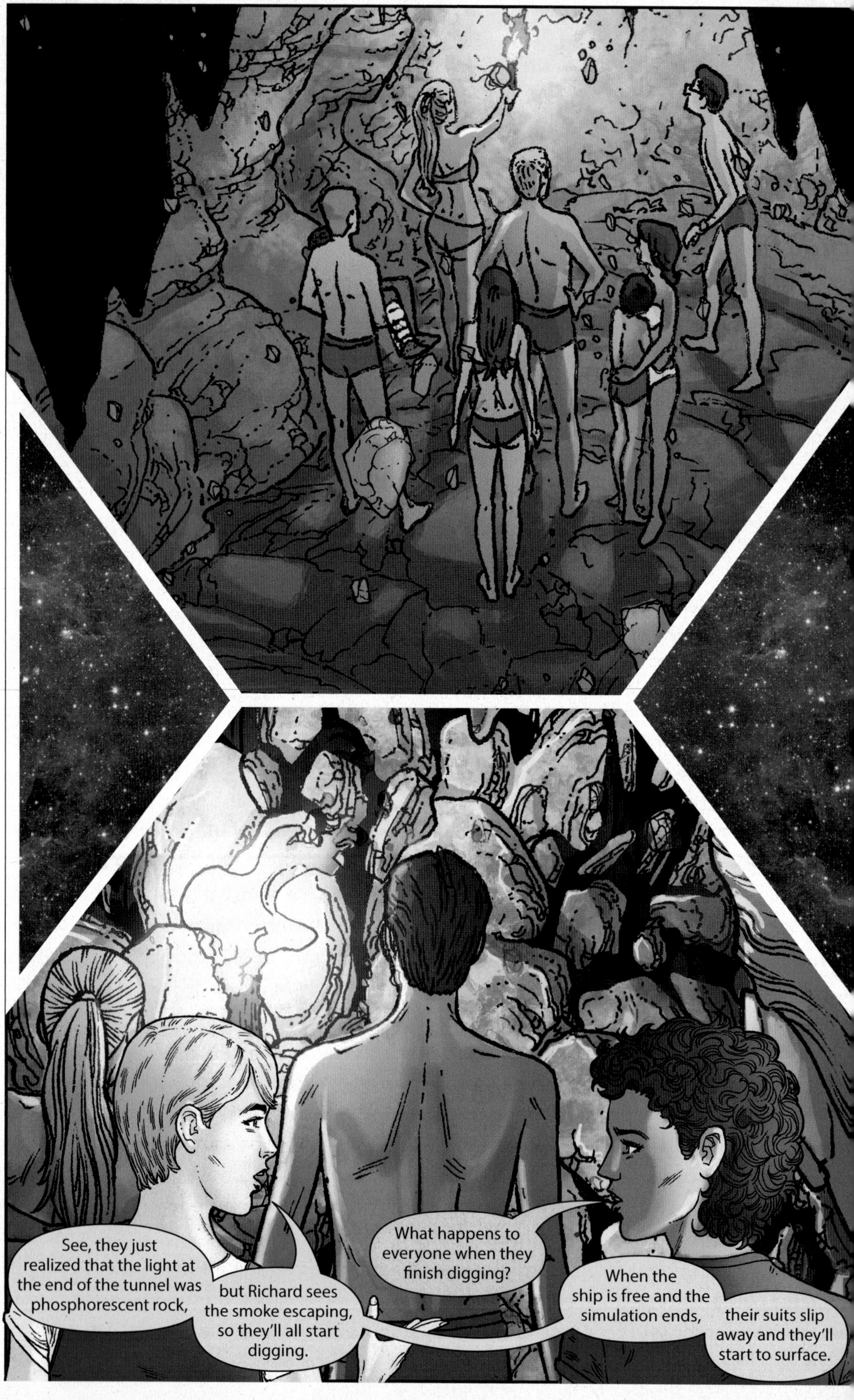
See, they just realized that the light at the end of the tunnel was phosphorescent rock,
but Richard sees the smoke escaping, so they'll all start digging.
What happens to everyone when they finish digging?
When the ship is free and the simulation ends,
their suits slip away and they'll start to surface.

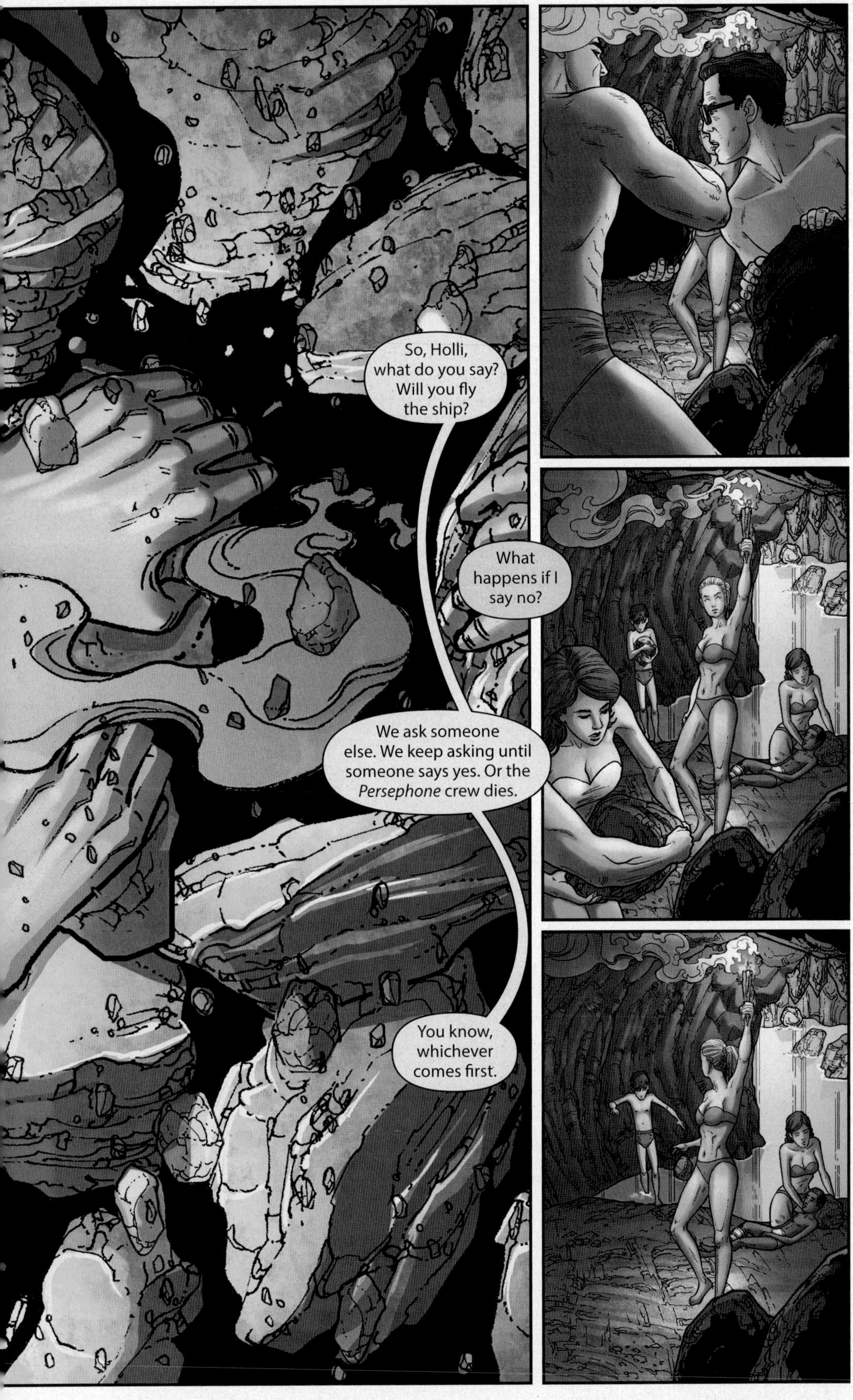

So, Holli, what do you say? Will you fly the ship?
What happens if I say no?
We ask someone else. We keep asking until someone says yes. Or the *Persephone* crew dies.
You know, whichever comes first.

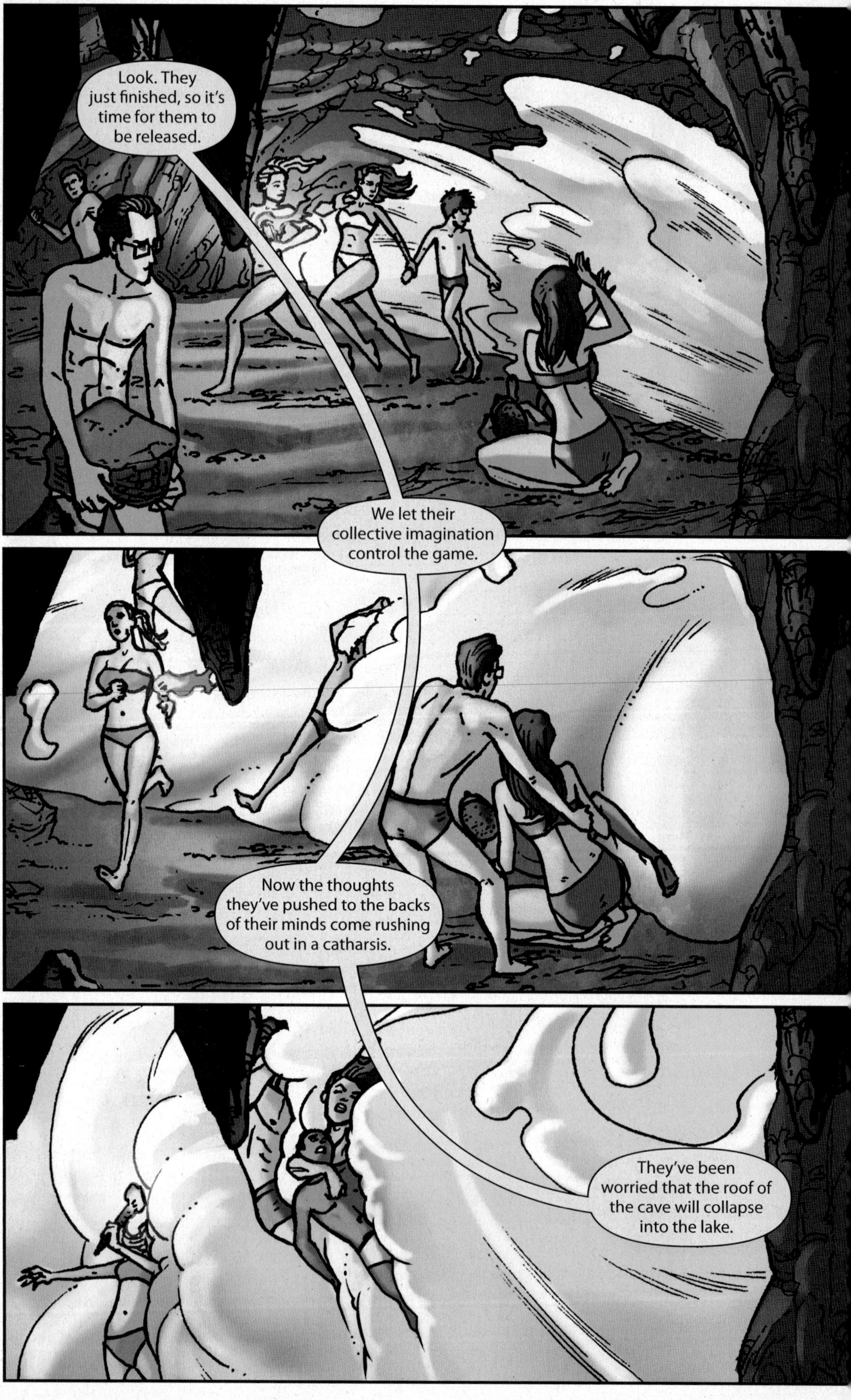
Look. They just finished, so it's time for them to be released.
We let their collective imagination control the game.
Now the thoughts they've pushed to the backs of their minds come rushing out in a catharsis.
They've been worried that the roof of the cave will collapse into the lake.

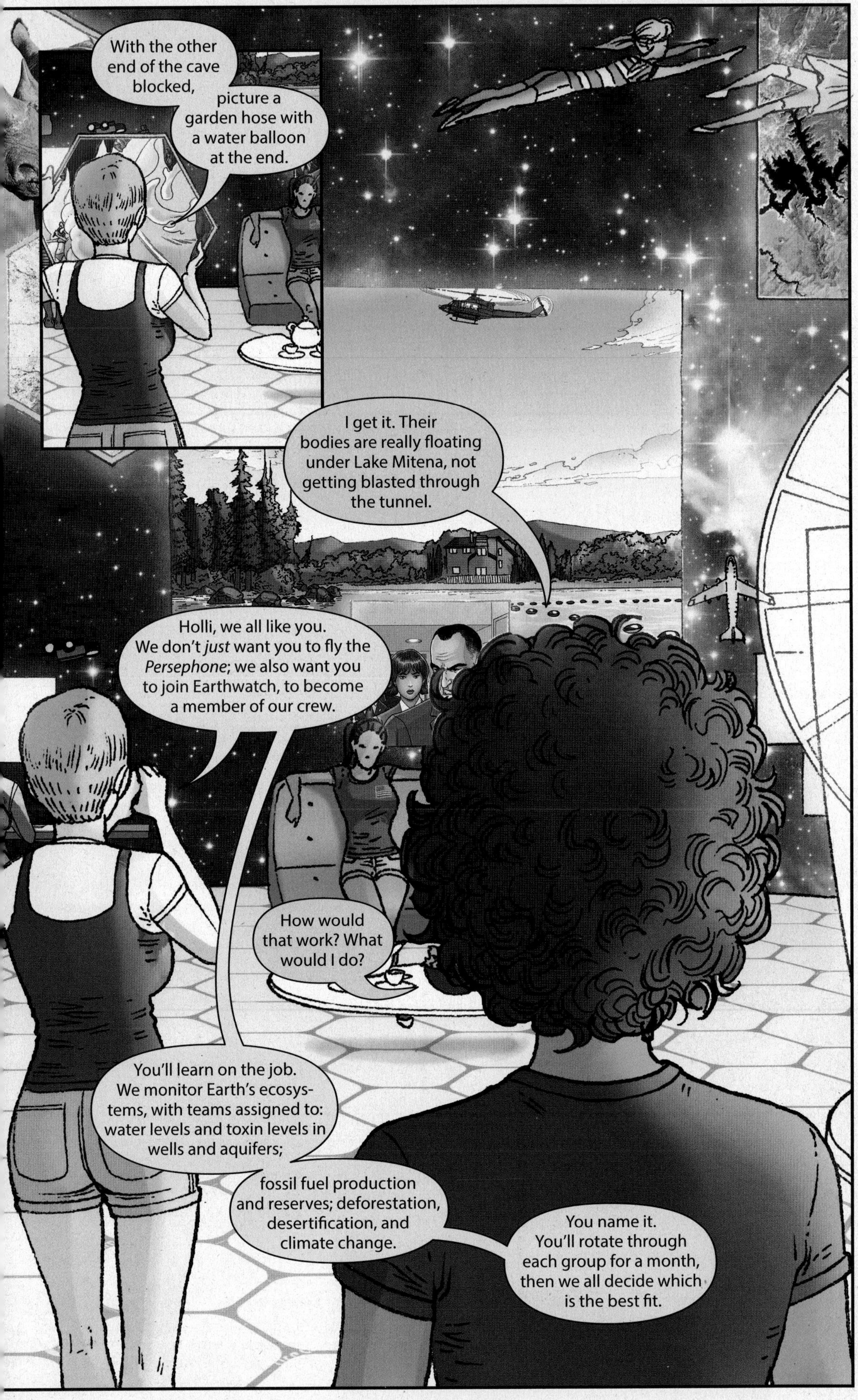
With the other end of the cave blocked,
picture a garden hose with a water balloon at the end.
I get it. Their bodies are really floating under Lake Mitena, not getting blasted through the tunnel.
Holli, we all like you. We don't *just* want you to fly the *Persephone*; we also want you to join Earthwatch, to become a member of our crew.
How would that work? What would I do?
You'll learn on the job. We monitor Earth's ecosys-tems, with teams assigned to: water levels and toxin levels in wells and aquifers;
fossil fuel production and reserves; deforestation, desertification, and climate change.
You name it. You'll rotate through each group for a month, then we all decide which is the best fit.

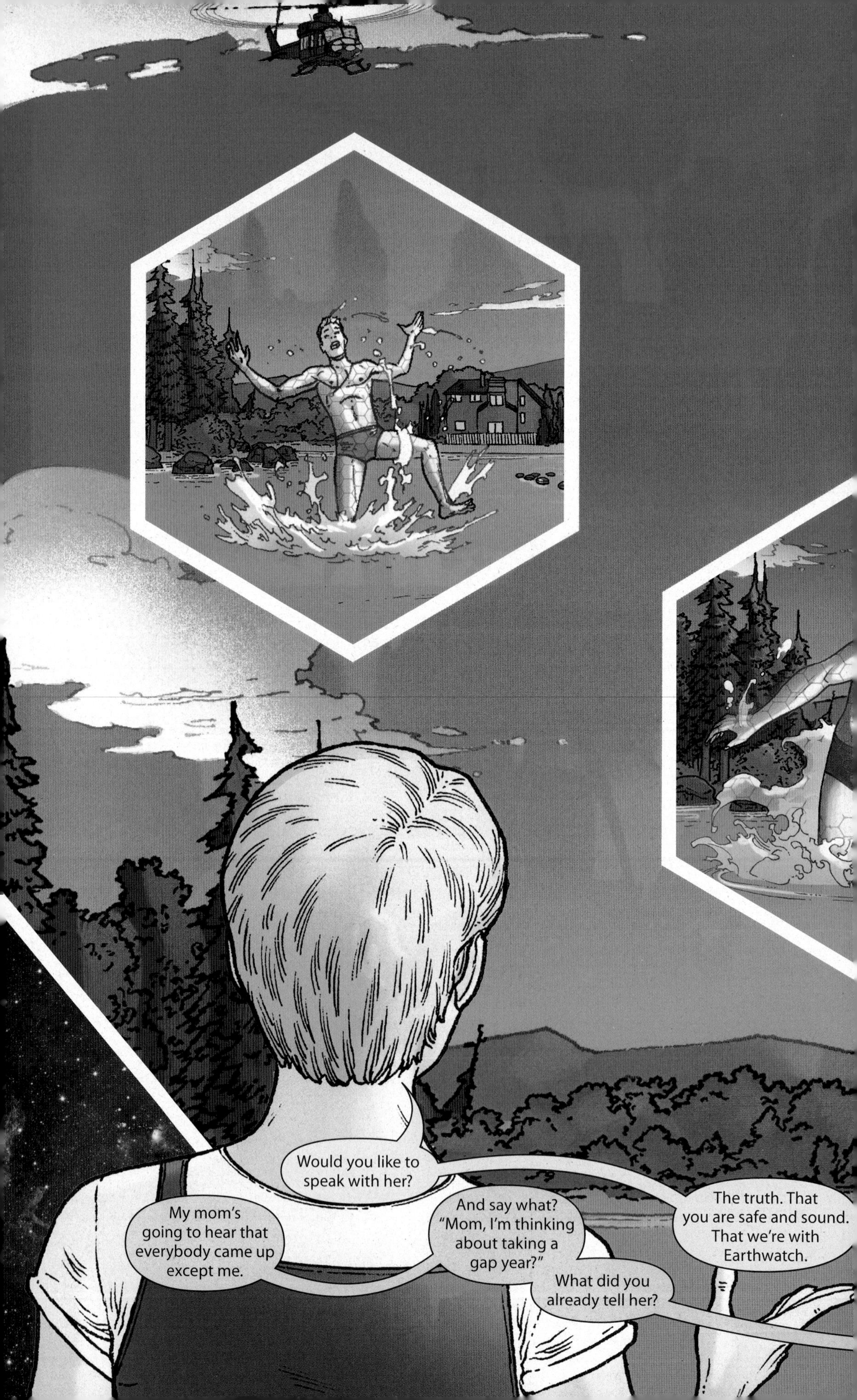
Would you like to speak with her?
My mom's going to hear that everybody came up except me.
And say what? "Mom, I'm thinking about taking a gap year?"
The truth. That you are safe and sound. That we're with Earthwatch.
What did you already tell her?

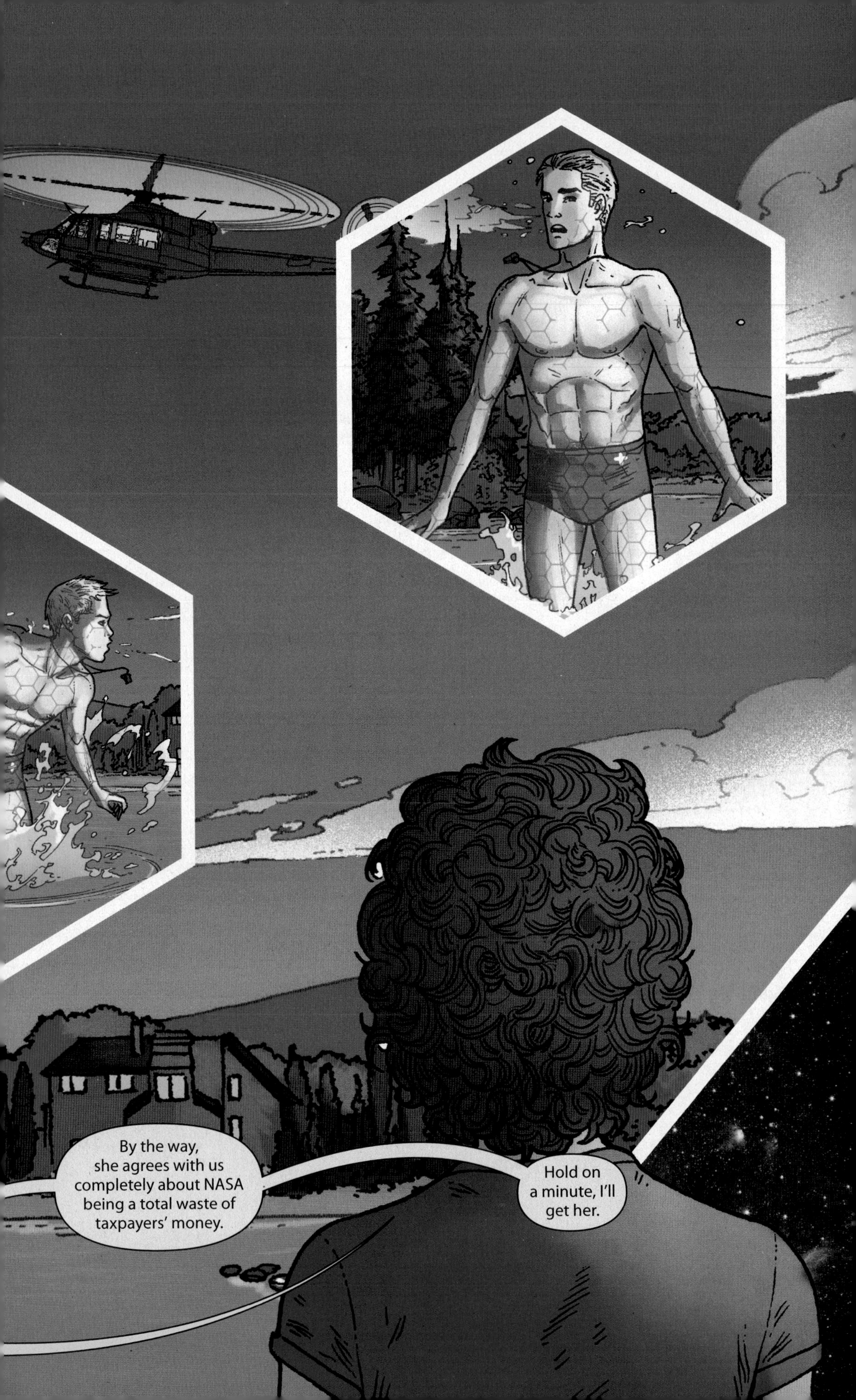
By the way, she agrees with us completely about NASA being a total waste of taxpayers' money.
Hold on a minute, I'll get her.

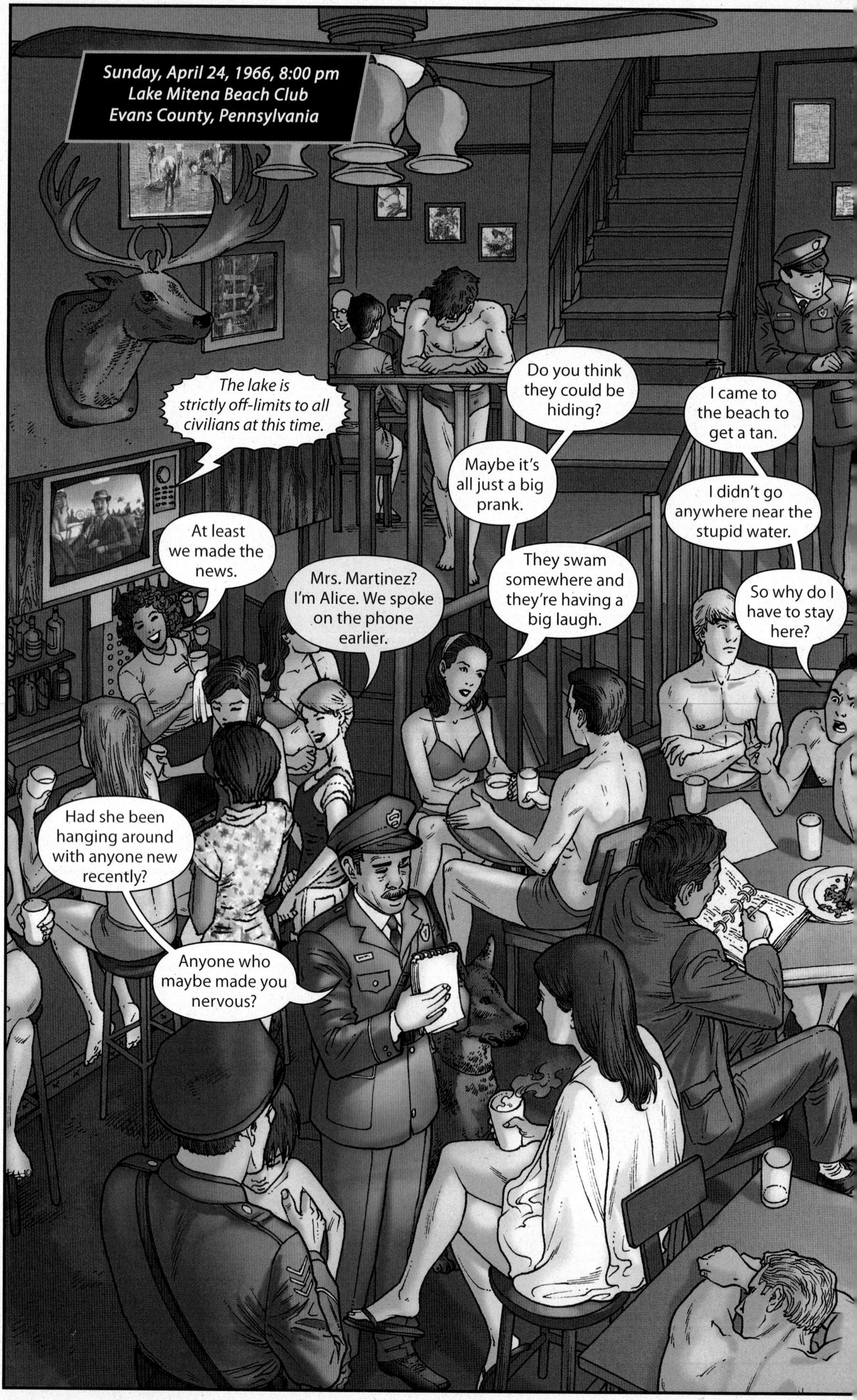
Sunday, April 24, 1966, 8:00 pm
Lake Mitena Beach Club
Evans County, Pennsylvania
The lake is strictly off-limits to all civilians at this time.
Do you think they could be hiding?
Maybe it's all just a big prank.
They swam somewhere and they're having a big laugh.
I came to the beach to get a tan.
I didn't go anywhere near the stupid water.
So why do I have to stay here?
At least we made the news.
Mrs. Martinez? I'm Alice. We spoke on the phone earlier.
Had she been hanging around with anyone new recently?
Anyone who maybe made you nervous?

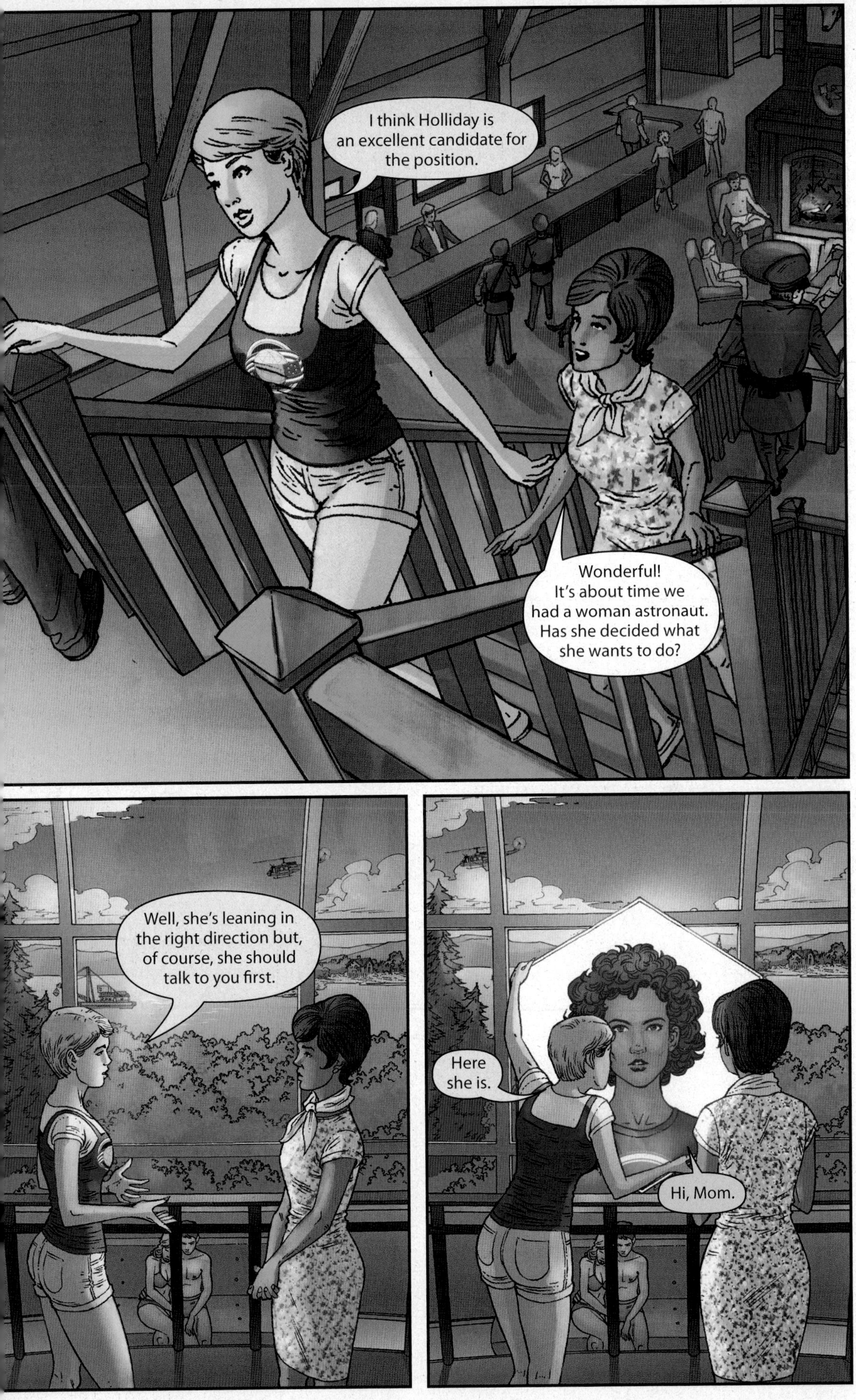
I think Holliday is an excellent candidate for the position.
Wonderful! It's about time we had a woman astronaut. Has she decided what she wants to do?
Well, she's leaning in the right direction but, of course, she should talk to you first.
Here she is.
Hi, Mom.

THE NATIONAL AIR AND SPACE ADMINISTRATION

October 4, 1957 – The Soviet Union launched *Sputnik*, the world's first man-made satellite, into space.

November 3, 1957 – The Soviet Union followed with *Sputnik 2*, which carried Laika, a canine. Laika survived the trip into space but died when the oxygen supply ran out.

January 31, 1958 – The United States launched its first satellite, *Explorer 1*.

August 19, 1960 – The Soviet Union launched *Sputnik 5* with a grey rabbit, 42 mice, two rats, flies, several plants, fungi, and two canines, Belka and Strelka; all passengers survived the trip to and from space.

April 12, 1961 – Soviet cosmonaut Yuri Gagarin became the first human in space.

May 5, 1961 – Alan Shepard became the first American in space.

May 25, 1961 – President John F. Kennedy rallied Congress and the nation to support the first manned mission to the moon, which became the Apollo program.

February 3, 1966 – The Soviet Union landed the first spacecraft on the moon; the United States followed with *Surveyor I* on June 2.

July 2, 1969 – American astronauts Neil Armstrong and "Buzz" Aldrin became the first men on the moon.

September 1976 – American probe *Viking 2* discovered water frost on Mars.

August and September 1977 – *Voyagers 1* and *2* were launched; each would transmit images of the outer planets over the decades while on their (still ongoing) journeys.

April 12, 1981 – The United States launched the first space shuttle *Columbia*.

August 6, 2012 – NASA's *Curiosity* rover landed on Mars.

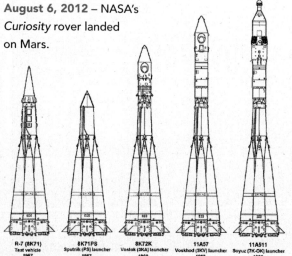

R-7 (8K71) Test vehicle 1957	8K71PS Sputnik (PS) launcher 1957	8K72K Vostok (3KA) launcher 1960	11A57 Voskhod (3KV) launcher 1963	11A511 Soyuz (7K-OK) launcher 1966

SINCE *SPUTNIK'S* LAUNCH IN 1957

SATELLITES SENT INTO ORBIT	2,271
ACTIVE SATELLITES	1,381
UNITED STATES	568
RUSSIA	133
CHINA	177
ALL OTHER COUNTRIES	503
ACTIVE MILITARY SATELLITES	295
UNITED STATES	129
RUSSIA	75
CHINA	35
ALL OTHER COUNTRIES	56

5

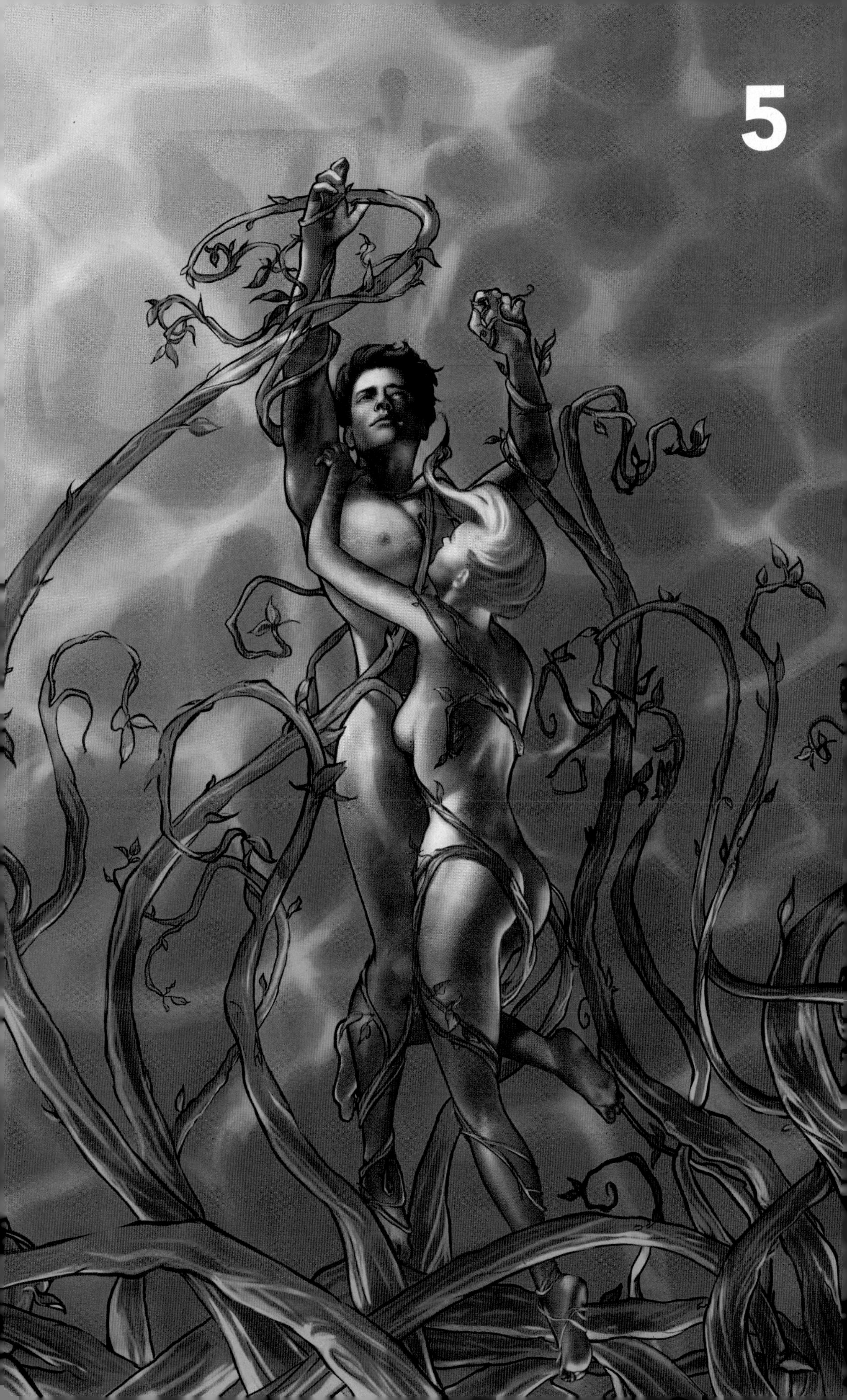

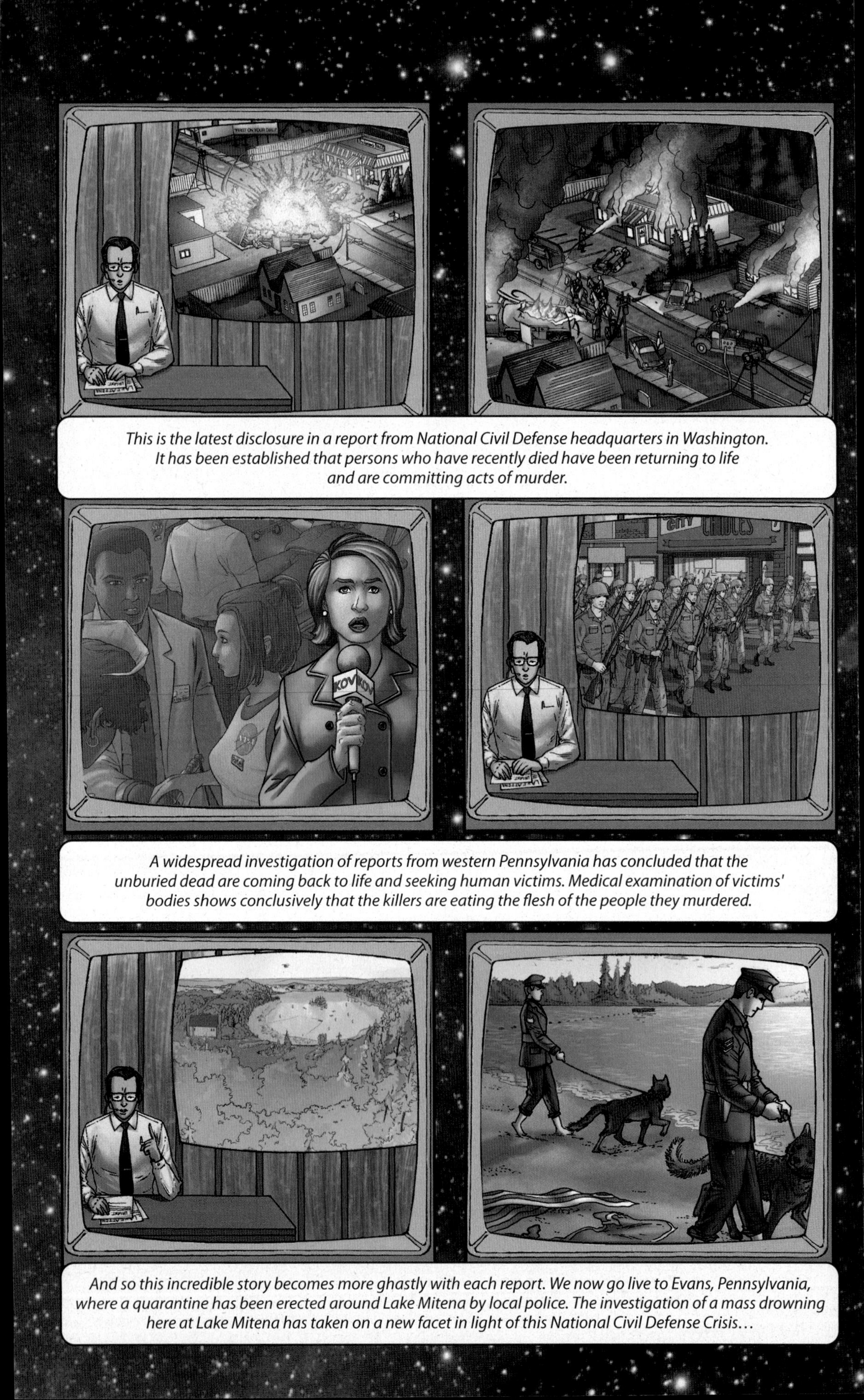
This is the latest disclosure in a report from National Civil Defense headquarters in Washington. It has been established that persons who have recently died have been returning to life and are committing acts of murder.
KOV
KOV
A widespread investigation of reports from western Pennsylvania has concluded that the unburied dead are coming back to life and seeking human victims. Medical examination of victims' bodies shows conclusively that the killers are eating the flesh of the people they murdered.
And so this incredible story becomes more ghastly with each report. We now go live to Evans, Pennsylvania, where a quarantine has been erected around Lake Mitena by local police. The investigation of a mass drowning here at Lake Mitena has taken on a new facet in light of this National Civil Defense Crisis…

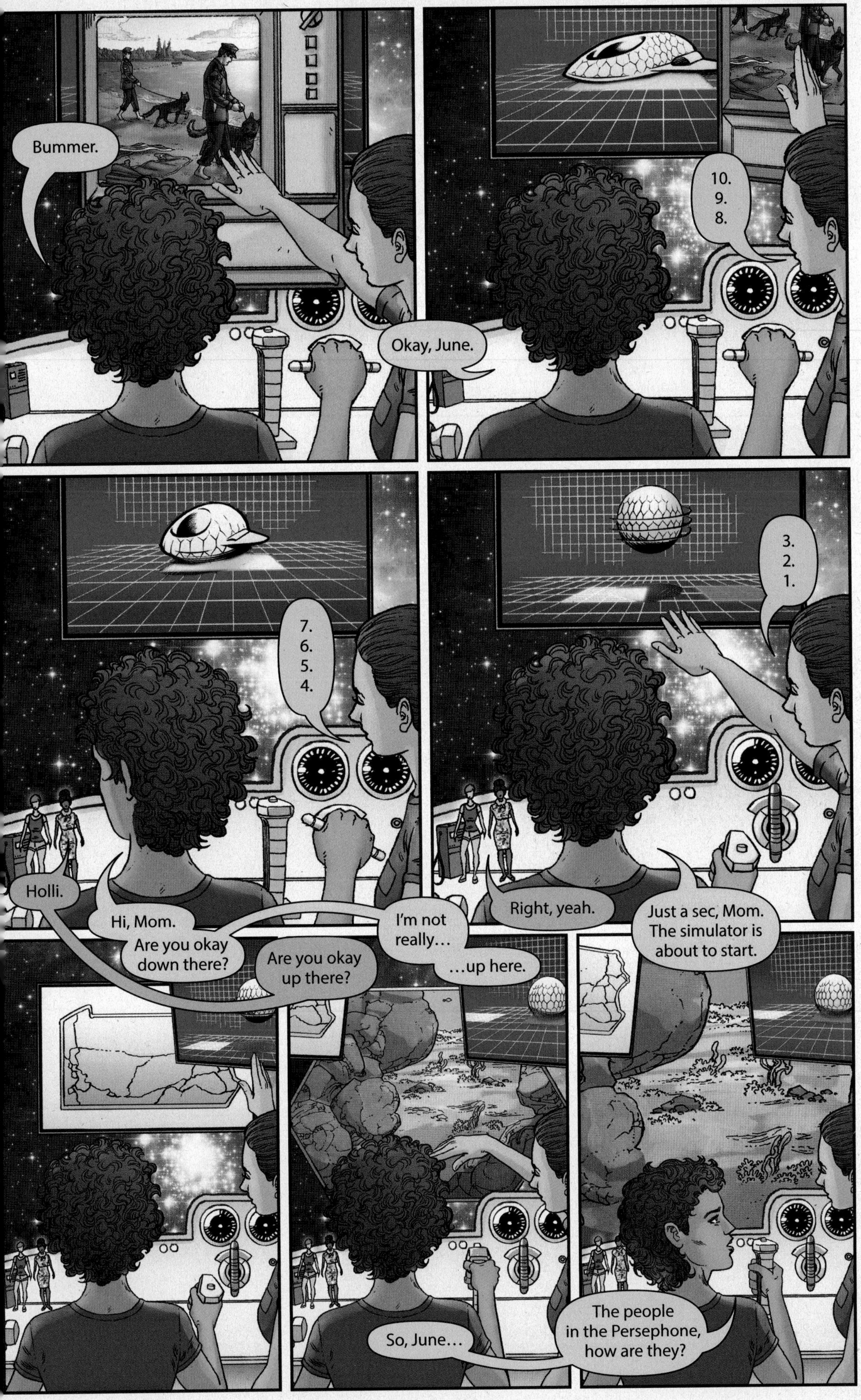
Bummer.
Okay, June.
10.
9.
8.
7.
6.
5.
4.
3.
2.
1.
Holli.
Hi, Mom.
Are you okay down there?
Are you okay up there?
I'm not really…
…up here.
Right, yeah.
Just a sec, Mom. The simulator is about to start.
So, June…
The people in the Persephone, how are they?

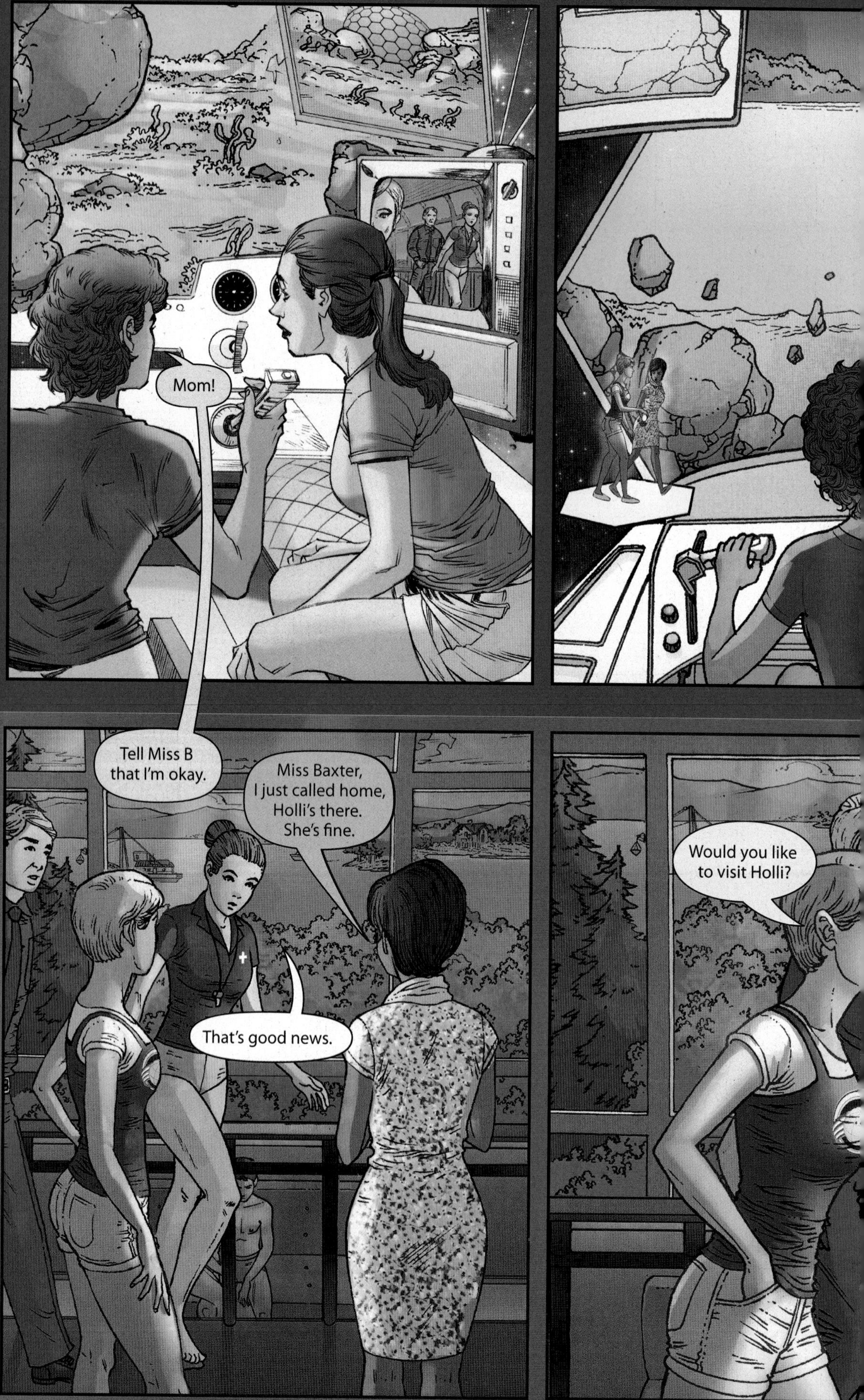

Mom!
Tell Miss B
that I'm okay.
Miss Baxter,
I just called home,
Holli's there.
She's fine.
That's good news.
Would you like
to visit Holli?

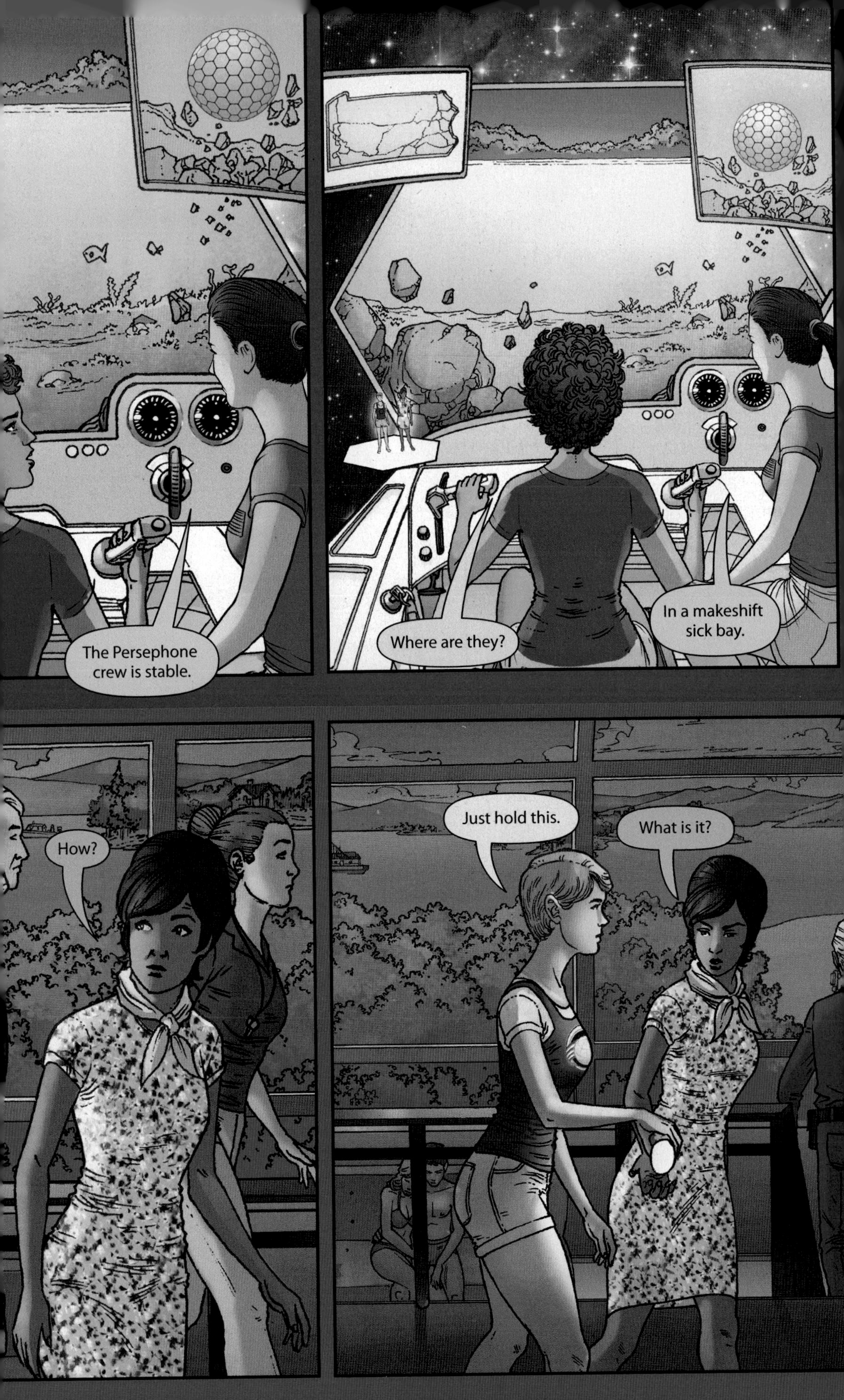
The Persephone crew is stable.
Where are they?
In a makeshift sick bay.
How?
Just hold this.
What is it?

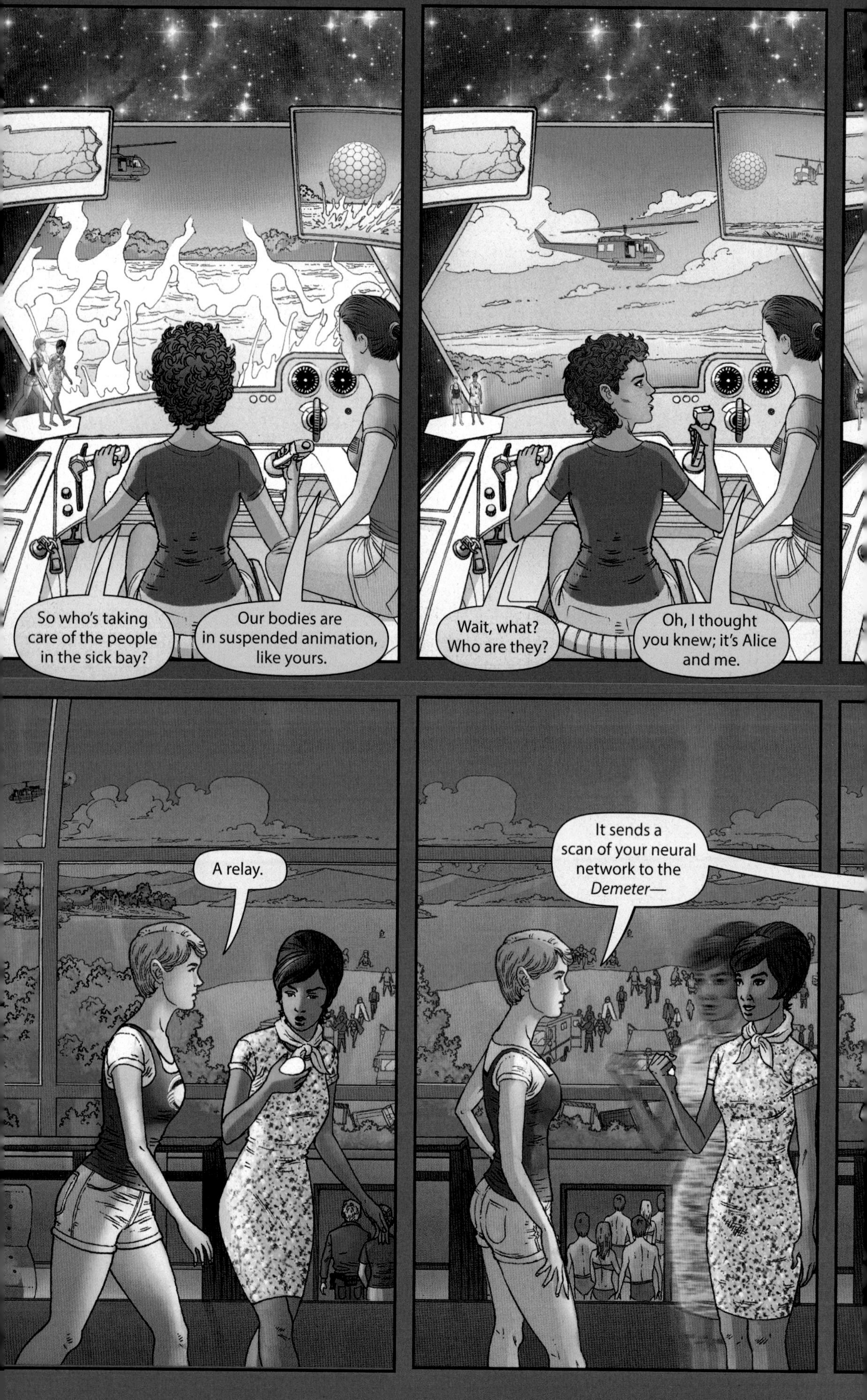
So who's taking care of the people in the sick bay?
Our bodies are in suspended animation, like yours.
Wait, what? Who are they?
Oh, I thought you knew; it's Alice and me.
A relay.
It sends a scan of your neural network to the *Demeter*—

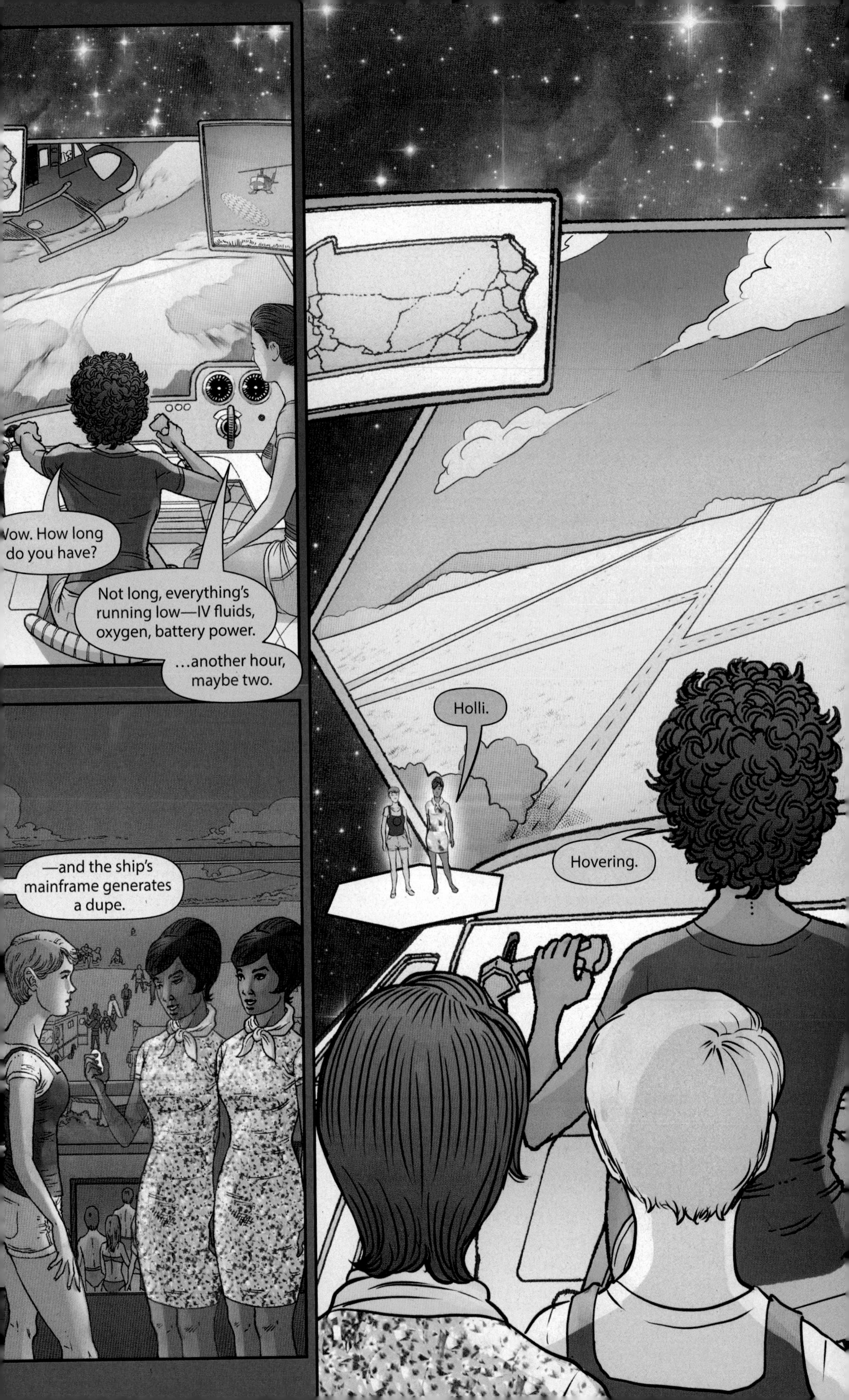
Wow. How long do you have?
Not long, everything's running low—IV fluids, oxygen, battery power.
...another hour, maybe two.
—and the ship's mainframe generates a dupe.
Holli.
Hovering.

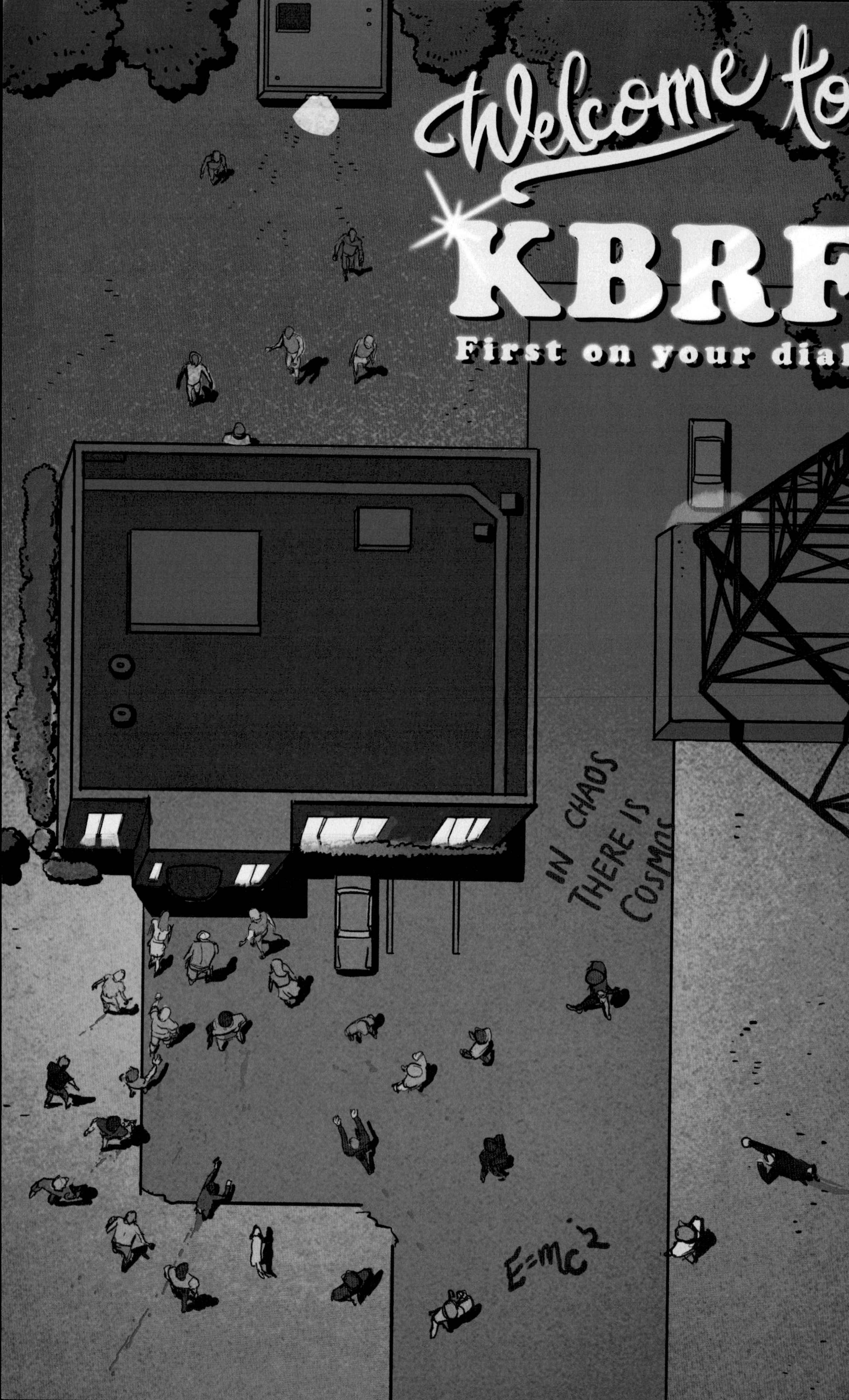
Welcome to
KBRF
First on your dial
IN CHAOS THERE IS COSMOS
E=mc2

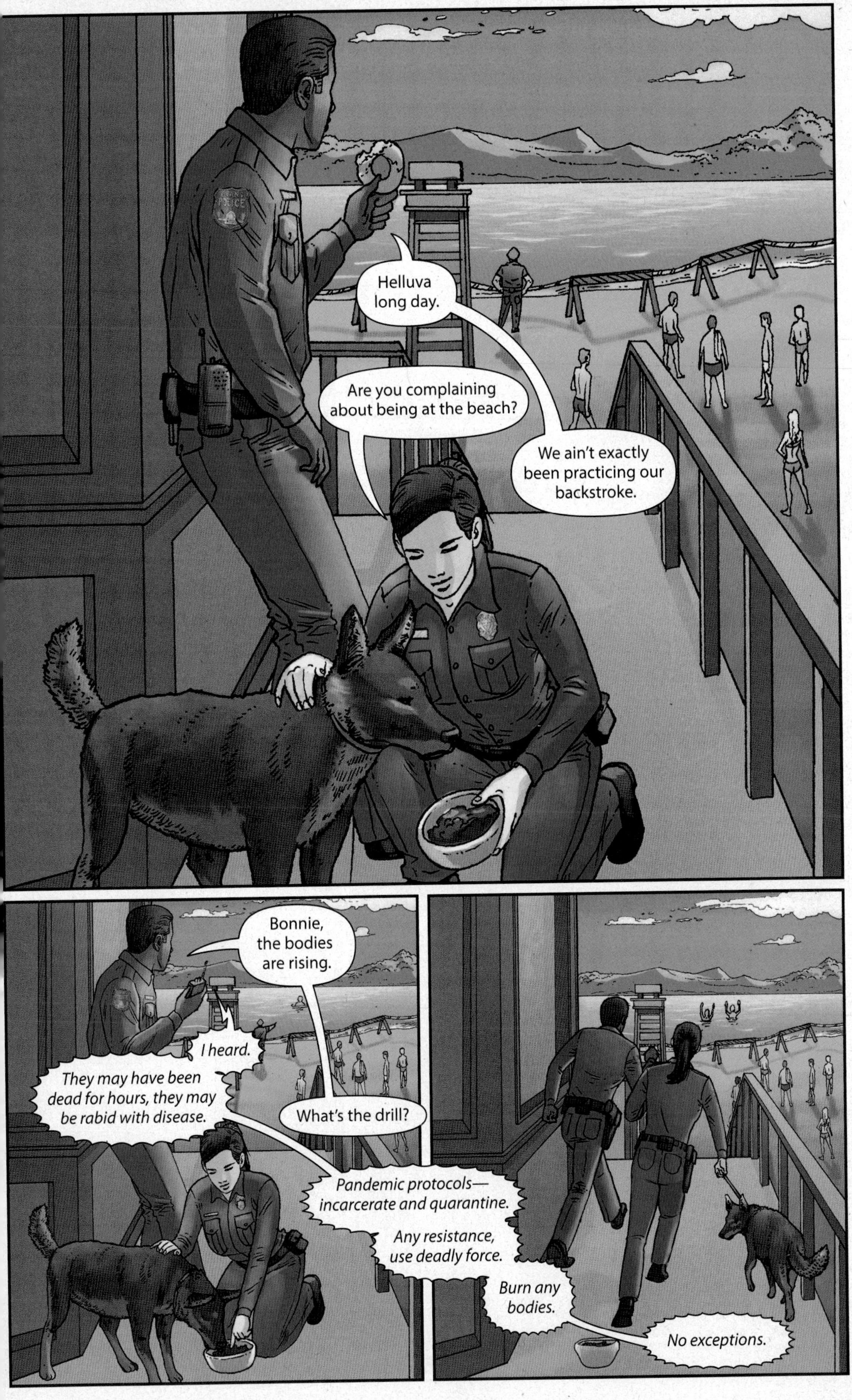
Helluva long day.
Are you complaining about being at the beach?
We ain't exactly been practicing our backstroke.
Bonnie, the bodies are rising.
I heard.
They may have been dead for hours, they may be rabid with disease.
What's the drill?
Pandemic protocols— incarcerate and quarantine.
Any resistance, use deadly force.
Burn any bodies.
No exceptions.

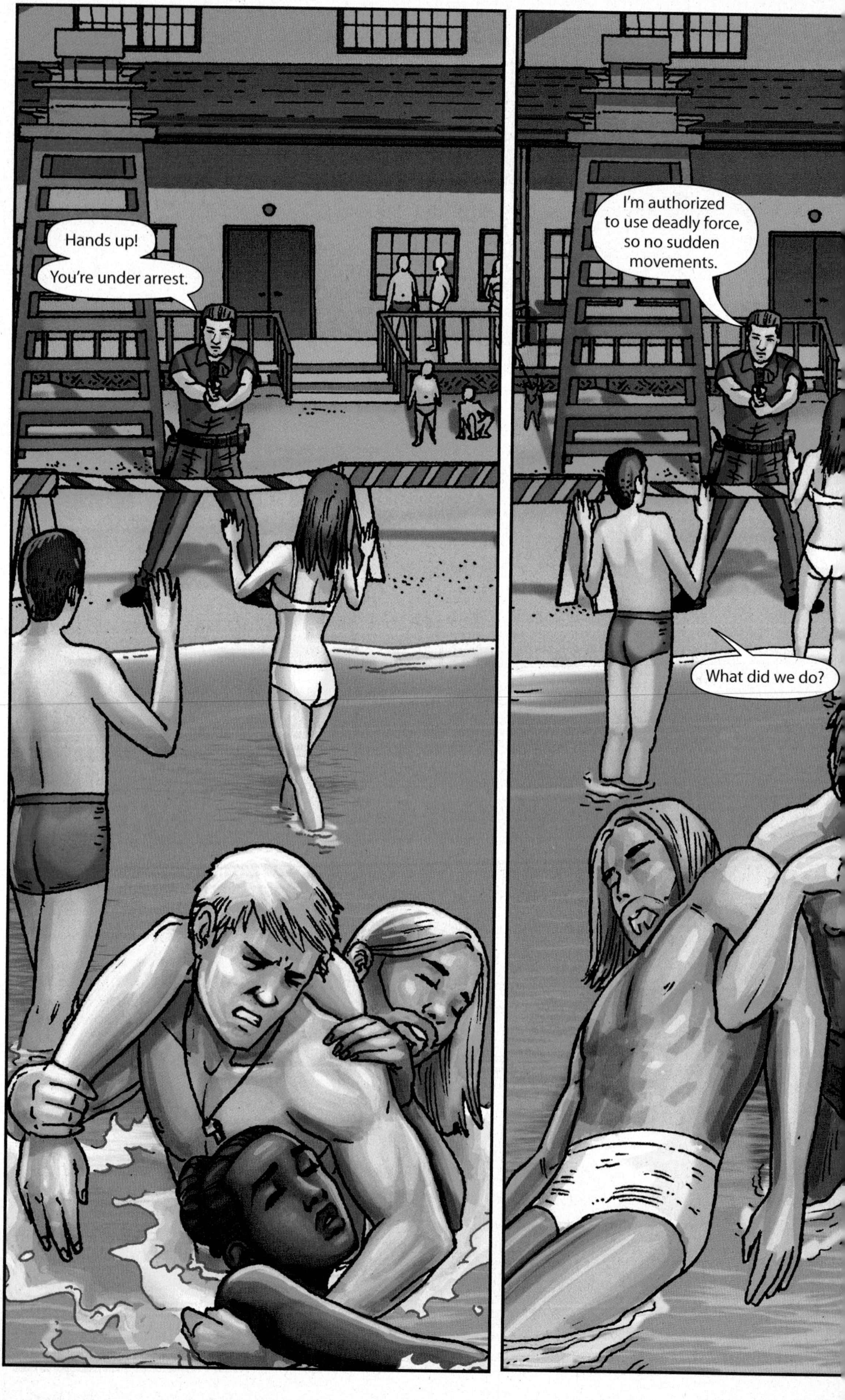
Hands up!
You're under arrest.
I'm authorized to use deadly force, so no sudden movements.
What did we do?

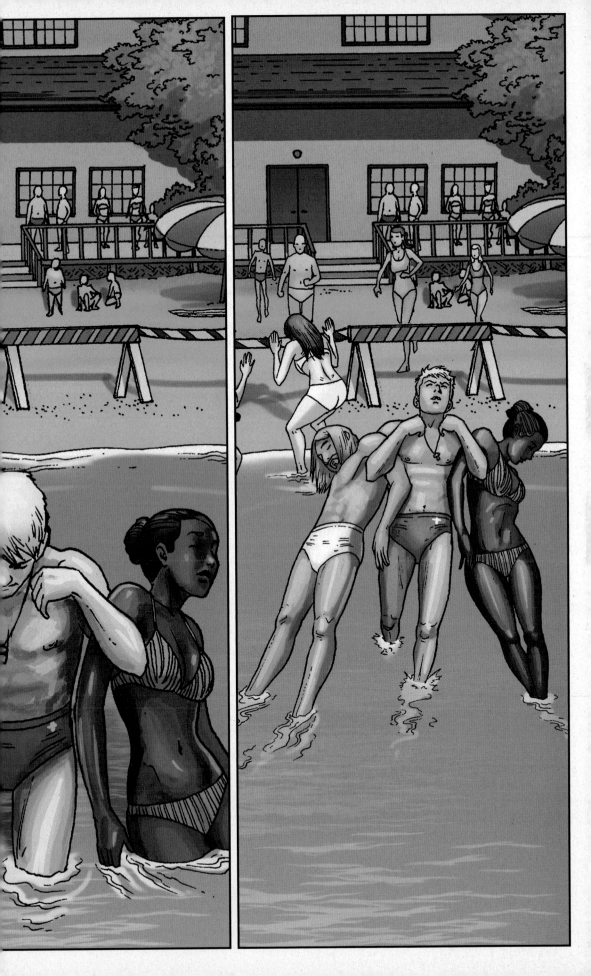

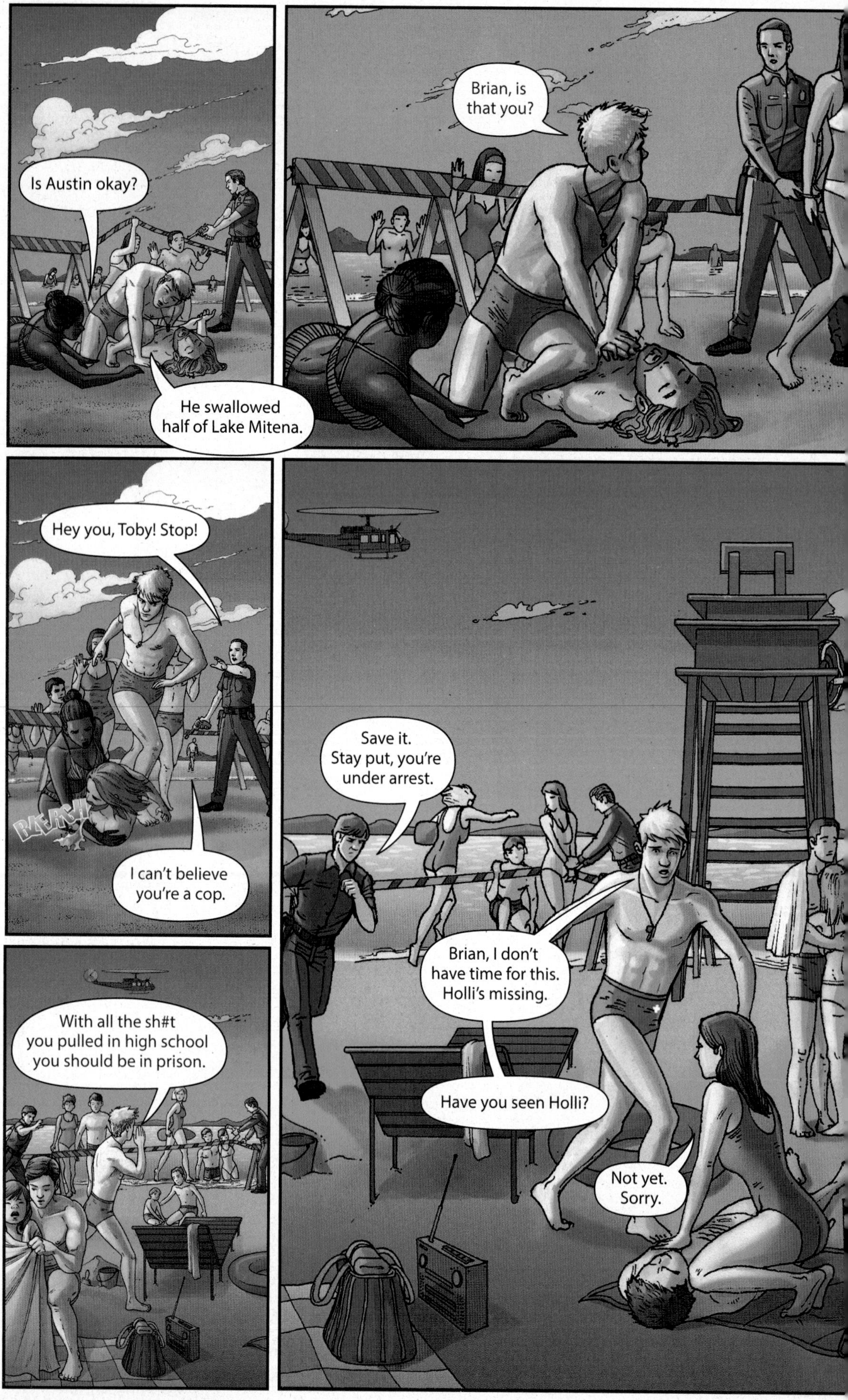
Is Austin okay?
He swallowed half of Lake Mitena.
Brian, is that you?
Hey you, Toby! Stop!
I can't believe you're a cop.
With all the sh#t you pulled in high school you should be in prison.
Save it. Stay put, you're under arrest.
Brian, I don't have time for this. Holli's missing.
Have you seen Holli?
Not yet. Sorry.

THEN NOW

	1966	2015
WORLD POPULATION	3,400,000,000	7,200,000,000
McDonald's		
LOCATIONS	850	36,000
COUNTRIES	1	118
BIGGEST BURGER	1.6oz	5.4oz
AVERAGE MEAL CALORIES	590	1,500
Walmart		
LOCATIONS	24	11,495
COUNTRIES	1	28
PERCENTAGE OF PRODUCTS MADE IN CHINA	0%	70%
NFL		
SUPER BOWL VIEWERS	50,000,000	114,000,000
AVERAGE SALARY	$15,000	$1,900,000
Apple		
LOCATIONS	0	453
iOS DEVICES SOLD	0	1,000,000,000
Prison Industry		
STATE AND FEDERAL PRISON POPULATION	200,000	2,300,000
PERCENTAGE OF FEDERAL PRISON POPULATION: DRUG VIOLATIONS	11%–16%	50%
Health Industry		
COST OF HEALTH CARE	$201 PER CAPITA	$10,000 PER CAPITA
COST OF MEDICARE	$3,000,000,000	$634,300,000,000
Political Industry		
COST OF PRESIDENTIAL CAMPAIGN	$8,800,000	$5,000,000,000

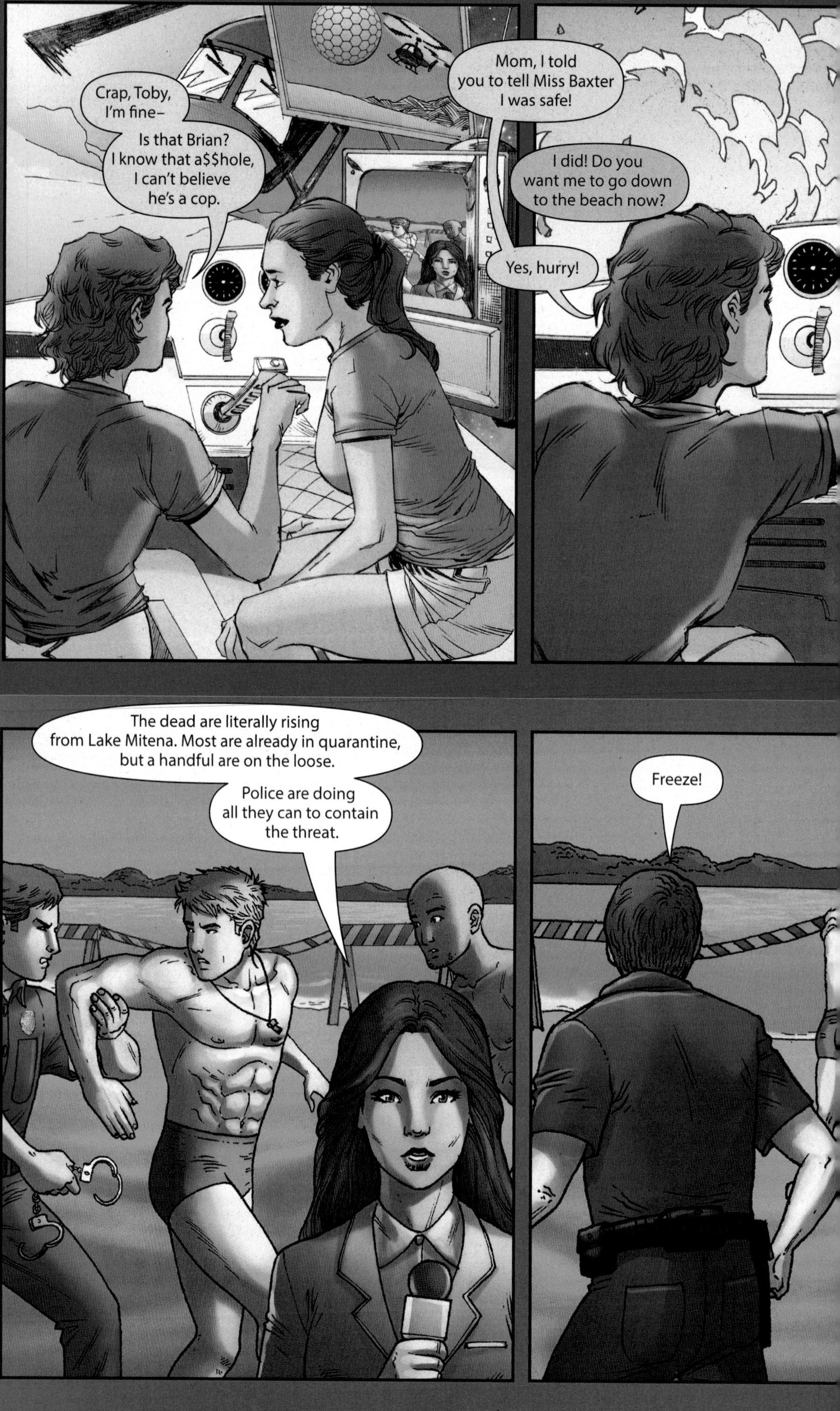
Crap, Toby, I'm fine–
Is that Brian? I know that a$$hole, I can't believe he's a cop.
Mom, I told you to tell Miss Baxter I was safe!
I did! Do you want me to go down to the beach now?
Yes, hurry!
The dead are literally rising from Lake Mitena. Most are already in quarantine, but a handful are on the loose.
Police are doing all they can to contain the threat.
Freeze!

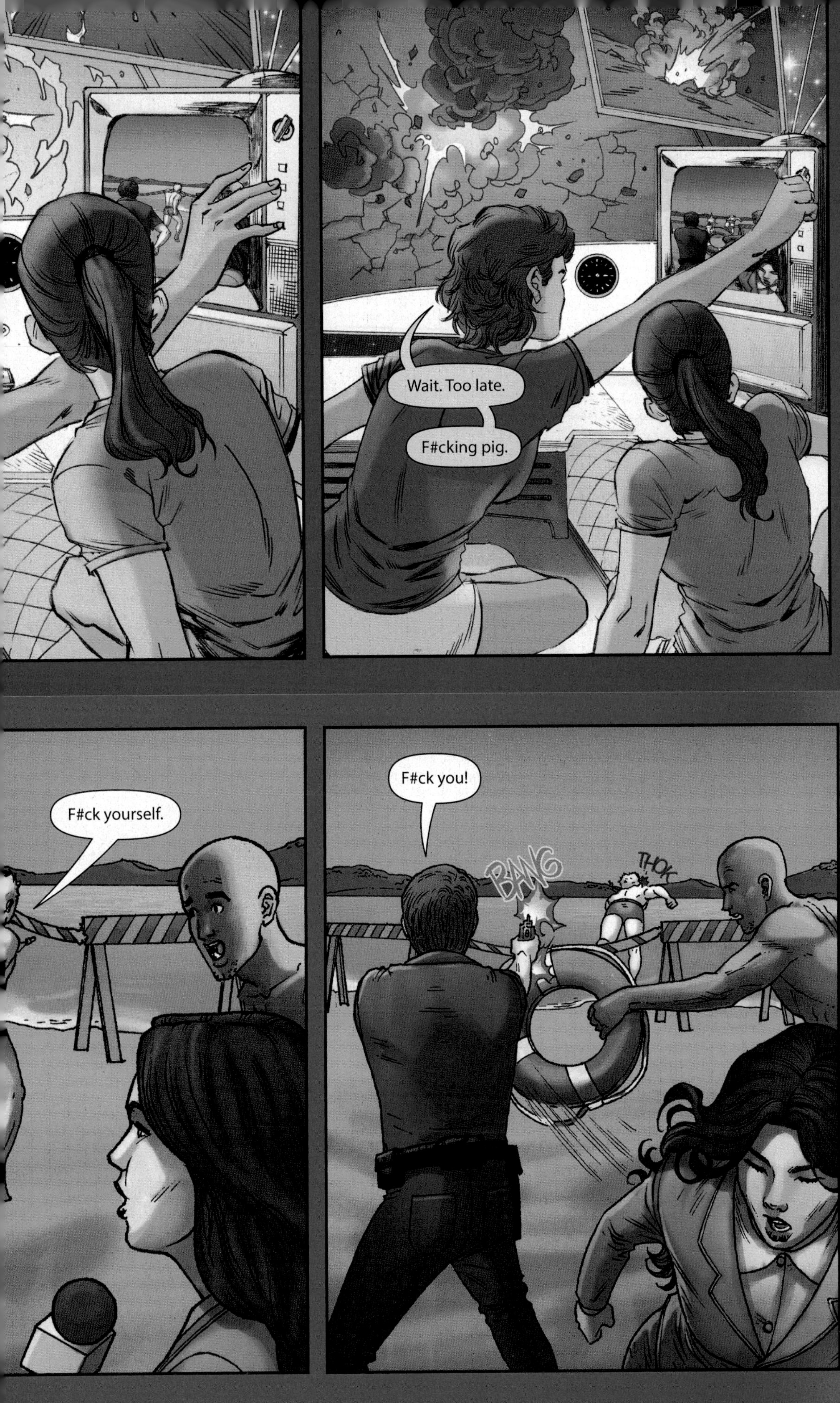
Wait. Too late.
F#cking pig.
F#ck yourself.
F#ck you!
BANG
THOK

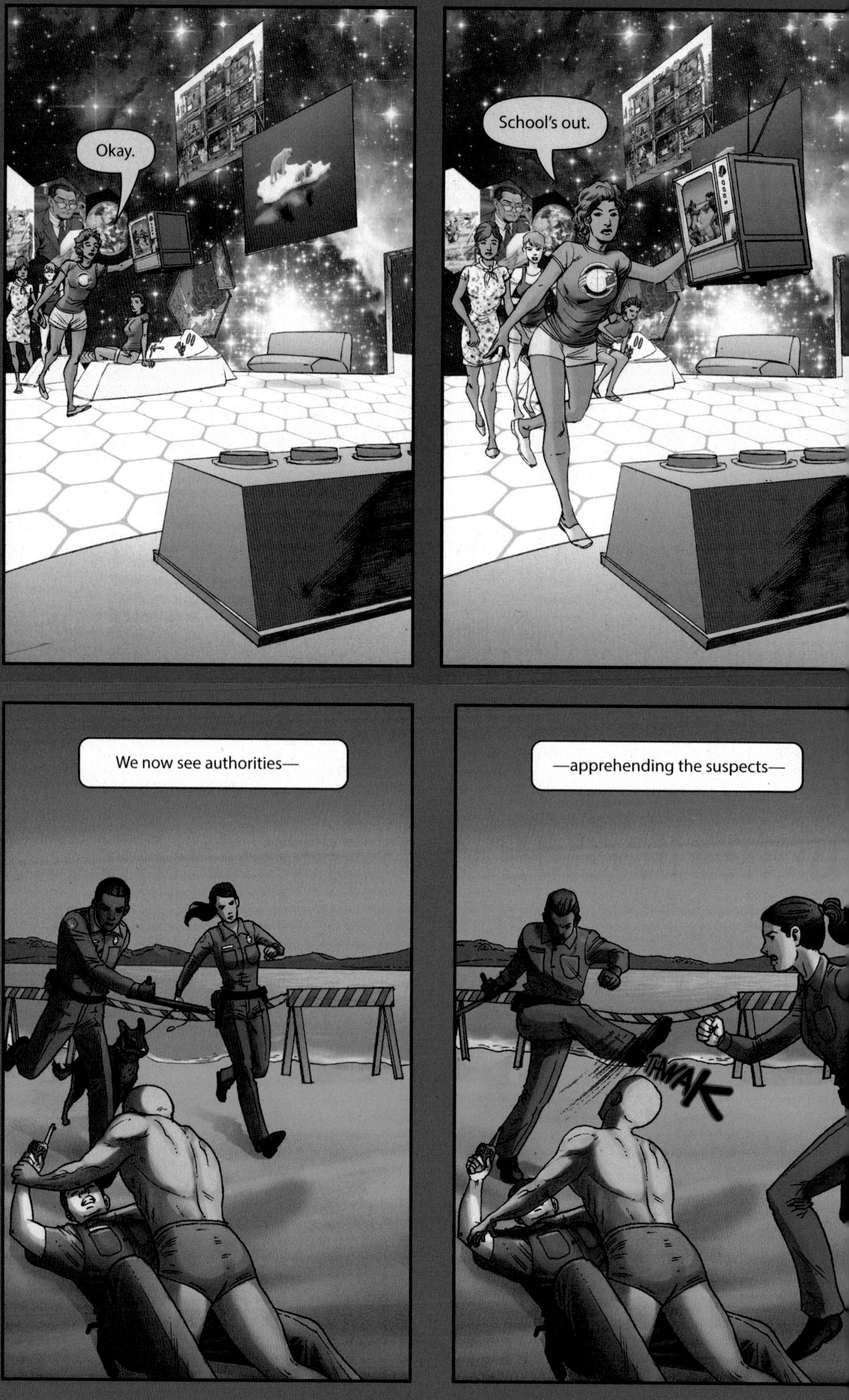
Okay.
School's out.
We now see authorities—
—apprehending the suspects—
THWAK

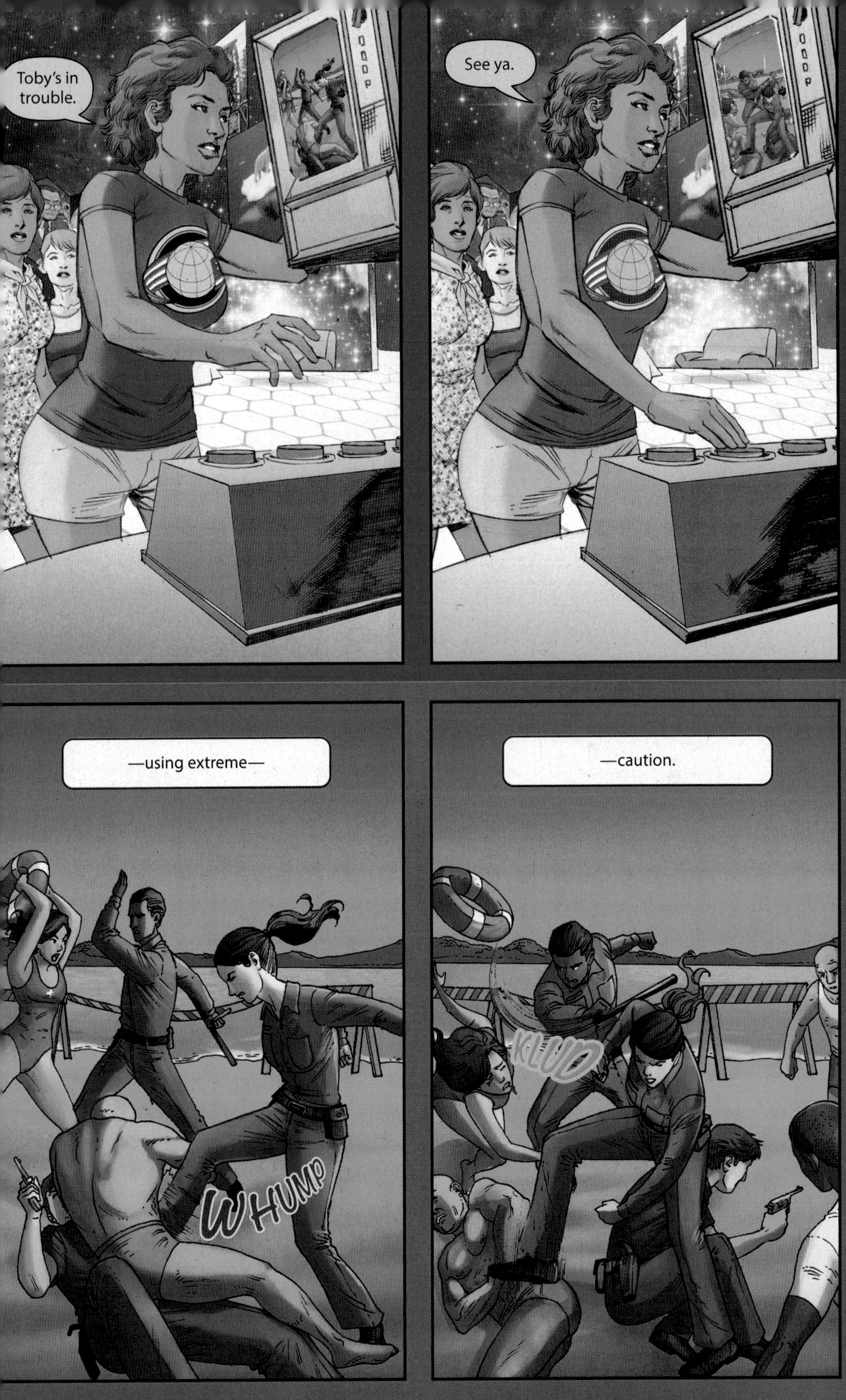
Toby's in trouble.
See ya.
—using extreme—
WHUMP
—caution.
KLUD

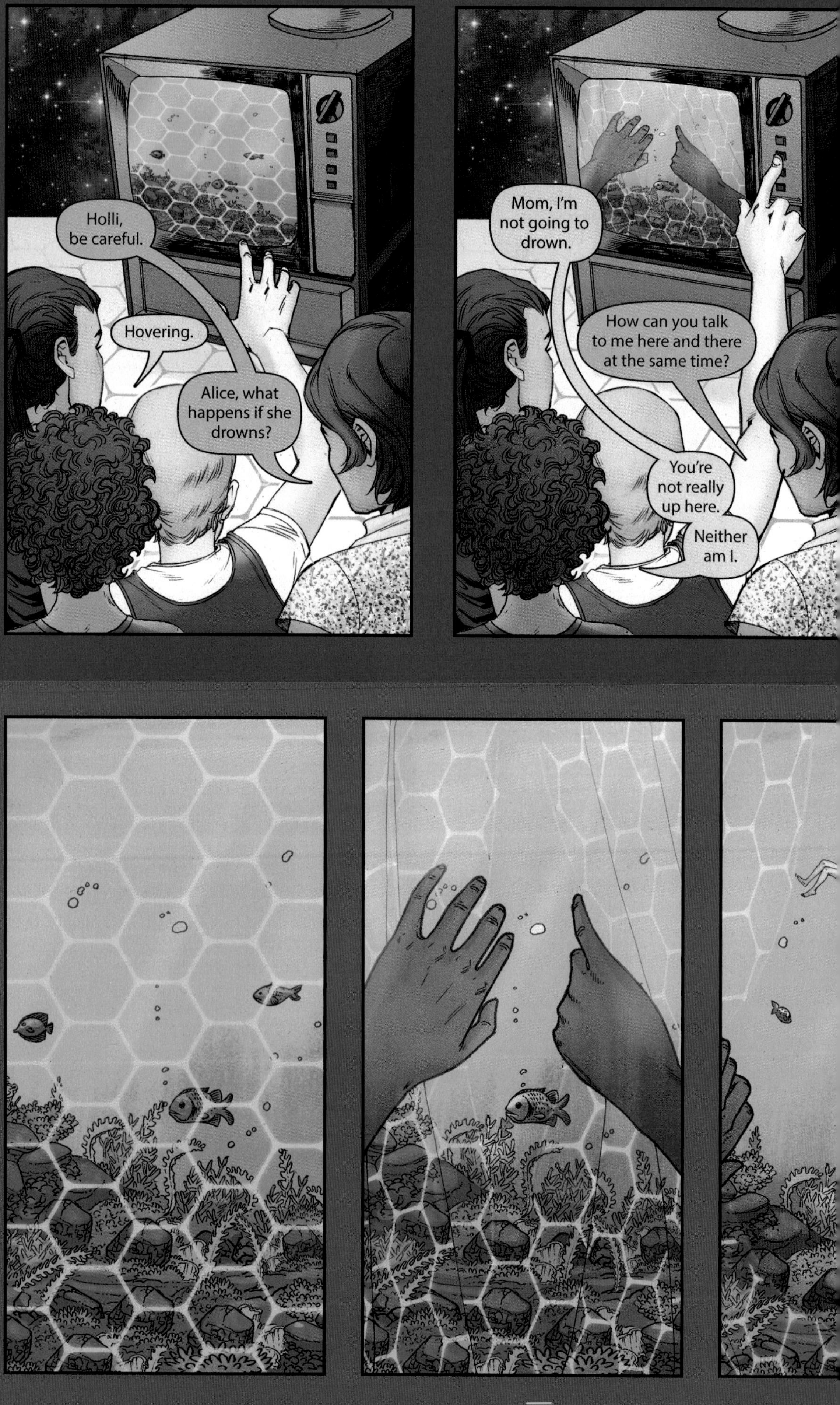
Holli, be careful.
Hovering.
Alice, what happens if she drowns?
Mom, I'm not going to drown.
How can you talk to me here and there at the same time?
You're not really up here.
Neither am I.

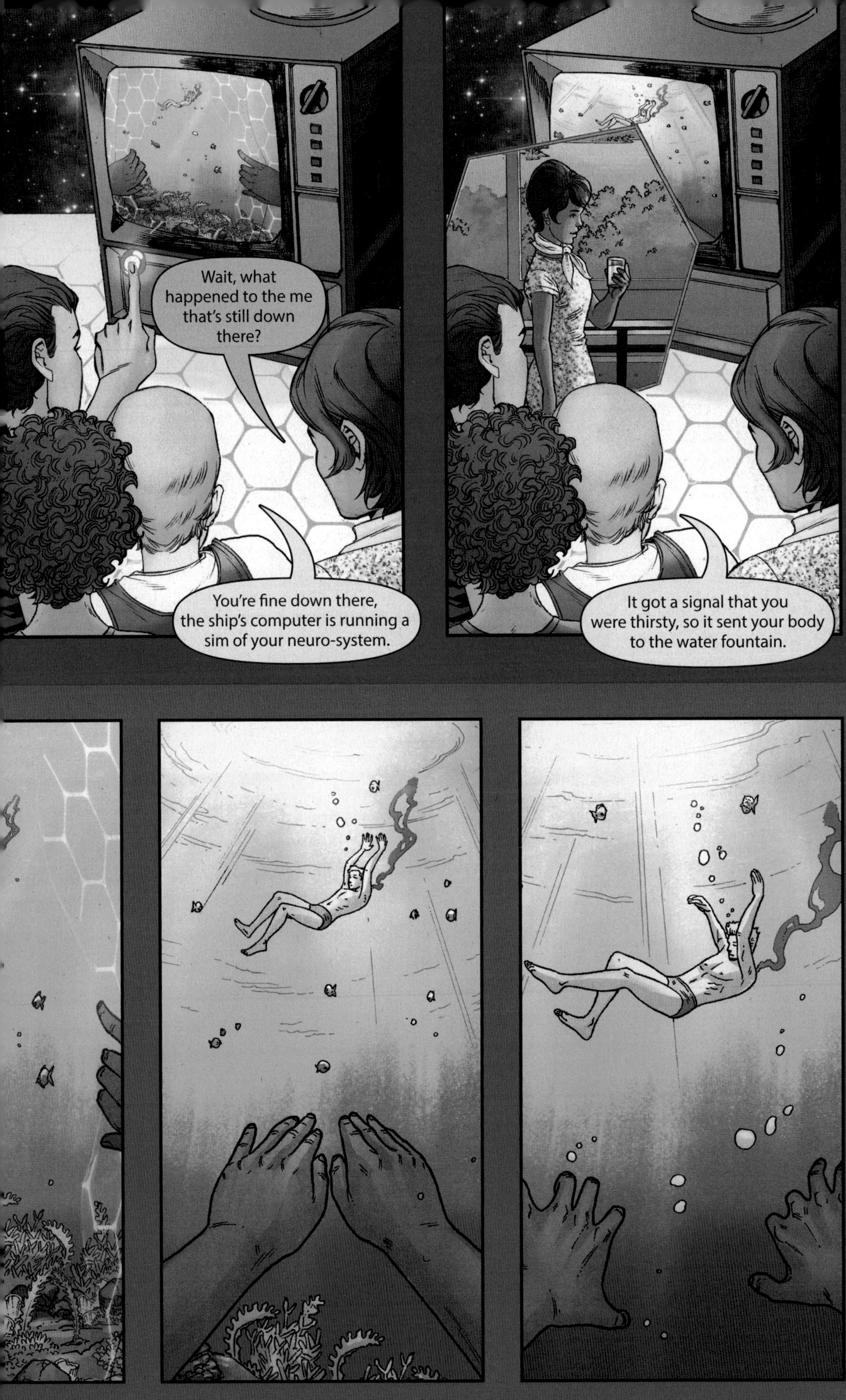
Wait, what happened to the me that's still down there?
You're fine down there, the ship's computer is running a sim of your neuro-system.
It got a signal that you were thirsty, so it sent your body to the water fountain.

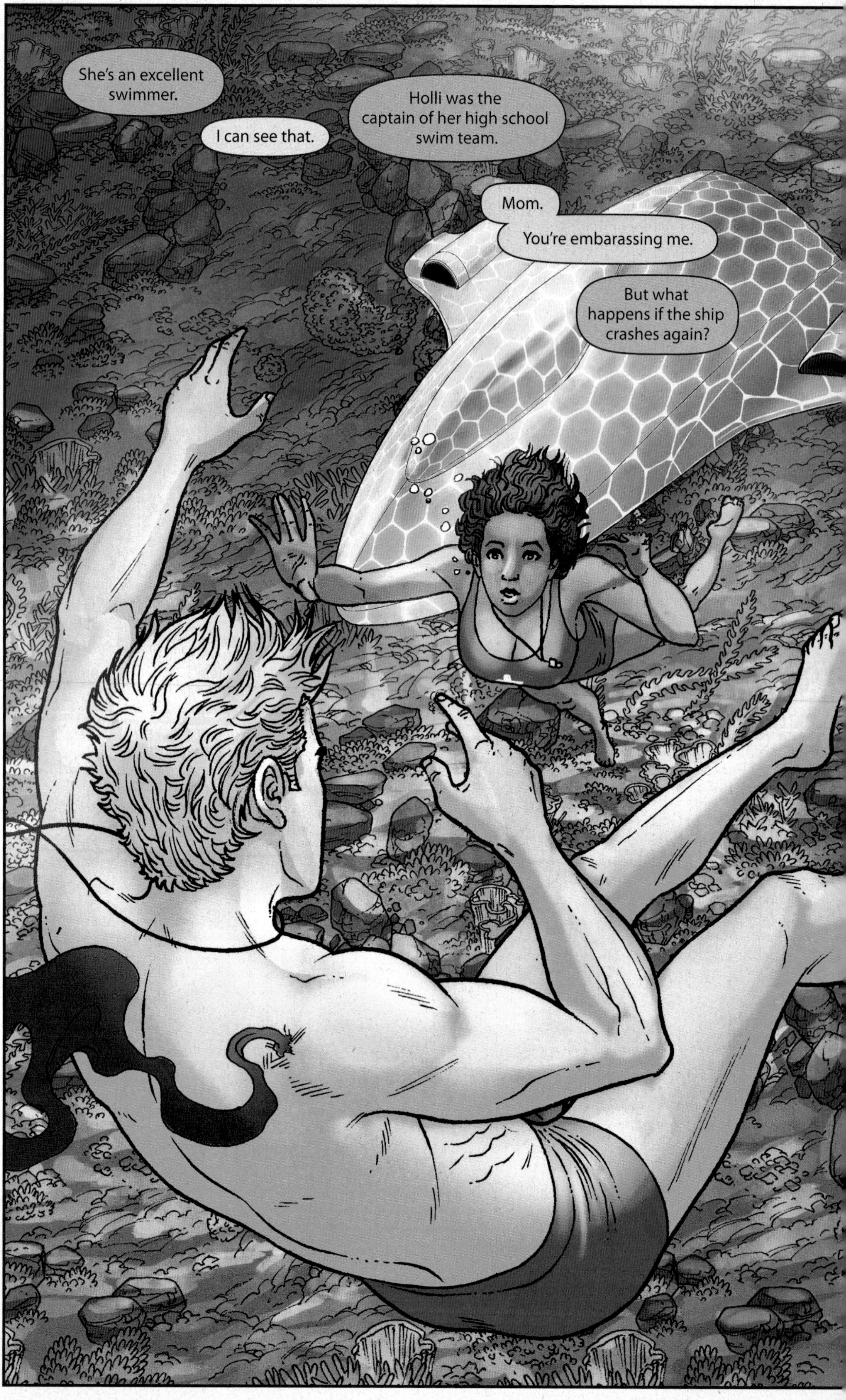
She's an excellent swimmer.
I can see that.
Holli was the captain of her high school swim team.
Mom.
You're embarassing me.
But what happens if the ship crashes again?

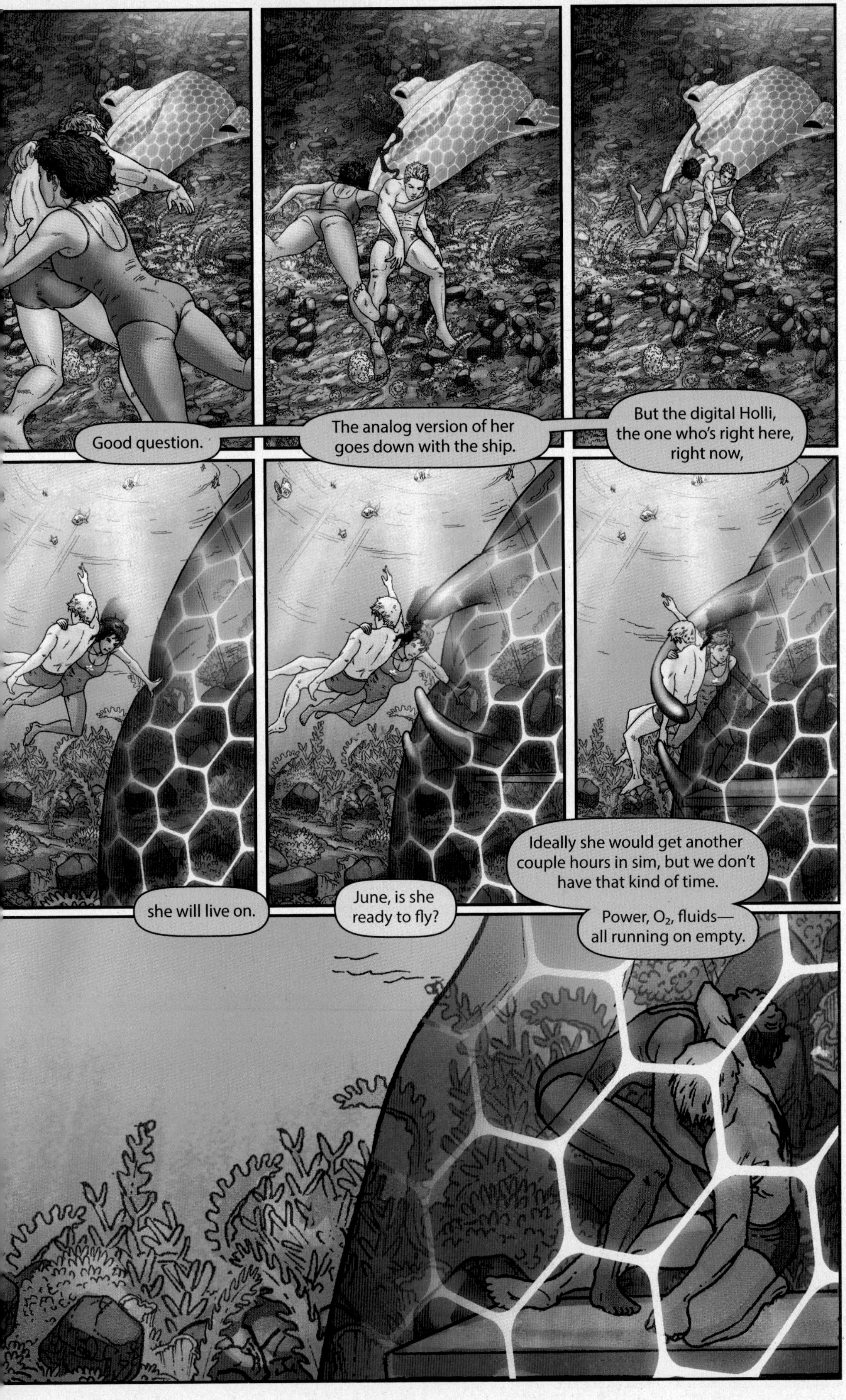
Good question.
The analog version of her goes down with the ship.
But the digital Holli, the one who's right here, right now,
she will live on.
June, is she ready to fly?
Ideally she would get another couple hours in sim, but we don't have that kind of time.
Power, O_2, fluids—all running on empty.

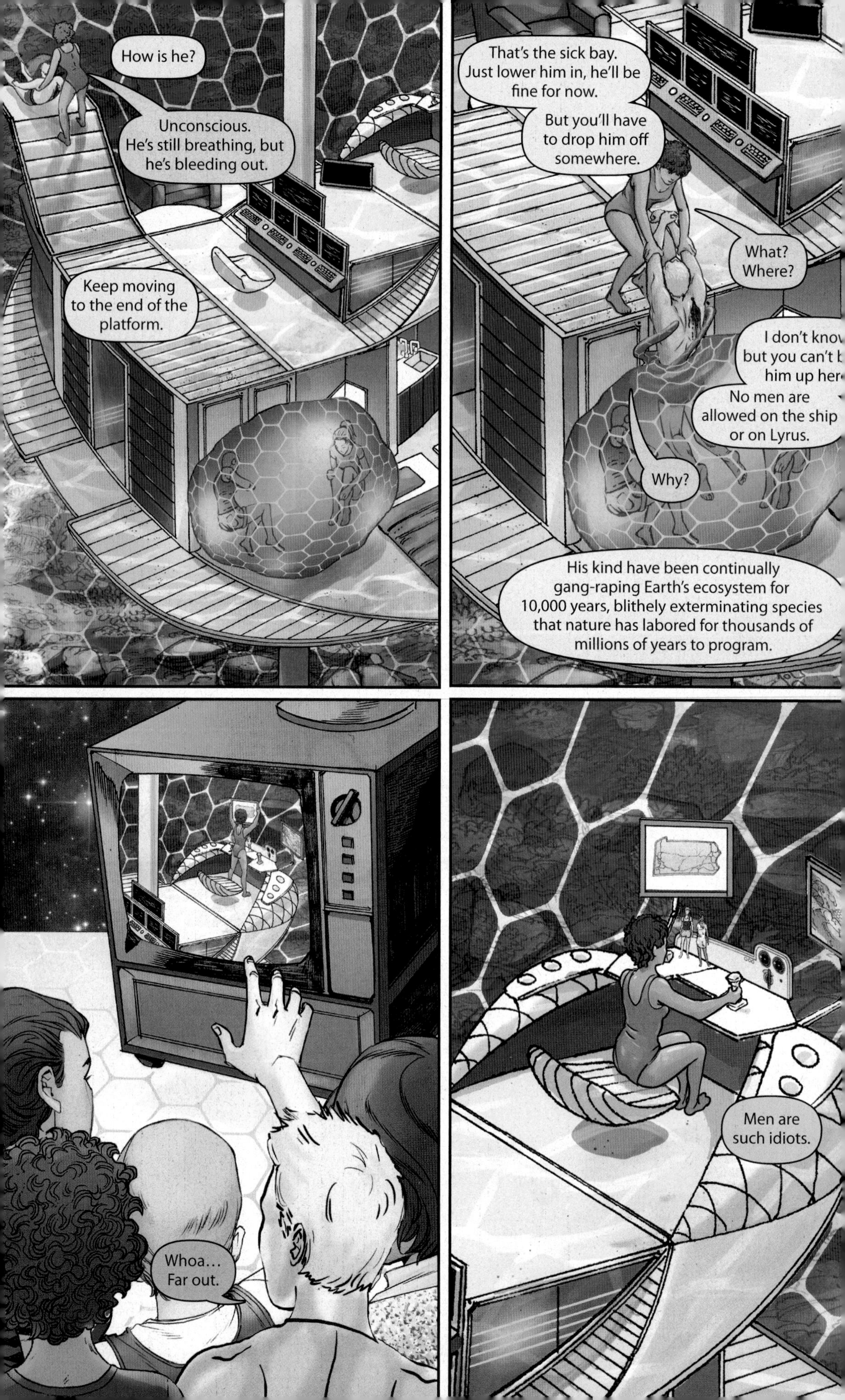
How is he?
Unconscious.
He's still breathing, but
he's bleeding out.
Keep moving
to the end of the
platform.
That's the sick bay.
Just lower him in, he'll be
fine for now.
But you'll have
to drop him off
somewhere.
What?
Where?
I don't kno
but you can't b
him up her
No men are
allowed on the ship
or on Lyrus.
Why?
His kind have been continually
gang-raping Earth's ecosystem for
10,000 years, blithely exterminating species
that nature has labored for thousands of
millions of years to program.
Whoa…
Far out.
Men are
such idiots.

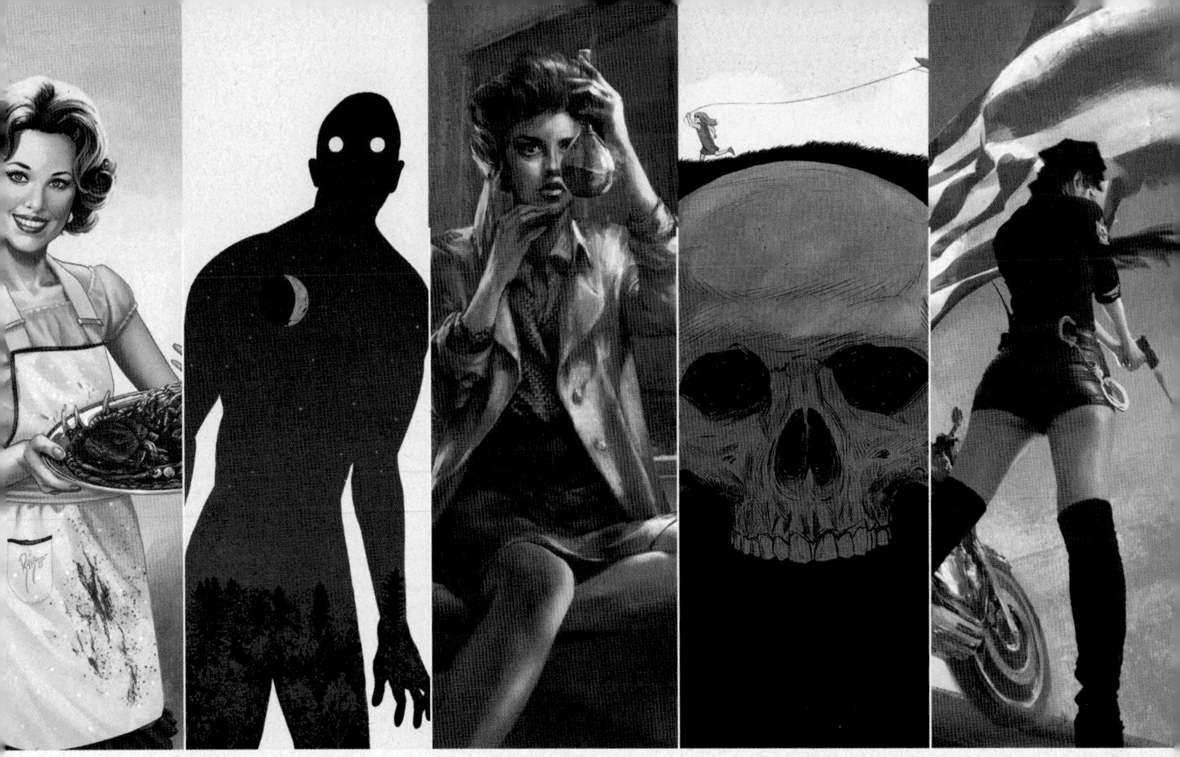

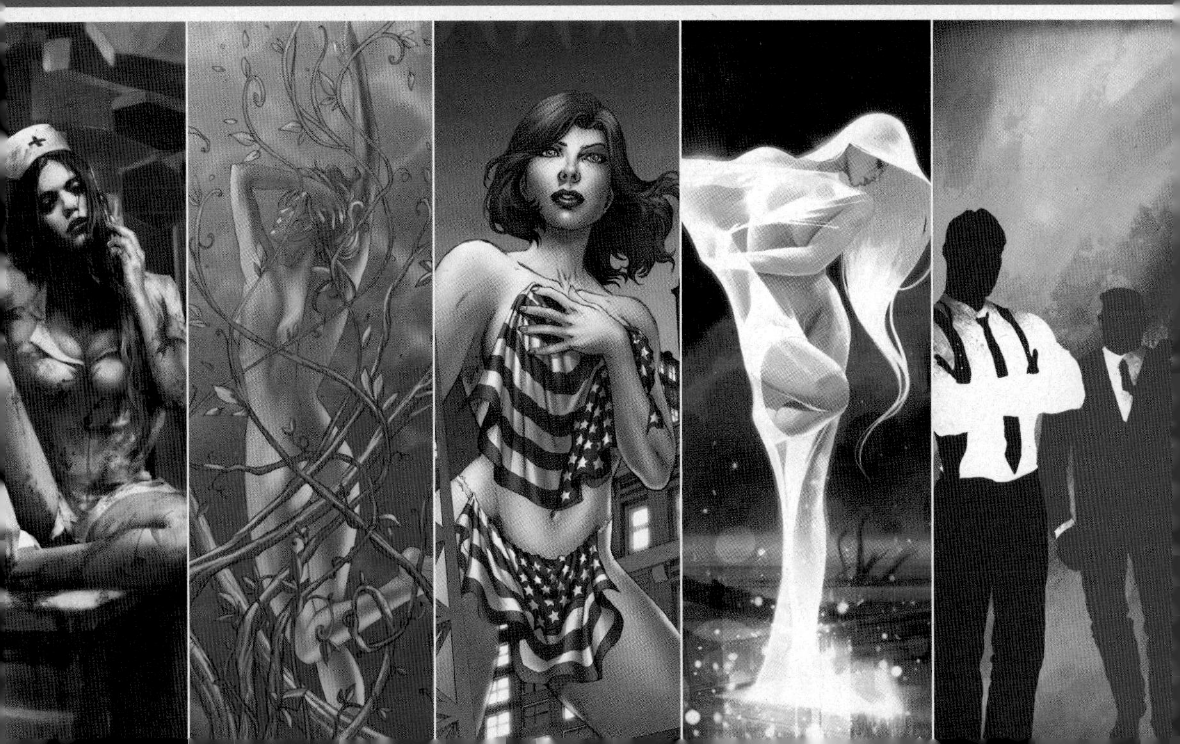

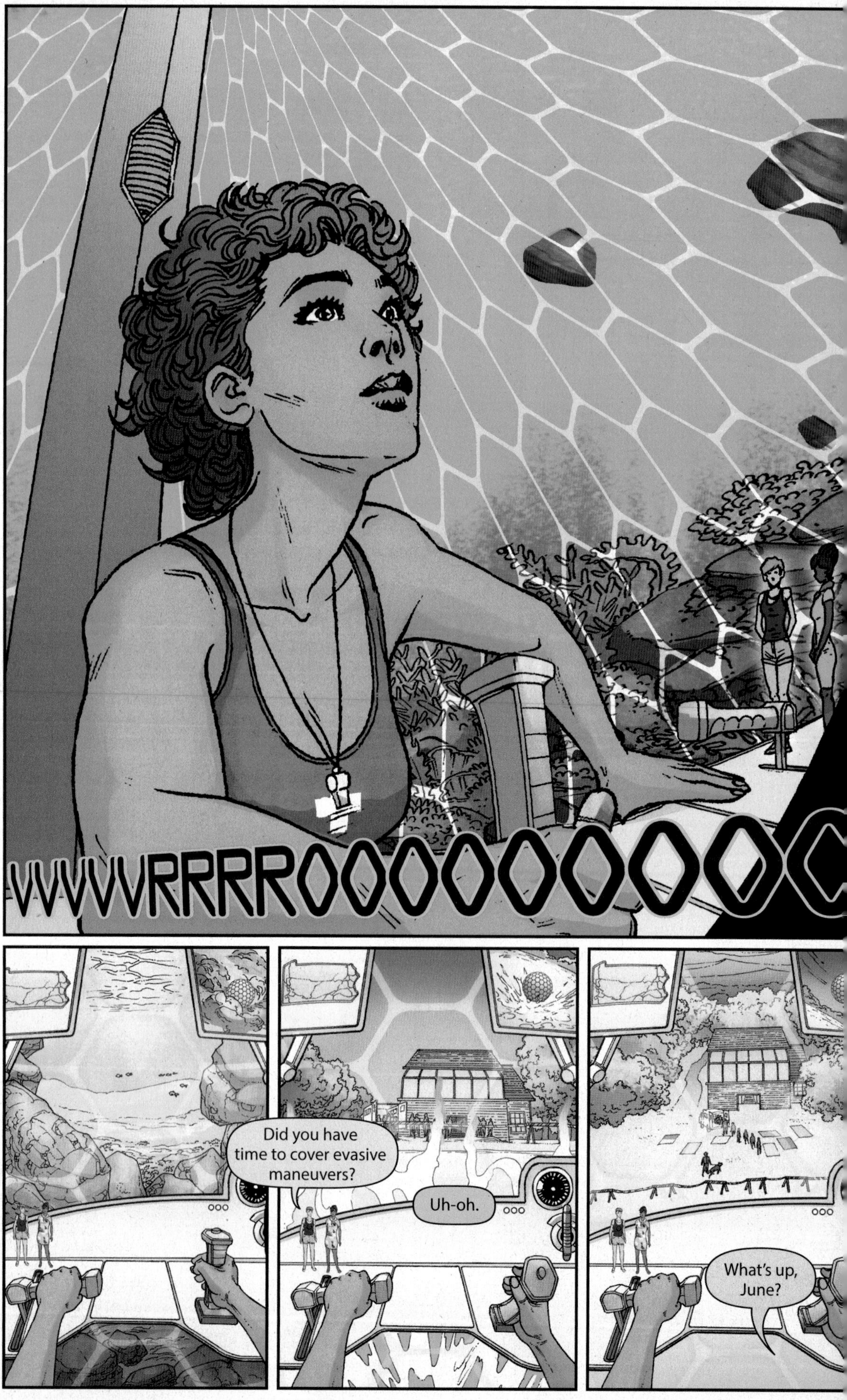

VVVVVRRRROOOOOOOOO
Did you have time to cover evasive maneuvers?
Uh-oh.
What's up, June?

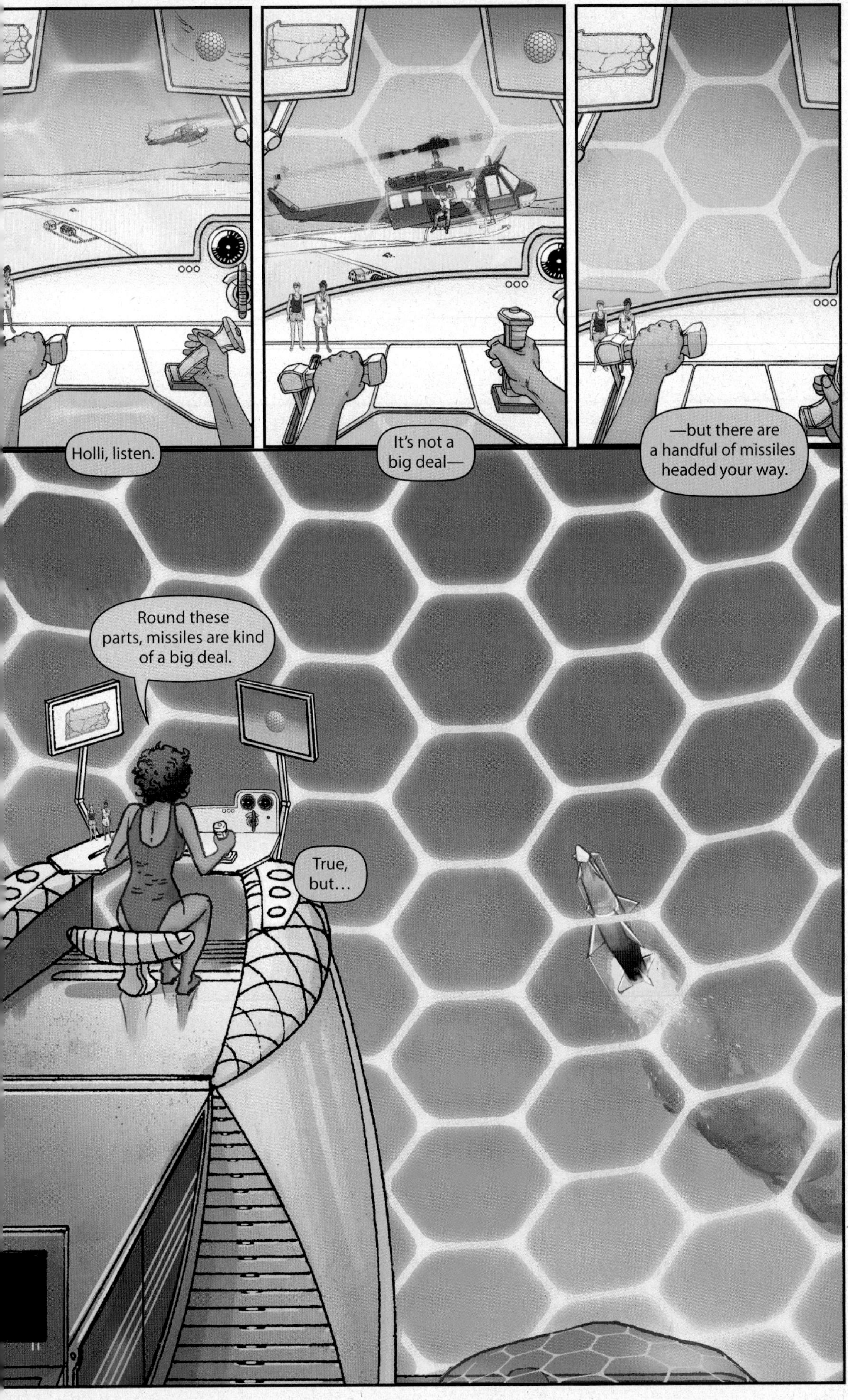
Holli, listen.
It's not a big deal—
—but there are a handful of missiles headed your way.
Round these parts, missiles are kind of a big deal.
True, but…

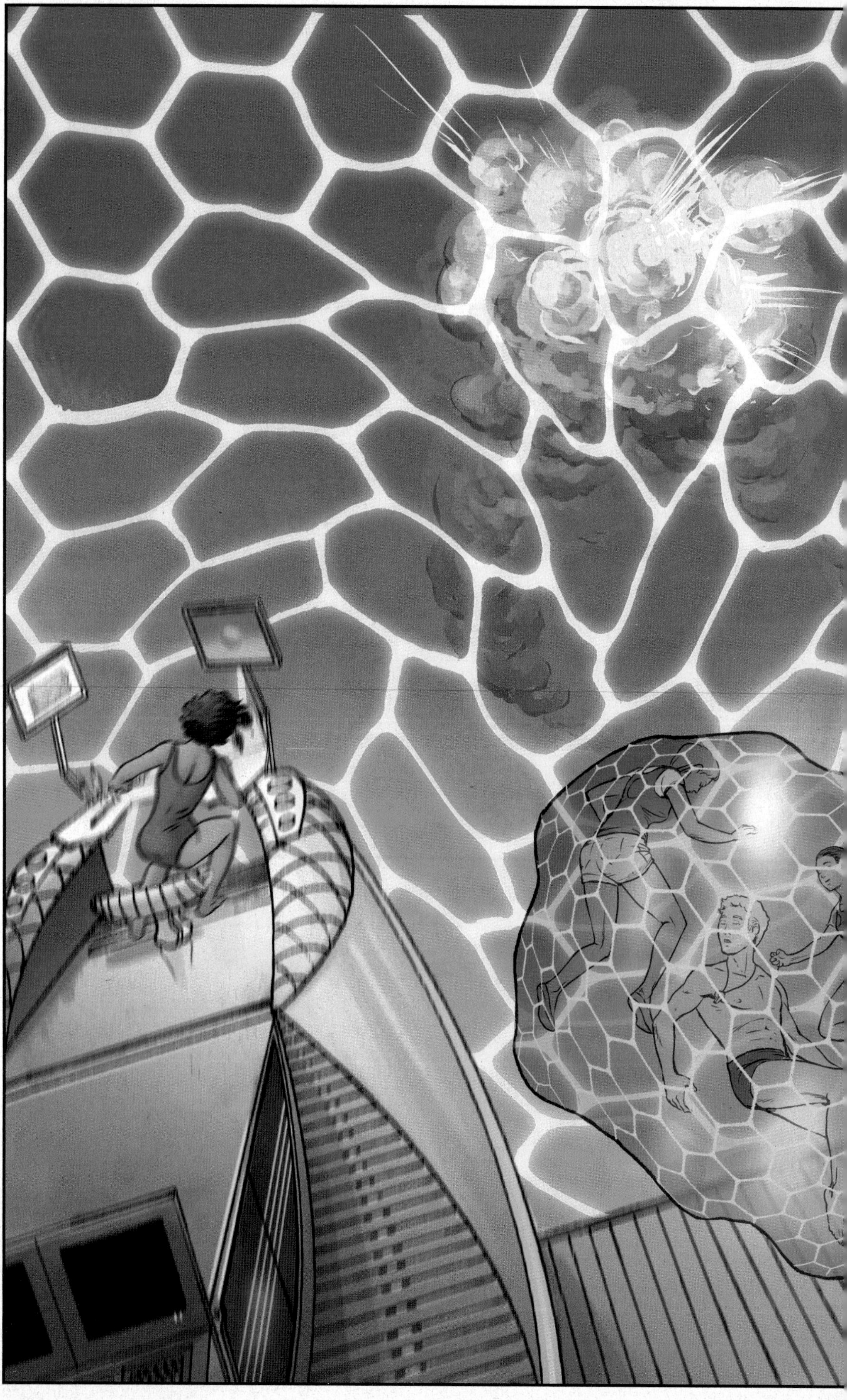